THE FOUR HOME RUNS CLUB

THE FOUR HOME RUNS CLUB

SLUGGERS WHO ACHIEVED BASEBALL'S RAREST FEAT

Steven K. Wagner

ROWMAN & LITTLEFIELD
Lanham • Boulder • New York • London

Published by Rowman & Littlefield
An imprint of The Rowman & Littlefield Publishing Group, Inc.
4501 Forbes Boulevard, Suite 200, Lanham, Maryland 20706
www.rowman.com

Unit A, Whitacre Mews, 26-34 Stannary Street, London SE11 4AB

British Library Cataloguing in Publication Information Available

Library of Congress Cataloging-in-Publication Data

Names: Wagner, Steven K., author.
Title: The four home runs club : sluggers who achieved baseball's rarest feat / Steven
    K. Wagner.
Description: Lanham, Maryland : Rowman & Littlefield, [2018] | Includes
    bibliographical references and index.
Identifiers: LCCN 2018008333 | ISBN 9781538115428 (cloth : alk. paper)
Subjects: LCSH: Home runs (Baseball)—History.
Classification: LCC GV868.4 .W35 2018 | DDC 796.357/26—dc23
LC record available at https://lccn.loc.gov/2018008333

∞™ The paper used in this publication meets the minimum requirements of American
National Standard for Information Sciences—Permanence of Paper for Printed Library
Materials, ANSI/NISO Z39.48-1992.

Printed in the United States of America

For Mom

CONTENTS

CONTENTS

PROLOGUE

It is, some believe, the most historic home run in baseball history, one that was first celebrated on October 3, 1951, at New York's Polo Grounds. Giants fans have been celebrating it ever since.

"The Giants win the pennant! The Giants win the pennant! The Giants win the pennant! The Giants win the pennant!" broadcaster Russ Hodges repeated over and over as New York Giants slugger Bobby Thomson jubilantly circled the bases following a dramatic ninth-inning walk-off home run served up by Brooklyn Dodgers pitcher Ralph Branca. "I don't believe it. I don't believe it. I *will not believe it.*"

Thomson's three-run blast, later dubbed the "Shot Heard 'Round the World," won the National League pennant for the Giants and catapulted them into the World Series. The Dodgers, meanwhile, quietly returned home to await the start of another season. Sadly for them, the slogan "Wait 'til next year" once again was in play, much to the vexation of weary Brooklynites.

Watching in stunned disbelief from his infield perch that day was Dodgers first baseman Gil Hodges, who only a year earlier had been on top of the baseball world after hitting four homers in a single game; on deck as Thomson started his home run swing was Willie Mays, who nine years later would hit four round-trippers in a ballgame. By the fall of 1951, Hodges's four shots seemed remote compared with Thomson's giant blast into immortality. Just an annotation in baseball history, is Hodges's collection of homers. Or, is it?

The definition of "home run" is, as Branca underscored that day, a perspicuous one: *a safe hit that allows the batter to touch all bases and score a run.*[1] In most instances the "touch" is easy. It's the "hit" that's the hard part.

(Unless you're Kirk Gibson of the Los Angeles Dodgers, whose swing and trot were both difficult at one moment in time. On October 15, 1988, in the first game of the World Series against the Oakland A's, the injured Gibson was asked to pinch hit with a runner on base and two men out in the last half of the ninth inning. His team was behind, 4–3, and Gibson was facing future Hall of Fame closer Dennis Eckersley, who was enjoying one of his finest seasons. Gibson, who was barely able to walk or swing a bat due to injuries, battled Eckersley for six minutes before drilling a home run into the right-field bleachers and limping around the bases to score the winning run. For Gibson, whose home run that day is ranked with Thomson's blast as one of the greatest ever, both hitting and circling the bases were difficult.)

In all of sports there are few skills more challenging than hitting a baseball thrown at high velocity. It is so difficult that baseball great Wilver Stargell, a former Most Valuable Player who hit almost 500 home runs during a 20-year career, described the act as succinctly as anyone ever has in a single oft-repeated quotation: "They give you a round bat and they throw you a round ball and they tell you to hit it square."[2]

During the 2017 major-league season a record 6,105 baseballs were hit "square" enough to clear the fences. Most players hit only one homer in a single game, although many hit two and a fair number hit three. The last time a player hit four home runs in the same game was in September 2017, when J. D. Martinez accomplished it for the Arizona Diamondbacks.

As a home run reference point, Giancarlo Stanton of the Miami Marlins led all major-leaguers with 59 blasts in 2017. Many players didn't hit one. Some didn't even dribble a single.

If hitting a round ball squarely is a difficult task, then hitting the ball square enough to send it sailing over an outfield fence planted more than a football field away is the ultimate in hitting success. Doing that four times in the same ballgame against the world's premier pitchers is an unthinkably difficult task.

Difficult, but not impossible.

Since Major League Baseball first began to entertain fans almost a century and a half ago, 18 players have hit four home runs in a ballgame, an average of about one every nine years. Some of those sluggers were legends—for example Hall of Famers Lou Gehrig and Mays. One, Pat Seerey, played only a few short seasons and has been all but forgotten. Still others fall somewhere in between—Mark Whiten and Bob Horner, to name a pair.

By most accounts, the stars must be in order for any player to homer four times in one game. It helps if your team is way ahead or way behind—if a game is out of reach there is less chance that a hurler will pitch around a home run hitter, depriving him of the one at-bat that might make the difference between three home runs and four. It also helps if a hitter is in peak health, although Mays accomplished the task while sick. Seerey, a lifetime .224 hitter, did it despite carrying 40 extra pounds. Rocky Colavito overcame a foamy start when an angry fan tossed a beer on him early in the contest—perhaps the sticky brew helped him grip the bat better during an era before pine tar and batting gloves were in vogue.

Members of the Four Home Runs Club come from all walks of life and nationalities. Shawn Green is Jewish. Josh Hamilton is a Christian. Hodges was Catholic. Ed Delahanty was a drunk.

There are Kansans, New Yorkers, and Ohioans. There are Easterners, Southerners, and Midwesterners. One player, Carlos Delgado, was born in Puerto Rico. Producing the most club members was, surprisingly, Ohio. None of the 18 hail from California despite the Golden State's rich baseball heritage.

Most remarkable, however, is what each player accomplished during his one special game, and individual statistics from the 18 games are surprisingly diverse. Green accumulated 19 total bases, a major-league record that still stands. Adcock hit a smash that struck the top of the wall and came within inches of being a fifth homer. Delgado was the only batter to connect for four home runs in just four at-bats. Mark Whiten drove in a record-tying 12 runs during his big game, while Mike Cameron drove in the minimum for a four-home run game: four. Delahanty's four home runs included two inside-the-park shots—no other club member hit even one home run that failed to clear a fence. Bobby Lowe hit two out in the same inning. Seerey hit homers in three consecutive innings and is one of only a handful of players—Mays and Green are others—to hit three home runs on another occasion. Oddly, Seerey hit only 86 home runs in six-plus seasons, almost 10 percent of them in those two games. Although he and Mays put up the best-ever two-game statistics with 31 total bases, Seerey is the third weakest home run hitter of the 18-member gang; Mays is the most prolific.

It goes to show that nothing in baseball, not even the ability to wallop four home runs on a given day, is predictable. As Ted Williams, one of the game's great hitters, once declared, "Hitting is 50 percent above the shoulders."[3] That may explain Seerey, who didn't possess the discipline nor the refined ability that others in the Four Home Runs Club did. But he did possess one essential quality: confidence in his ability to hit balls for distance, especially when it counted. Unfortunately, below his cranium were 40 extra pounds.

What about other members? What enables a man to hit four home runs in a game and never again smack even three? Perhaps it's something intangible, a hidden motivator. "I'd rather hit home runs," slugger Dave Kingman said. "You don't have to run as hard."[4]

Maybe that's the answer. On their one extraordinary day did any of those 18 players simply not feel like running hard? Or, were they wound up enough to want to run the extra distance that four home runs required, a total of 1,080 feet, or two-tenths of a mile? Or, was each fortunate to face pitchers in the twilight of their careers who no longer had what it took to get a slugger out? In many instances that was the case, although Hodges's game contradicts the notion: He hit the first of his four home runs against a budding superstar—the great Warren Spahn.

Nor was height a factor, nor heft. Three players were 6-foot-4, and three were 5-foot-10. The heaviest player was 240 pounds, while the lightest weighed only 150.

When it comes right down to it the ingredients required to hit four home runs in a single game probably vary from player to player. Or, maybe there are no special ingredients. Babe Ruth never socked four home runs in a game and he was arguably the greatest hitter ever. Good old concentration and a swing that was better than ever on one particular day may be the only requisite that is needed. No one will ever know for sure.

What *is* known are the details of those 18 ballgames and the players who authenticated them—who was pitching that day, to which fields each ball was hit, how the game turned out, how each player's remaining years in baseball played out, and how the media celebrated each mind-boggling accomplishment. Or, in some cases, how some players were later eulogized. After all, seven of the 18 players have since succumbed—the oldest member of the club is Mays, who is now 86, and right behind him is Colavito at 84. At age 27 Scooter Gennett is the youngest of the group.

Eighteen is the story of baseball exceptionalism, one that reintroduces 18 players who accomplished more offensively in one game than many players do in a career (catcher William Holbert, who finished his career with the Brooklyn Bridegrooms, forerunner of the Dodgers, batted 2,000 times in his career without hitting a single home run). It's about a select fraternity of men who, on a given day, played the game as well as it can possibly be played. If throwing a perfect game is the ultimate achievement for a big-league pitcher, then hitting four home runs in a game is the essence of what it means to be a great hitter—at least for a day.

Perhaps Jay Justin Clarke, who hit eight home runs in leading his Class D Corsicana Oil Citys (*sic*) team to a 51–3 win over the Texarkana Casketmakers in a June 15, 1902, Texas League contest, portrayed it best.

Babe Ruth. *National Photo Company Collection (Library of Congress)*

"I remember it as though it were yesterday," Clarke, who on that day hit more home runs than in his entire nine-year major-league career, told a reporter 25 years later.[5] Obviously such achievements aren't erased by the cataract of time.

Nor will those of Gehrig, Seerey, Colavito, and the rest of the four-home run gang be erased by the passage of years. Their achievements are far too monumental to pass away, and they'll certainly be discussed and debated as long as men swing bats and balls fly far and away. Because home runs sometimes are too memorable for words.

What follows on these pages are words that discuss the improbable greatness of 18 men, players who comprise what I call the Four Home Runs Club. It's a fraternity of excellence, a society of fanaticism, a club of conundrum. And Giants hero Bobby Thomson, despite the cataclysm of an unlikely home run more than 65 years ago, will never be a member. He was, you might say, no Pat Seerey.

Still, he cherished the adulation and even notoriety that his achievement attracted. "It was the best thing that ever happened to me," Thomson later told an inquiring reporter. "It may have been the best thing that ever happened to anybody."[6]

That may be true; however, the 18 batsmen described on these pages, beginning with Lowe and ending with Martinez, might just give Thomson a pretty good argument.

ACKNOWLEDGMENTS

W ith gratitude I acknowledge the following people and organizations for their contributions to the preparation of this book. Without them it would have been difficult, if not impossible, to complete this project, nor would I have been able to do justice to the 18 ballplayers portrayed on these pages:

Ken Roussey, formerly the photo archives assistant with the National Baseball Hall of Fame, and John Horne, currently coordinator of rights and reproductions for the Hall, who made available for my use many of the photographs contained herein.

The San Francisco Giants, who graciously contributed a photograph of New York and San Francisco Giants great Willie Mays.

The Texas Rangers, who provided a photograph of Josh Hamilton.

Photographers Jerry Coli, Minda Haas, Keith Allison, and Rafael Amado Deras, who graciously permitted me to use their photographs—some through the image bank Dreamstime.

The Library of Congress, which provided photographs of the great Babe Ruth and Lou Gehrig.

Dennis Seerey, who sent me photographs of his father, Pat Seerey.

The unknown sportswriter who retrieved one of the photos of Pat Seerey from a trash bin and provided it to the family many years ago.

Baseball Almanac, Baseball Encyclopedia, and Baseball-Reference.com, whose statistical data was instrumental in defining many of the players described herein.

A special thanks goes to the dozens of major-league ballplayers, including members of the Four Home Runs Club, who were willing to share with me their recollections of those 18 landmark games, two of whom played alongside Pat Seerey when he joined the fraternity as far back as 1948. These include the following:

Paul Bako
Frank Bolling (All-Star)
Bret Boone (All-Star)
Mike Buddie
Tim Burke (All-Star)
Chis Bushing
Mike Cameron (All-Star)
Vinnie Chulk
Rocky Colavito (All-Star)
Billy DeMars
Carl Erskine (All-Star)
Scott Feldman
Shawn Green (All-Star)
John Halama
Aubrey Huff
Howie Judson
Jim Lonborg (Cy Young Award)
Larry Luebbers
Andy McGaffigan
Troy Patton
Albie Pearson (Rookie of the Year)
Mel Roach
Mark Whiten

The firsthand remembrances of each of those players were instrumental in helping me to capture as accurately as possible what it may have been like to experience or witness the heroic individual achievement of hitting four home runs in a Major League Baseball game.

BOBBY LOWE
May 30, 1894

In 1894, Bobby Lowe proved unequivocally that neither Ruthian brawn nor Goliathan stature are necessary to achieve home run superiority. For 18 years Lowe played within the confines of his modest, far-from-towering build but often carried a big stick. On the playing field, especially on May 30, 1894, little more mattered.

Of all the players who have hit four home runs in a game, Lowe was both the shortest and the lightest. Still, his accomplishments that day loom giant, like Goliath. There are the four home runs in one game, something no one had done before. Two of those were hit in the same inning, a feat that only one player had accomplished previously. He also eclipsed the National League record for total bases in a game, a mark that would stand for six decades. Perhaps most important, more than a century after he retired Lowe is still regarded as a genuinely nice guy, unspoiled by the fame and riches of baseball.

In fact, if nice guys finish last, Bobby Lowe was a true gentleman. While usually a winner on the baseball diamond, he did finish virtually last in one historically important category: the number of career home runs hit by a nonactive member of the elite Four Home Runs Club (Scooter Gennett, who remains active, will likely pass him next season, fixing Lowe at the bottom of the pile). Playing in the Deadball Era prior to 1919, Lowe finished next to last among those 18 players. By today's standards he is not even considered a home run threat.

Of all the men who powered four home runs, few were weaker home run hitters than one-game home run wonder Lowe, who was revered by fans and fellow players but was hardly considered a slugger at the plate.

Bobby Lowe. *National Baseball Hall of Fame*

"As a model for young players to copy, Lowe is to be highly recommended," wrote the *Pittsburgh Press* in a 1913 article published after Lowe had completed his short tenure as a baseball scout for the Detroit Tigers. "His playing career was honorable, and he saved his money so well that when he retired he could have lived a life of ease had he desired to do so."[1]

Statistics underscore Lowe's lack of long-ball power. In 1894, the year that he performed the unlikely feat of hitting four home runs, "Linc," as he was affectionately known due to his presidential middle name, Lincoln, hit only 17 home runs during the entire season. Granted, the celebrated Deadball Era, when home runs were a premium commodity for nearly every major-league club, was still in play and would remain so for another quarter-century—until Babe Ruth came along and hit a then-head-scratching 29 homers for the Boston Red Sox in 1919, his breakout season as a power hitter. Prior to the prodigious Bambino's conversion from pitcher/slugger to full-time slugger the following season, 17 home runs was considered a mother lode for one man in one season, as evidenced by the meager 96 blasts that a man for whom home runs have paradoxically become synonymous, John "Home Run" Baker, posted during a career that began in 1908 and lasted 15 years. (Baker led the American League for four consecutive years, never hitting more than 12 in a season. In 1914 he led the league with nine.)

As it turned out, 17 homers was the career high-water mark for Lowe, who also hit 14 balls over big-league fences in 1893 but no more than seven in any other season either before or after that. And while he did play almost two decades in the major leagues, most of that time with the Boston Beaneaters, Lowe averaged fewer home runs per season (3.9) than he hit in that one momentous game for the Boston club.

Many of Lowe's other numbers also were uninspiring. With a lifetime batting average of .273, he averaged just 107 hits and 55 runs batted in during his long career, fewer than most hitters whom the passage of time has conferred the descriptor of greatness upon. The only time he ever led the league in anything, and it was hardly a high-profile offensive category, was in 1894, the year of his four-home run barrage. That season Lowe officially came to bat 613 times (not counting 50 walks and nine sacrifice bunts) in only 133 games, more than any other player in the National League. With that high number of at-bats he still managed to register a career-best .346 batting average. The Gay Nineties, retrospectively recalled as a prosperous period of gaslights and Gibson girls, were his bread-and-butter years.

Despite often weak offensive numbers compared with other players in the exclusive four homers coterie—he hit under .250 seven times—Lowe was a mainstay with the Beaneaters, formerly the Red Stockings and later to become the

Boston Braves as baseball stormed toward maturity. He played 12 uninterrupted seasons with the National League club and for good reason: Despite his failure to earn a coveted spot in the National Baseball Hall of Fame when its first selectees were inducted in 1939, Bobby Lowe is considered one of the finest second basemen ever to wear a baseball uniform. That said, when he retired from the game in 1907 he did so with only 71 homers to his credit—6 percent of them blasted during that one memorable game. When he died in 1951 Lowe's obituary easily might have boasted that he was the "first player to hit four home runs in a single game" and a "fine defensive player"—and nothing more.

Lowe's defensive skills notwithstanding, no one can take away The Game, which occurred on May 30, 1894, at the Beaneaters' temporary Congress Street Grounds in downtown Boston. The weather that day was pleasant, summer was just around the corner, and Lowe was enjoying the best season he would have as a player, a campaign that would see him bang out 212 hits. Little did he know that the ballgame that day against the lowly Cincinnati Red Stockings, who would finish near the cellar in the National League, would be his finest moment as a major leaguer and the one that would etch his name forever in the annals of baseball history.

Robert Lincoln Lowe was born in Pittsburgh, Pennsylvania, to Robert L. and Jane Lowe on July 10, 1865, just months after the assassination of Abraham Lincoln—perhaps explaining his unusual middle name. He grew up on Bluff Street in nearby New Castle during the post–Civil War Reconstruction period, when slaves were free but economic transformation of the Southern states was far from it. There are few references to his baseball exploits prior to the middle teen years, when Lowe was selected to play in a pickup baseball game between local physicians and printers. Then working as an apprentice at a print shop, a not-uncommon trade during the fast-evolving heyday of newspapers and magazines, he asked organizers to give him an opportunity to participate in the game along with some of his peers. After mulling it over they granted the boy's request and planted him—where else?—in right field to see what he could do. The year was 1881 and Lowe was just 16 years old. History records that despite his age, inexperience, and the absence of modern-day ball gloves, he did all right.

"Before the game was fairly commenced, the kid had won all the honors in the field and at bat," wrote author George V. Tuohey in his definitive history of baseball in Boston. "The next year he played with a strong amateur team in New Castle [Pennsylvania]."[2]

Unfortunately, Lowe's tenure as a player with the New Castle Archie Reeds was interrupted for several years shortly after it began. As sole provider for his mother and sister, he left the team the following year and returned home to help support his family, leaving baseball behind—albeit only temporarily. By that time baseball was in his blood, just as the eventual national pastime would soon be in the country's blood, and the young man reversed course and began looking for ways to return to the game in a meaningful role.

Lowe joined a newly organized New Castle team at the age of 21 in 1886, led the club in hitting as a catcher/third baseman, and then moved over to the Eau Clair Lumbermen of the Northwestern League in 1887, where he played through the following season before joining the Milwaukee Brewers of the Western Association in 1889. By that time, his talents with the bat and glove had become conspicuous to the major-league Beaneaters, who at the request of manager Frank Selee offered him a contract. On April 19, 1890, at the age of 24, Lowe made his major-league debut with the team.

It was certainly a historic period during which to play baseball in Beantown. The Boston Marathon began in 1897, won by John J. McDermott. City officials were boldly beginning to ban theatrical plays and literary works that offended them, giving rise to the phrase "banned in Boston." And whispers of a coming automobile age were being heard citywide, resulting in establishment of the Porter Motor Co. as one of the first car manufacturers anywhere. The company advertised its Porter Stanhope as the "only perfect automobile."

Playing in the outfield, Lowe started strong with the Beaneaters, hitting a respectable. .280 during his rookie season. He then came of age, batting .346 in 1894, the year of his four-home run game, an accomplishment author Tuohey dismissed in a single inglorious paragraph.

"Lowe, on May 30, 1894, on the Congress Street Grounds, made four home runs in succession and topped off the day's batting with a single, making a total of 17 bases in five times at bat," he wrote. "The opposing pitcher was [Elton P. "Ice Box"] Chamberlain of the Cincinnatis."[3] Period.

Although records from the period are incomplete, history notes that there was much more to Lowe's storied achievement that day than simply four free trots around the diamond, in particular his inaugural membership in the Four Home Runs Club and the superlative third inning. His achievements that day may have been largely owed to the fact that the game was played at what is widely regarded as a hitter's ballpark, one that just four years after it was built had already outgrown its usefulness as a major-league venue.

After fire destroyed their regular home ballpark, known as South End Grounds, Lowe and his fellow Beaneaters moved to temporary quarters at Congress Street Grounds just two weeks prior to his historic game. At least for

Lowe the fire and subsequent move proved to be propitious. Congress Street Grounds was a double-deck stadium that had opened in 1890,[4] and the ballpark's fences measured a mere 250 feet down the left-field foul line and 255 to right[5]—perfect for a line-drive hitter who had home run power. If the 5-foot-9, 155-pound Lowe, or anyone else for that matter, had any designs toward going on a home run spree, Congress Street Grounds, with dimensions down the lines that only slightly exceeded a Little League ballpark, was the perfect place to do it.

Lowe had two opportunities to break from the gate strong that day, as the Beaneaters, who had won the National League pennant the previous three seasons, were playing a split doubleheader—morning and afternoon games with a long lunch break in between—against the Cincinnati Reds. In front of a crowd of only 8,500 fans, Boston had won the opener, giving the hometown team four victories in a row and setting the stage for Lowe to make baseball history.

In the second game Boston started its top hurler, Charles "Kid" Nichols, who had pitched his way to 30 or more wins the previous three seasons and was on his way to a fourth-straight 30-victory season and enshrinement in the Hall of Fame. With even fewer fans in attendance for the nightcap—approximately 3,000—the Reds greeted Nichols with a home run in the top of the first inning to take an early 2–0 lead. After making his only out of the afternoon leading off for Boston in the bottom half of the first, Lowe quickly made up for his inauspicious beginning only a couple innings later when he went to work as a one-man wrecking crew, leaving the Reds far behind with two powerful swings of the bat.

With the score tied 2–2 in the bottom half of the third inning, Lowe came to bat again and blasted a hard smash over the short left-field fence for his first home run of the game, a solo shot. After he touched home plate and returned to the dugout, Boston strung together a series of singles in addition to a hit batter, a walk, and a sacrifice, enabling the Beaneaters to bat through the lineup and Lowe to come to the plate for a second time in the inning. Just as he had 30 minutes earlier, Lowe again hit a shot over the left-field fence for his second home run of the inning, another solo blast that enabled the Beaneaters to increase their output in the inning to nine runs and post an insurmountable 11–2 lead before any of the Boston players had even broken a sweat.

"Two homers in one inning, that must be a record," manager Selee, who was seated in the Beaneaters' dugout, commented as his second baseman happily circled the bases to the applause of the relative handful of fans in attendance.[6] As the words left Selee's mouth, starting pitcher Nichols walked over and graciously extended his hand to Lowe after his teammate crossed home plate and headed for his seat on the bench.

At that point, Lowe's hand was certainly worth shaking. With just two innings completed the kid from Pennsylvania was enjoying a slugfest that would culminate in the greatest individual performance that the relatively young enterprise of Major League Baseball had ever seen. The game was only beginning.

The Reds pulled to within five runs of the Beaneaters, at 11-6, in the top of the fifth before Lowe came to bat in the bottom of the inning looking for his third home run of the game. He wasted little time collecting it, once again stroking a drive over the left-field fence for his third solo shot in four at-bats. That home run marked only the seventh time that a player had hit three home runs in a big-league game.

With Boston leading, 12-6, Lowe came to bat in the bottom half of the sixth inning for the fifth time and again made his swing count. His next big blow occurred with two teammates on base. After Lowe dug in at the plate he promptly socked his fourth home run of the day, a three-run blast over the short left-field fence, dutifully touching the bases as fans cheered the new record and showered their hero with coins. When all of the numismatic contributions had been collected, Lowe's purse for the afternoon totaled $160, a tidy sum by nineteenth-century standards and roughly one-third the average annual income for wage earners during that year, when a dozen eggs cost 25 cents and a gallon of milk even less than that.

Perhaps as an anticlimax Lowe came to bat once more in the game, during the eighth inning, with a chance to hit his fifth home run of the ballgame, something that has never been achieved. By then the Reds had his number, and Lowe managed only a single. Nonetheless he finished the day 5-for-6 with six RBI and 17 total bases, the latter mark setting a National League standard that seemed insurmountable. The final score that day: Boston 20, Cincinnati 11, with all of the Reds' runs charged to Boston's winning and much-beleaguered pitcher, ace Kid Nichols.

After the game a public controversy arose concerning the fact that all of Lowe's home runs were hit over the short left-field fence in a cracker box of a stadium; however, one sportswriter attempted to put the issue to rest. "[Lowe's] home runs were on line drives far over the fence and would be good for four bases on an open prairie," wrote Tim Murnane of the *Boston Globe*.[7] End of controversy.

Bobby Lowe would play in the major leagues for 13 more seasons, joining the Chicago Orphans (1902), who became the Chicago Cubs a year later, the Pittsburgh Pirates (1904), and the Detroit Tigers (also in 1904). During his last seven seasons of professional baseball, from 1901 through 1907, Lowe hit just four home runs, equal to the number he hit on May 30, 1894. After hitting 17 home runs in 1894, his biggest season of four-baggers after that was five in 1897, although he did continue to pile up RBI. By the last five years of his major-league career the one-time, one-game slugger had become little more than a singles hitter, with an occasional double, triple, or home run thrown in for good measure. His final game was on October 6, 1907, when Lowe was 42 years old, and he departed the sport as a beloved favorite of local baseball scribes. One wrote,

> For a grand player, Lowe is seldom given the credit often dished out to his inferiors. His work does not appeal to the bleachers and grandstand like the less-natural and clumsy player, who is often seen floundering around like a fish out of water while the crowd enjoy the effort and go home to tell what great playing they saw. He is a hard worker, you will hear them say. Bobby Lowe is not only a hard worker, but [also] a conscientious player and an artist of the first magnitude.[8]

Added the *Detroit News*, "Lowe was one of the greatest and is today one of the most popular ballplayers ever in the game. There is no better type of the gentleman in baseball, and no one ever heard ought but words of praise for him."[9]

In 1904, toward the end of his career, Lowe served as player-manager for the Detroit Tigers. The position proved to be a good training ground for the soon-to-become-well-traveled Lowe, who in 1907 was named baseball coach for the University of Michigan Wolverines, where despite his immersion in college ball he still managed to take note of the rising popularity of professional baseball.

"There is more interest being taken in baseball in different league towns than ever before," he said.[10]

After leaving the university he signed to coach the minor league Grand Rapids Wolverines of the Central League the next year, but that position too was short-lived. Finally, in 1909, he was hired as baseball coach at Washington & Jefferson College in his home state of Pennsylvania, and he finished up his baseball career as a scout for the Detroit Tigers in 1912. Lowe finally retired from the game to live in Michigan, where he settled with his wife, Harriet, and held down a number of different jobs in the public and private sectors. For Bobby Lowe, baseball, which had come of age with the advent of the twentieth century and, in 1903, something called the World Series, had become a dear memory.

Although long retired from the game, Lowe did make a curious personal appearance in 1932. After New York Yankees slugger Lou Gehrig hit four home runs in a game on June 3 of that year, becoming the first American League player to do so, Lowe posed awkwardly in his Boston uniform alongside the popular first baseman. The smiling Gehrig appeared delighted to be in the presence of such an esteemed player, while Lowe, at 67, looked miscast and somewhat uncomfortable. Nonetheless it was made clear afterward that Lowe was pleased to pose for pictures with such a highly regarded athlete, someone who rose to fame as a ballplayer during another period of relative austerity: the Roaring Twenties.

"I feel complimented to share the record with so grand a boy," Lowe was quoted as saying.[11]

Although clearly aging and almost four decades older than future Hall of Famer Gehrig, Lowe would live 10 years longer than the revered Iron Horse. On December 8, 1951, a decade after Gehrig had succumbed to the ravages of amyotrophic lateral sclerosis, Lowe died quietly at his home in Detroit at the age of 86 and was buried at nearby Evergreen Cemetery. A quirky obituary appeared in newspapers the following day:

> Robert L. Lowe, former Major League Baseball player, died yesterday at the age of 83. He was the first of four men in baseball history to hit four home runs in a regulation nine-inning game . . . Lowe hit his four homers on the afternoon of Memorial Day, 1894, in the second of two games played against Cincinnati on the old Congress Street Grounds in Boston. Boston won the morning game, and Bobby celebrated by treating his wife to a fish dinner at the North Boston Railroad Station.
>
> When he came to bat in the first inning in the afternoon, he was still feeling the effects of the generous meal and was an easy out. First up in the third inning, he smacked the ball over the left-field fence and repeated the stunt when a prolonged rally brought him to the plate for the second time that inning. He hit his third and fourth homers, also over the left-field fence, in the fifth and sixth innings, and ended with a single in the eighth. After his fourth homer, the fans tossed $160 in coins onto the diamond.[12]

Today, more than 60 years after his death, Bobby Lowe remains a baseball footnote, an ideogram of what an able hitter who lacks overwhelming power can accomplish if everything is working right at the proper moment in time. And while 17 other players have since hit four home runs in a game, it was Lowe who set the standard by doing it during a period when baseballs didn't rise as meteorically as they do today. Some might argue that despite his staying power, of all those in the Four Home Runs Club, Lowe was one of the least powerful offensive players of the lot. Even if he was Lowe nonetheless founded the distinguished four home runs brotherhood, an accomplishment for which he deserves—and has rightly received—big-league credit.

2

ED DELAHANTY

July 13, 1896

In the summertime, Niagara Falls is a frothing mass of churning water, a cacophony of energy so powerful that those reckless enough to transgress its liquid borders often suffer dire consequences.

In 1903, when searchers pulled Ed Delahanty's body from a swirling, foamy cauldron miles downstream from the perennial newlywed getaway, many questions were left unanswered. Most pressing to the Washington Senators, who had been established just two seasons earlier, was who would fill the large shoes and sparse, formless leather glove that were unexpectedly vacated by the team's volatile left fielder, the American League's reigning batting champion, when death visited just months before the first-ever World Series was played? After all, the 35-year-old left fielder was one of the finest contact hitters that baseball has known. He was hitting a solid .333 at the time his body was pulled from the chilly waters of Niagara just halfway into his 16th season after having hit an even more formidable .376 during the previous campaign when he won the American League batting crown. In fact, the fiery, hard-drinking Delahanty, who dressed with an elegance characteristic of upscale, turn-of-the-century Boston, had not hit below .300 since 1891, his fourth big-league season, and had batted over .400 a remarkable three times during the 1890s, when he emerged as a bona fide star. His highest average ever was .410 in 1899, the year he led the National League in base hits, doubles, RBI, and batting average.

In the hardscrabble, rough-and-tumble world of early twentieth-century professional baseball, where the names of teams—Boston Beaneaters—sounded puerile to many present-day Americans and players rubbed elbows with Pullman porters, night watchmen, and, occasionally, police dispatchers, there were few players better at their craft than the handsome Delahanty, who during 15 seasons playing for the Philadelphia Quakers, Philadelphia Phillies, Cleveland Infants, and Senators led the league in doubles five times, RBI three times, home runs twice, triples once, and, perhaps just for the fun of it, stolen bases once. He also captured two batting titles—one in

Ed Delahanty. *National Baseball Hall of Fame*

each league—while recording a lifetime batting average of .346, fifth on the all-time list behind such baseball luminaries as feisty Ty Cobb, surly Rogers Hornsby, enigmatic Joe Jackson, and flamboyant Lefty O'Doul. His career average surpassed some of baseball's greatest hitters, including Tris Speaker, Ted Williams, Babe Ruth, Tony Gwynn, and Pete Rose, who amassed 19 batting titles among them.

Still, one accomplishment stands out from the others: On July 13, 1896, while playing at Chicago's long-ago-demolished West Side Grounds, sometimes referred to as West Side Park, Delahanty, known as "Big Ed" or simply "Del," became only the second big-league player to hit four home runs in a game. Competing in a rectangular ballpark that seated only 16,000 fans, many of them dressed in suit, tie, and fedora, but whose center-field fence was a whopping 560 feet from home plate, Delahanty hit two inside-the-park home runs and two shots that cleared the fences en route to a 5-for-5 game and seven RBI.[1] Big Ed, also known affectionately as the "King of Swat," had a career day.

Edward James Delahanty, the oldest and most highly regarded athlete of five baseball-playing brothers, four of whom eventually made it to the major leagues, was born October 30, 1867, in Cleveland, Ohio, population 92,000. His parents were James and Bridget Delahanty, who had emigrated from Ireland to the United States toward the end of the Civil War. Like many nineteenth-century immigrants, the boy's father worked several low-paying jobs while his mother turned the family's large home on Phelps Street into a residential boardinghouse in hopes of making ends meet and jump-starting Ed to a good beginning in life. The couple apparently succeeded, as four more sons—Tom, Joe, Frank (known as Pudgie), and Willie—were born in slow succession in the 15 years following Ed's birth during the post–Civil War years.

The Delahanty boys spent most of their early years doing what many boys did before television, video games, and cellular phones: They played baseball, either at the ball field adjacent to a local firehouse or at nearby sandlots. The pastime eventually paid big dividends, mostly for Ed.

"We were given bats instead of rattles," he once said of his early years growing up in Cleveland.[2] Baseball certainly was at the forefront of his life from the beginning.

When it came to baseball, Ed Delahanty stood tall above his younger siblings, and at age 20, after graduating from Cleveland High School and completing a stint at a local college, his hitting enticed scouts to recruit the young man for a semipro team known as the Cleveland Shamrocks. Before long he was earning as much as 13 dollars per week in the Ohio State League, and he finished out the 1887 season hitting an eye-popping .351 for Mansfield (a minor-league team situated in Ohio—the team had no nickname), a first-year club. Before even setting out for Mansfield he made his career intentions clear to his mother.

"I'm goin' to quit you and play ball in Mansfield," he said, to which his mother replied, "Drat baseball—it's ruinin' the family."[3]

After raising his batting average 60 points to .412 playing for the Wheeling, West Virginia, Nail Cities in early 1888, Delahanty's contract was purchased by the Phillies for the grand sum of $2,000. Ed Delahanty was on his way to fame, fortune, and, eventually, an unsympathetic demise.

At 6-foot-1 and weighing only 170 pounds, it took a while for Delahanty to prove himself against journeymen big-league pitchers, who had few limitations on what pitches they could throw—including, in that era, spitballs. An undisciplined swinger and slightly underweight for his formidable frame, Delahanty hit only .228 during his rookie season in 1888, collecting just one home run in almost 300 at-bats for the Phillies.

"If I could only hold myself like that old crab [Cap] Anson, I would be better than he ever did," Delahanty said of the future Hall of Famer, with a twinge of jealousy in his tone.[4]

The following season his average climbed to .293 and Delahanty increased the number of hits, doubles, and triples he recorded in his rookie season, although he still trailed Anson, his exemplum for success, in the batting average department by more than 50 points that season. The higher average may have been the impetus for him to move on, and he jumped ship to the Cleveland Infants of the Players League for the 1990 season. There he batted .296 with 153 hits and 64 RBI, demonstrating the hitting brilliance that would become his trademark as a big-league ballplayer.

Delahanty returned to Philadelphia after the short-lived Players League failed, hitting a disappointing .243 in 1891 but with a respectable 86 RBI, a total that landed him in eighth place among the league leaders in that category. Despite the modest batting average it was clear that Delahanty could hit baseballs for distance and drive in runs with the best of his peers. Still young and exceedingly strong, he was in the major leagues to stay.

His breakout season came in 1892 when Delahanty, who following four relatively obscure seasons had recommitted himself to success and worked diligently to achieve it, hit .306 with six home runs and 91 RBI at a time when long-ball shots were rare. He also collected 21 triples, the only time in his career he would lead the league in that department despite finishing 13th on the all-time major-league triples list. Perhaps most important, he also led the league in slugging percentage that season, something he would repeat four more times despite hitting only 101 lifetime home runs. While considered a slugger in the early days of baseball, Delahanty's career home run total is mediocre by today's standards.

For his outstanding effort in 1892, the now-defunct weekly newspaper *Sporting Life* applauded Delahanty for his "hard and timely" hitting.[5] He was just getting warmed up.

Playing for the Phillies in 1893, Delahanty slugged 19 home runs and drove in 146 runs, leading the league in both categories while posting a .368 batting average. He also popped 35 doubles and 18 triples among his 219 hits. With numbers like those he was certainly looking forward to the 1894 season.

Meanwhile, Delahanty's younger brother Tom was beginning to make some noise of his own on the baseball diamond, and on September 29, 1894, he made his major-league debut as his brother Ed's stock was continuing to soar. Also a member of the Phillies, Tom was fortunate to have begun his career as a teammate of his highly respected older sibling, whose watchful eye had to be an encouragement for the green, 22-year-old novitiate as he got his feet wet facing big-league pitchers.

Unfortunately, Tom's success in the majors would not compare with that of his older brother. In three big-league seasons the 5-foot-8 younger Delahanty would play for four different clubs, finishing with a "lifetime" batting average of .239 and zero home runs. Frank Delahanty and, of course, Ed would play more seasons in the major leagues than brothers Tom and Joe, who each completed three campaigns in the circuit. Ironically, Frank was killed in a fall at his home in 1966, 63 years after Ed took his own catastrophic and highly publicized fall.

As Tom's fortunes continued to ebb during the mid- and late 1890s, Ed kept getting better. Between 1894 and 1899 he hit over .400 three times and just under that coveted marker once. In a little more than a decade he had convinced everyone that he might just be one of the greatest major-league hitters of all time, a distinction many believe today.

Delahanty proved that in spades to the amazement of fans on a warm summer day in 1896. Playing against the Chicago White Stockings, later to become the Cubs, he put on a show of hitting prowess that Major League Baseball had only seen once before: at the hands of Bobby Lowe.

On July 13 the Phillies arrived in Chicago, likely by train rather than stage-coach as earlier teams in baseball history had, in the midst of a winless road trip despite a hitting streak by Delahanty that had climbed to 19 games. The team was fighting off a number of key injuries, one of which was Delahanty's recently dislocated shoulder, and the weather that day at West Side Grounds was uncommonly hot—more than 100 heat-related deaths were reported in the Windy City alone on the day of the game.[6] Hurt, hot, and slumping, the odds were stacked against the Phillies as the team opened a series against the White Stockings.

Delahanty was hot too, but in a very different way. Facing veteran curveball artist William "Adonis" Terry, so nicknamed during early baseball's proliferation of curious nicknames because of his box-office looks, Delahanty batted cleanup that afternoon as only an estimated 1,000 fans watched from the stands, a number held down by the sweltering 100°F heat and high humidity. In the top of the first inning, after a walk to Dick Cooley and a sacrifice that moved the runner along, Delahanty came to bat with two out and promptly blasted an outside pitch to deep right field, churning all the way around the bases to score the Phillies' first runs as right fielder Jimmy Ryan ran down the baseball.

Two innings later Delahanty smashed a shot toward shortstop that flattened infielder Bill Dahlen in his tracks and rippled into left field for a single.

Delahanty's third at-bat was almost predictable. With two men on base he hit a bullet that flew over the scoreboard in right field, coming to roost across a nearby street amid a flock of clucking chickens. The home run ball was retrieved by a youngster who fled the scene followed in hot pursuit by a determined Chicago police officer. As far as history records, no arrest was made.

Down 9–6 in the seventh inning, Delahanty came to bat once again with two home runs and a single under his belt. He promptly drilled a fastball over center fielder Billy Lange's head, the ball rolling toward the outfield clubhouse. As Lange ran after the ball and ultimately retrieved it, Delahanty sprinted around the bases like a man being chased for his second inside-the-park home run of the day and his third home run.

By the ninth inning of a long and operose game, with the hometown Cubs leading 9–7, fans were paying little attention to the outcome and only wanted to see Delahanty hit one more time before heading toward the turnstiles. Hit he did, driving a long blast that exploded off his bat and carried some 450 feet over the center-field fence. Those in attendance gave Delahanty a standing ovation after he glided around the bases following his fourth home run of the afternoon, a solo blast that pulled the Phillies to within one run of the Cubs, 9–8. According to one news report, if it hadn't been for Delahanty's hitting exhibition, Chicagoans who witnessed the slugfest would likely have "cursed the day baseball was invented,"[7] a likely reference to the unbearable temperature on that hot July afternoon.

By the time the game ended, Delahanty had achieved something only one other player—Bobby Lowe of the Boston Beaneaters two years earlier—had done in the quarter-century that Major League Baseball had been in existence: slugged four home runs in a game. He had done it in the unlikeliest fashion, with two inside-the-park home runs. Of the 16 other men who eventually would be equal to hitting four home runs in a game, only Delahanty accomplished it with at least one home run that failed to clear the fences, let alone two.

"Today, they came just right," Delahanty said of the pitches he managed to hit for home runs. "Tomorrow, I probably would not get a hit. Those things can't be explained."[8]

Even with his accelerating greatness the newspapers continued to misspell his name, spelling it "Delehanty." The indignity irritated him.

"My name is spelled D-e-l-*a*-h-a-n-t-y," he'd remind them. "I do not think it fair that a man who has won fame as a swatter of shoots and benders (fastballs and curves) should have his name misspelled just because some fellows think it easier to make an *e* than an *a*."[9]

Unfortunately, Delahanty played in a municipality that by then was becoming known as contented with corruption, one ruled by a formidable GOP political web. As a ballplayer living in a community that gave birth to his country, Delahanty sought his own form of personal corruption in a growing metropolitan area that had no shortage of drinking establishments.

Despite the four-home run day and a series of highly productive seasons after 1896, by the turn of the century Delahanty's personal life was beginning to erode, and along with that his professional life. While playing for the lowly Senators, a charter member of the American League, in 1902 and 1903, he began drinking and gambling to excess. Eventually, as his gambling intensified, he began asking fellow ballplayers to help out with his debts and even threatened suicide if they failed to come through with the needed cash. Delahanty was on a downward plunge.

"Next to a base hit, Del likes a straight tip," one sportswriter said of Delahanty. A second scribe ingloriously dubbed him the "ranking chief of the horsey boys."[10]

Despite his mounting woes, as the pressure intensified Delahanty continued to hit the ball with power. In 1902, his final full season in the major leagues, he clubbed 43 doubles to lead the league and knocked in 93 runs, winning the American League batting title with a .376 average. Personal problems aside, Delahanty appeared headed toward another fine season in 1903 and an opportunity to participate in baseball's first-ever World Series.

"A ballplayer's standing is dependent on what he does on the ball field, and I propose to do my best," he said before the season began. "If I have good luck in batting, I'll fare all right."[11]

It was not to be, and Delahanty's personal and professional problems finally came to a head halfway through the 1903 season. Perhaps that shouldn't be surprising, as the 1890s, also known as the Naughty Nineties, were characterized by decadence and social scandal. Broke, binge drinking, out of shape, fussing with management, and caring for a sick wife all at the same time, Delahanty seemed to walk in step with the times, abruptly leaving the team on July 2 headed on a journey that would satisfy his dangerous excesses.

Boarding a train headed for New York, perhaps to discuss possible future employment with Giants manager John McGraw, Delahanty began causing problems, drinking excessively, smoking in prohibited areas, and inadvertently breaking the glass casing that protected a cabinet containing emergency tools. After entering the wrong sleeper berth and causing a kerfuffle among passengers, he was ordered to leave the train at Bridgeburg, Ontario, on the Canadian side of Niagara Falls.

"I don't care whether I'm in Canada or dead," a man believed to be Delahanty was heard to say as he was escorted off the train.[12]

As the train left him behind and sped across a railway bridge over the Niagara River headed for Buffalo, New York, Delahanty reportedly ambled onto the bridge and stood precariously at its edge, a lonely character staring pathetically toward the black water far below. Fearing he might be a smuggler, a night watchman briefly scuffled with the slugger, dragging him to the center of the bridge; however, the watchman stumbled during the altercation and Delahanty ran off. Within minutes, just before 11:00 p.m., Delahanty either fell through an open draw or jumped into the Niagara River 25 feet below. His body was found several miles downstream on July 10, 1903. He was 35 years old.

An article the following morning recounted the tale of Delahanty's tragic death:

> The body of Edward Delahanty [name misspelled even in his obituary], the right fielder of the Washington baseball team of the American League, who fell from the International Bridge last Thursday night, was taken from the river at the lower Niagara gorge today. Relatives of Delahanty arrived here this afternoon and positively identified the body as that of the missing baseball player. Delehanty's body was mangled. One leg was torn off, presumably by the propeller of the Maid of the Mist, near whose landing the body was found.[13]

Perhaps writer Robert Smith explained Delahanty's success in baseball and his tortured final days the best of anyone in a 1903 article. Smith wrote, "Men who met [him] had to admit he was a handsome fellow, although there was an air about him that indicated he was a roughneck at heart and no man to temper with. He had that wide-eyed, half-smiling, ready-for-anything look that is characteristic of a certain type of Irishman. He had a towering impatience too, and a taste for liquor and excitement. He created plenty of excitement for opponents and spectators when he laid his tremendous bat against a pitch."[14]

Services for Delahanty were held at Immaculate Conception Church in Cleveland, and in attendance that day was none other than McGraw; Delahanty was buried at nearby Calvary Cemetery. His grieving family eventually filed suit, seeking $20,000 in damages from the Michigan Central Railway Co.; however, a jury determined that his widow, Norine, and the couple's young daughter should receive only $5,000 in damages—an inglorious sum.

As time passed, life—and baseball—returned to normal. Without their dependable slugger at the helm the Senators finished in last place in the American League, a surprise to no one. Frank Delahanty made his major-league debut two years later and brother Joe two years after that. But neither made the kind of splash that their older sibling had. By 1915, when Frank retired after six seasons in the major leagues, all of the Delahanty brothers were finally out of baseball after almost three decades. As a testament to Ed's greatness, Frank left baseball with a lifetime batting average more than 120 points below that of his troubled sibling, who was long gone but certainly wouldn't be forgotten. In 1945, as the war years ended and almost a half-century after his untimely and controversial demise, Delahanty was inducted into the National Baseball Hall of Fame.

Pitcher Philip "Red" Ehret, who faced Delahanty for seven seasons in the National League, said the big left fielder was the "hardest man in the league for pitchers to puzzle."[15] Sam Crawford, an outfielder/first baseman for 18 seasons, offered a similar tribute, calling Delahanty the "best right-handed hitter I ever saw."[16]

The Chicago White Stockings, who watched with interest as Delahanty scurried around the bases with four home runs, would doubtless have agreed with those assessments. By virtue of his special game against the White Stockings, a rare moment in baseball history when power, fate, and luck converged with the best of all possible results, Delahanty presented one of the finest hitting exhibitions of all time. Today, more than a century later, the memory of that day and his great career lives on in the hallowed Hall of Fame at Cooperstown, New York, where the greatest players the world has known are enshrined. Delahanty's Hall of Fame plaque reads, fittingly, "One of baseball's greatest hitters."

3

LOU GEHRIG

June 3, 1932

For some people, fame is accrued through exemplary deeds or bold actions. Others might utter a simple phrase that is long remembered—perhaps a sentence or two spoken in a moment of deep emotion. The late New York Yankees first baseman Lou Gehrig accomplished both in his abbreviated lifetime: His memorable deeds, most of them performed on the ball field, are well documented and long remembered. And, his lasting words, articulated on one unforgettable day in 1939, are etched in stone. Or, perhaps, hickory.

It was one sentence, uttered calmly through tears as his world—primarily, the Yankees and their ardent fans—looked on in sorrow, that immortalized the great "Iron Horse," engraving his accomplishments on the hearts and minds of baseball fans forever.

"Today I consider myself the luckiest man on the face of the earth," Gehrig spoke into a microphone at Yankee Stadium on July 4, 1939, head bowed as he chewed on a stick of gum between deep breaths that fought back his emotions. Few know what he said or did either before or afterward on that summer day, but almost everyone has heard those 13 words repeated many times on their television sets and radios.

For most people, Gehrig's short peroration continues to reverberate three-quarters of a century after his premature death in the Bronx, New York. Others, most notably the sportswriters and photographers who were assigned to cover his departure from baseball, also felt a keen sense of sadness. "You talk about sadness," the great sportswriter Shirley Povich said in a televised interview a half-century later. "That's the day I saw photographers crying."

Few people suffering from amyotrophic lateral sclerosis (ALS), a progressive neurodegenerative disease that causes patients great suffering and eventually results in a slow and methodical death, would consider themselves lucky under similar circumstances. But Gehrig was a unique individual. Kind, contented, humble, appreciative, and immensely talented, he recognized the blessing of his rich life and was grateful for having been fortunate enough to experience it. Even if he was facing the imminent dégringolade of his prized body and a grim death, he was still able to publicly acknowledge the great fame and overwhelming fortune that had come his way during the 37 years he had lived. Unbeknownst to him, as of that moment he had just two more years—two very challenging years—to live before ALS would slam the lid shut on his incomplete life.

Despite his shyness, Gehrig spoke reassuringly to the 62,000 fans who had packed Yankee Stadium on Lou Gehrig Appreciation Day to both thank him and bid him farewell: "I might've been given a bad break, but I've got an awful lot to live for," he concluded, wiping away tears with a handkerchief before turning to walk away from his position at home plate, where trophies and gifts had been placed to honor him. "Thank-you."

What made his words affecting were his on-field exploits and undeniable adulation, which until then had been lavished upon him as a player. Because Lou Gehrig, perhaps the most feared member of the 1927 Yankees and their acclaimed Murderers' Row, was, to put it unambiguously, a Gehrigian figure. A giant, a legend. A superstar before the word truly entered the lexicon. In light of his accomplishments and the exaltation that came his way he really did have a lot to live for. His words, presented to 62,000 fans, underscored the man's character:

> For the past two weeks you've been reading about a bad break I got. Yet today I consider myself the luckiest man on the face of the earth. I have been in ballparks for 17 years and have never received anything but kindness and encouragement from you fans. Look at these grand men. Which of you wouldn't consider it the highlight of his career just to associate with them for even one day? Sure, I'm lucky. Who wouldn't consider it an honor to have known Jacob Ruppert? Also, the builder of baseball's greatest empire, Ed Barrow? To have spent six years with that wonderful little fellow, Miller Huggins? Then to have spent the next nine years with that outstanding leader, that smart student of psychology, the best manager in baseball today, Joe McCarthy? Sure, I'm lucky. When the New York Giants, a team you would give your right arm to beat, and vice versa, send you a gift, that's something. When everybody down to the groundskeepers and those boys in white coats remembers you with trophies, that's something. When you have a wonderful mother-in-law who takes sides with you in squabbles with her

Lou Gehrig. *Harris & Ewing Collection*
(Library of Congress)

own daughter, that's something. When you have a father and a mother who work all their lives so you can have an education and build your body, it's a blessing. When you have a wife who has been a tower of strength and shown more courage than you dreamed existed—that's the finest I know. So, I close in saying that I might have been given a bad break, but I've got an awful lot to live for.

Consider what he accomplished during those 17 years that Gehrig wore Yankee pinstripes. Between his rookie season in 1923 and his final season in 1939, Gehrig slugged 493 home runs, drove in 1,995 runners, scored 1,888 runs, and finished his career with a lifetime batting average of .340. He also was awarded two American League Most Valuable Player Awards, won a batting title, and earned a Triple Crown. He was named to the All-Star Team seven times (it would have been more if the All-Star Game had been in existence prior to 1933) and hit more grand slam home runs (23) than anyone in baseball history.

During the course of his long and brilliant career, Gehrig led the league at various times in hits, doubles, triples, home runs, RBI, and numerous other offensive categories. He was truly a great player, someone so talented at hitting baseballs that even in his final illness-shortened season and the early stages of his debilitating disease, when it clearly was affecting his ability to strike a baseball, Gehrig managed to slap four hits and drive in a run before calling it quits. What's more, he struck out only once in 28 at-bats during that last fateful season, when he batted just .142.

Gehrig rose to baseball prominence in the toughest of times, especially during the 1930s. The Wall Street crash of 1929 had roiled the economy, and a Great Depression would settle in from coast to coast and throughout the world. In the West, winds of tremendous force would create a Dust Bowl of awe-inspiring proportions. And a different kind of force—Nazism—would lead the world toward a war of massive and widespread implications before the decade was over. Baseball, it seems, was a timely diversion for a country facing unrest.

Through it all, baseball was king. With his career winding down, Babe Ruth would nonetheless hit almost 200 homers during the shortened decade. And other Yankee future greats were beginning to make a stir, men like Joe DiMaggio and Bill Dickey.

Of all the statistics that Gehrig managed to amass for the greatest of all baseball organizations, perhaps two resonate above all others. The first is his mark of 2,130 consecutive games played, a streak that stood for 56 years until Cal Ripken broke it in 1995. The second is one that most fans probably aren't even aware that he accomplished. On June 3, 1932, playing against the Philadelphia Athletics at Shibe Park in the City of Brotherly Love, Gehrig was anything but brotherly, slugging four home runs in a single game to become the first person ever to achieve that in baseball's modern era. Almost as if attempting to delineate himself from Ed Delahanty and Bobby Lowe, the two men who had accomplished the same thing before him, Gehrig narrowly missed a fifth home run when a towering blast was caught at the wall in the deepest part of cavernous center field. There would be no "five" on that day—four would have to suffice for the soft spoken, likable, always optimistic Lou Gehrig.

Said Brooklyn Dodgers first baseman Gil Hodges, who duplicated the four home runs feat many years later on August 31, 1950, "Gehrig had one advantage over me. He was a better ballplayer."[1]

Gehrig might argue the point—it would have been well within his nature to diminish his own accomplishments in order to elevate those of another player. Of all the ballplayers in the history of the sport, few were as talented yet humble as Larrupin' Lou, who by virtue of both his numerous on-field accomplishments and his death at such an early age—he was only 37—emerged as a true American hero, one who in death may loom even larger than he had before his life ended on June 2, 1941. In death, in a mere heartbeat, Gehrig soared from superstar to legend.

Henry Louis Gehrig was born Ludwig Heinrich Gehrig on June 19, 1903, in the Yorkville section of Manhattan to Heinrich and Christina Gehrig, German immigrants who had moved to the area only a few years before their son was born. From the outset the couple strove to make sure the boy succeeded in life, although as an immigrant the elder Heinrich struggled to find work as a sheet metal worker. That, coupled with his chronic poor health and tendency to drink, made things difficult for the Gehrig family, and Christina soon took on odd jobs, including house cleaning, laundering, and cooking for wealthy New York residents in an effort to help make ends meet. Although beset by other hardships along the way, including the childhood deaths of Gehrig's two sisters, Anna and Sophie Louise, and an unnamed infant brother, the working-class family somehow managed to scrape by.

While her husband struggled at times, Christina was intent that young Louis should receive an education, and he did just that. As a young man Gehrig excelled in sports, especially football and baseball, after enrolling at Commerce High School in 1917. He at first refused to play on the high school baseball team because he was shy about appearing in front of crowds; however, with prodding from his coach the young man finally relented, landing at first base after demonstrating clumsiness in the outfield and control issues as a pitcher.

Despite those early shortcomings it was in high school that people first started taking notice of the young man's ability to play, and Gehrig eventually blipped onto the radar screen of the New York Giants, who offered him a try-out that he ultimately failed despite hitting six consecutive home runs. He was dispirited, but the indomitable Gehrig soon recovered.

Baseball aside, at least for the moment, Gehrig enrolled at Columbia University in 1921 with a football scholarship. His goal at that time? Rather than play football or baseball professionally he wanted to become an engineer.

As a freshman Gehrig played fullback, performing well enough. He continued playing football during his sophomore year at college, and in the spring of 1923 he joined the college baseball team as a first baseman/pitcher, once striking out 17 players in a single game and earning the nickname "Columbia Lou." Gehrig was so good in college that he drew the attention of a Yankees scout, and in April 1923 he signed his first professional baseball contract. For nothing more than signing his name Gehrig received a hefty $1,500 bonus from the Bronx Bombers—big money at that time and his family's ticket out of Manhattan to the New York suburbs. At last Gehrig was on a path to greatness.

After signing the Yankees contract Gehrig withdrew from Columbia in 1923 and joined a minor-league team in Hartford, Connecticut, which played in the Eastern League. It was there that he hit a respectable .304 during his one and only season of minor-league ball—good enough to earn him a one-way ticket to the majors.

"We were mighty short on infielders in those days," Gehrig said years later with typical modestly.[2]

His early seasons in the majors were dispiriting ones, even though his numbers—what numbers he had—were good. During his first season with the Yankees Gehrig was primarily used as a pinch-hitter, and he performed notably, hitting at a solid .423 clip with one home run in 29 at-bats. His reward was even fewer at-bats the next season when he hit .500—6-for-12—in 1924. While his offense had been limited to just 41 at-bats during his first two campaigns with the Yankees, the following year—1925—his name would for the first time enter the conversation for Most Valuable Player.

For Gehrig, everything seemed to be happening at full throttle: a brief stint at the Ivy League's Columbia University, an even shorter period with the Hartford Senators minor-league team, and a brief learning curve with the New York Yankees, every player's dream, before settling in as a star playing alongside the likes of Babe Ruth, Bob Meusel, Earl Combs, Herb Pennock, and Waite Hoyt. During the next few years, Gehrig would continue to progress as both a player and a person, and by 1927 he was recognized as a feared member of the elite Murderers' Row and an instrumental player on one of the greatest teams the sport has ever known.

In 1925, his first season as a regular position player, Gehrig hit a reassuring .295 with 29 runs and 68 RBI. After that there was no stopping the big Bronx slugger: He hit .313 with 16 home runs in 1926; .373 with 47 home runs in his 1927 MVP season; .374 with 27 home runs in 1928; .300 with 35 home runs in 1929; .379 with 41 home runs in 1930; and .341 with 46 home runs in 1931.

"Irrespective of any other players on our club, I am the man to whom the team looks as a pacesetter," he said. "Every year I am told I am the hitter who must lead the Yankees to the pennant. That suits me fine."[3]

Perhaps his greatest individual accomplishment occurred in 1932, the season when Gehrig—sports columnist Jim Murray once called him a "symbol of indestructibility, a Gibraltar in cleats"—notched the finest game of his brilliant career.[4] As if he needed it, the game, a 20–13 drubbing of the Athletics in front of their home fans, would embed him forever as one of the finest ballplayers who ever played the game.

Shibe Park in North Philadelphia was designed by the Athletics' primary owner, Ben Shibe, and his longtime and legendary manager, Connie Mack. Completed for a cost of about $300,000, the ballpark opened for business in 1909 when Lou Gehrig and the World Series he would eventually come to dominate were just six years old. Almost immediately Shibe Park was recognized as a template for the next generation of major-league ballparks. Seating 23,000 fans, the stadium was entirely built of steel and concrete and boasted an elaborate front entrance and a double-deck grandstand with walls that sported a French Renaissance portico comprised of brick and featuring arches.

The ballpark dimensions also were imposing: 378 feet from home plate to the left-field bleachers, 340 feet to the right-field fence, and an incredible 515 feet to straightaway center field,[5] where baseballs went to die. Those who saw the vast territory between right and left field might have correctly assumed that an airplane would be needed to carry a ball over the center-field fence, something Gehrig nearly achieved without the extra air power during that one-game home run derby of 1932.

Batting against starter George Earnshaw, a veteran who had won 20 or more games in three of his first four seasons in the big leagues, Gehrig came to bat in the first inning with a man on base and promptly drilled a ball over the left-center-field fence for a two-run home run. Just like that—Yankees two, Athletics nothing.

Philadelphia tied the score in the bottom half of the first, then held the Yankees scoreless until Gehrig came to bat again in the top of the fourth inning. Again facing the 6-foot-4, 210-pound right-hander, who earned the nickname "Moose" with his sturdy build, Gehrig hit another long drive, this time clearing the right-field wall for his second home run of the afternoon.

While Gehrig appeared to have Earnshaw's number, the Athletics meanwhile were pounding away at Yankees starting pitcher Johnny Allen, leading 8–4 after four innings. Then Gehrig came to bat in the top of the fifth with a chance to turn things around, facing Earnshaw for the third time. Gehrig welcomed the opportunity, lashing another shot that cleared the left-field fence; when the dust settled the Yankees had closed the gap to 8–7 and Earnshaw was headed for the showers. His line score that day included five innings pitched and three home runs surrendered to the great Lou Gehrig.

The Yankees continued battling, scoring two more runs in the sixth inning but still trailing the Athletics, 10–9, when the seventh inning rolled around. By then the crowd was aware that something historic might be unfolding, and coming to bat was the reason for that notion: Lou Gehrig, this time facing reliever Rube Walberg, a 10-year veteran who would win 155 games before his career would end. Gehrig wasted little time welcoming the big left-hander in the vein of his predecessor Earnshaw, notching his fourth home run of the contest, a solo shot over the right-field wall, putting him in the record books as having tied the American League mark for total bases in a major-league game with 16.

Prior to the home run, manager Connie Mack had ordered Earnshaw to sit next to him on the bench as reliever Walberg attempted to shut down the red-hot Gehrig, perhaps hoping the youngster would learn a thing or two from his more experienced relief pitcher. While Walberg had no more luck than Earnshaw getting Gehrig out, he did force the slugger to hit the ball to a different part of the ballpark.

"I see," Earnshaw sarcastically said to Mack. "Made him change direction."[6]

Four at-bats, four home runs. Gehrig wasn't through, however, not by—figuratively speaking—a long shot. After grounding out in the eighth inning the big first baseman had one more chance to achieve something no one else had been able to do: hit five home runs in a major-league game. Facing Ed Rommel, the Athletics' fifth pitcher, Gehrig rose to the occasion and hit his hardest ball of the afternoon, driving a shot to the deepest part of center field where future Hall of Famer Al Simmons caught it at the wall.

After a true donnybrook the Yankees had won the battle 20–13, led by Gehrig's four-homer attack. When the game finally ended, Gehrig's teammates razzed him about costing the league a bundle of cash by hitting four balls where they couldn't be retrieved for reuse, an apparent Depression era no-no. As always, Gehrig responded modestly. After the game he hugged the great Babe Ruth, under whose shadow he had labored for a good portion of his brilliant career.

"There will never be another guy like the Babe," Gehrig said. "I get more kick from seeing him hit one than I do from hitting one myself."[7]

After his one-man show Gehrig played another seven seasons before hanging up his spikes, all but the final one offensively successful. During that multiyear stretch he led the league twice in home runs and once in RBI, and he won a second batting title in 1936—three years before he abruptly retired from the game.

"I am a slave to baseball and only because I really love the game," he said. "[I] hate to think of taking even one day away when we are playing."[8]

Soon he would take many days away. His final illness-shortened season aside, when unbeknownst to him a menacing disease was already racing to take its toll, Gehrig slugged 32 doubles in 1938 to go along with six triples and 29 home runs, driving in 114 runs and batting .295—an outstanding season by any measure. But the next season would be something far different altogether.

Like bankruptcy, which writer Ernest Hemingway described as something that occurs gradually, then suddenly, so ALS struck down Gehrig, gradually at first and then suddenly and with a vengeance. Finally, after voluntarily ending his own consecutive games streak on May 2, 1939, and removing himself from the Yankees lineup for the first time in more than 13 years, Gehrig was through—he never played again.

"Joe, I'm out of the lineup," Gehrig told Yankees manager Joe McCarthy. "I'm just not doing the team any good."[9]

"I haven't been a bit of good to the team since the season started," Gehrig was also reported as having said. "It would not be fair to the boys, to [McCarthy], or to the baseball public for me to try going on. In fact, it would not be fair to myself."[10]

The Yankees announced his retirement the following month and Gehrig entered an endless maze of doctor appointments, hospital tests, and honorary appointments to jobs he'd be unable to fulfill. Finally, on a spring day in 1941, Lou Gehrig passed to the ages. Services were held at Christ Episcopal Church in the Bronx and Gehrig was buried in Kensico Cemetery in Valhalla, New York. Honorary pallbearers that day included Yankees manager Joe McCarthy, catcher Bill Dickey, and famed dancer Bill "Bojangles" Robinson.

In its story announcing his death, one writer said Gehrig died at 10:10 p.m. at the slugger's home, 5204 Delafield Avenue in the Bronx. The article described him as a man believed by some to have been the greatest player ever but someone whose career was cut short by a type of chronic paralysis that left Gehrig homebound during his final month of life, a time when his weight continued to drop and, for the final two weeks, he was confined to bed. Gehrig, the newspaper reported, lost consciousness just before he died with his wife and parents at his bedside.[11]

In the weeks before he died, the rapidly failing Gehrig had spent countless hours seated at home in an easy chair next to his front window, gazing out at the street and wondering. Up until the end one of his most prized possessions was a trophy with a bronze baseball at the top given to him by his teammates; each of their names was etched on the front. Also inscribed was a poem written by pallbearer John Kieran. While the trophy cost about five dollars, Gehrig cherished it more so than many of his other possessions. The inscription reads,

> We've been to the wars together, we took our foes as they came,
> And always you were the leader, and ever you played the game.
> Idol of cheering millions, records are yours by sheaves,
> Iron of frame they hailed you, decked you with laurel leaves.
> But higher than that we hold you, we who have known you best,
> Knowing the way you came through . . . every human test.
> Let this be a silent token . . . of lasting friendship's gleam,
> And all that we've left unspoken—your pals of the Yankees team.[12]

One of those teammates, the hard-living Ruth, paid Gehrig an understated tribute: "I never knew a fellow who lived a cleaner life. He was a clean-living boy, a good baseball player, a great hustler. He was just a grand guy."[13]

Before he died, Gehrig paid Ruth the ultimate compliment. "I'm not a headline guy," he said, adding,

> I always knew that as long as I was following Babe to the plate I could have gone up there and stood on my head. No one would have noticed the difference. When the Babe was through swinging, whether he hit one or fanned, nobody paid any attention to the next hitter. They all were talking about what the Babe had done.[14]

In the seven decades since his death, 15 men have matched Gehrig's single-game mark of four home runs in a game. Few came closer than he to hitting a fifth home run, something the slugger certainly would have accomplished had the game been played in a ballpark with slightly more normalized dimensions. In the end it didn't matter—four home runs or five, Gehrig would have been the same old Biscuit Pants, a man to whom records were of secondary importance when stood against the people he met and interacted with along the road of life.

Perhaps as a testament to Gehrig's searing modesty the headstone on his grave lists nothing of his baseball accomplishments nor the kind of man he was—just his name, an incorrect date of birth, and the year that he died. However, as a fitting tribute to an early member of the Four Home Runs Club, visitors regularly place bats, balls, and caps at the base of his grave marker.

4

CHUCK KLEIN

July 10, 1936

What he lacks in name familiarity, slugger Chuck Klein of the Philadelphia Phillies more than made up for on July 10, 1936, when he single-handedly demolished the Pittsburgh Pirates, 9–6, at the Bucs' Forbes Field. His brilliant performance, including six RBI in five at-bats, expanded membership in the Four Home Runs Club from three players to four, gave the National League a 3–1 membership edge, presented the Phillies with their second affiliate of the coveted fraternity and a 50 percent stake, and more than assured everyone that Klein (the National League's Most Valuable Player in 1932) would never be forgotten.

Certainly, winning an MVP Award, while prestigious in itself, gives no assurance of lasting remembrance. Phil Cavarretta of the Chicago Cubs won the award in 1945, although he failed to make the All-Star Team that same season—perhaps a reflection of his unremarkable numbers the previous year and his even less remarkable statistics during almost every season prior to that one. Little known Jim Konstanty won an MVP Award for the Philadelphia Phillies five years later, in 1950, the only year in 11 seasons that he made the All-Star Team.

In the American League, Jackie Jensen of the Boston Red Sox, hardly a household name, was named MVP in 1958, only his third—and final—year as an All-Star. And what about Bobby Shantz, who as a pitcher was named MVP for the Philadelphia Athletics in 1952? Hardly anyone except, perhaps, those who cheered them on during their heydays, remembers much about those MVP winners.

Counterpose that with others. Yankees ironman Lou Gehrig won two MVP Awards *and* hit four homers in a game to become the only American League

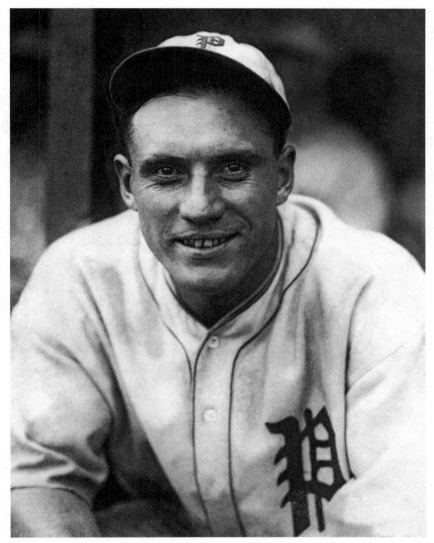

Chuck Klein. *National Baseball Hall of Fame*

player in the club through the date of Klein's 1936 enshrinement and is still revered. Willie Mays of the New York and San Francisco Giants posted similar accomplishments, rising to the occasion to slug four home runs in a ballgame in 1961—seven seasons after his first MVP Award and four seasons before his second and final one. More than a half-century after Mays accomplished the four-home run feat and eighty years after Gehrig did it, everyone still remembers the duo, even those who weren't around when they were busting down fences with their mighty blasts.

Klein hit a few mighty shots himself before hanging up his cleats. During a 17-year career that ended in 1944, he hit 300 home runs, drove in 1,201 runners, and finished with a lifetime batting average of .320. Not bad for a guy whose blue-collar forename—Chuck—is as bland as white bread.

Throughout the years he also kept good company. Of all the players who recorded 100 or more extra-base hits in a season, Klein is tied for third with Barry Bonds, at 107—something he accomplished in 1930 and a historical position that follows behind the likes of Babe Ruth (119) and Gehrig (117). Ranking behind Klein in single-season RBI production are a Who's Who of baseball luminaries, including Stan Musial and Hank Greenberg (103), Rogers Hornsby (102), and Jimmie Foxx (100). Klein is the only player ranking among the top 10 twice, as he also smacked 103 extra-base hits in 1932 to tie Greenberg and Musial.

Finally, only a handful of players have batted .350, driven in at least 150 runners, and hit 40 or more home runs in the same season. Klein is one of them. Also on that list are Ruth, Gehrig, Foxx, Hornsby, and Hack Wilson.

As a testament to the curiosity that is Chuck Klein, in 2009 the website Listverse credited his 1930 season as the fourth-best campaign in major-league history, behind those of Albert Pujols (2003), Joe DiMaggio (1937), and Stan Musial (1948). Justifiably so. During that heroic season he batted .386, hit 40 home runs, drove in 170 runners, hit safely 250 times (including 59 doubles), and scored 158 runs en route to posting an astronomical .687 slugging percentage. Still, separate evaluations by other organizations fail to list any of his individual seasons among baseball's top 50, a slight that can only be explained by his relative anonymity.

Instead, to this day, some 60 years after his death, Klein is most remembered for his four-home run game, and the perpetual asterisk beside his name is a stark reminder that he'll never entirely be forgotten. Not so long as membership in the Four Home Runs Club remains a baseball rarity of the highest order.

Charles Herbert Klein was born on October 7, 1904, in Indianapolis, Indiana. His parents were Frank and Margaret Klein, immigrant farmers who had come to the United States just as the nineteenth century was coming to an end. Like many immigrants, Klein's father worked hard at what he did—farming—and he became successful on several fronts. He not only owned a small corn farm near the state capital, but also worked as a deputy sheriff.

At the age of six Klein entered grade school, but his interest in studying was hampered by a fascination with other things, namely baseball. "I avoided as much work as possible in the classroom but did all the work possible on the ball field," he once told an interviewer.[1]

By his own admission Klein was a committed loafer, at least where school was concerned. "I worked on a farm. [I] played ball and loafed along the fishing and swimming holes of the White River, and my boyhood was not a lot different from that of other youngsters," he said.[2]

His efforts on the baseball diamond paid off, although that wouldn't happen for years. Klein enrolled at Southport High School in 1919 and was quickly acknowledged as the finest ballplayer on campus. By 1920 he had become an outstanding pitcher and a sturdy, dependable hitter, and although the local media recognized his abilities, scouts in the area were either oblivious or disinterested.

It was after high school that his lack of diligence in the classroom really began to hold Klein back. Unable to attend college, in part because of his mediocre performance in the classroom, Klein worked on a highway road crew and later at a steel mill, where he toned his muscles hefting hot steel into burning ovens six days a week. He later attributed his great strength to the back-breaking labor he performed at the mill day in and day out during the 1920s.

"There is one thing I can say about working in a steel mill," he told an interviewer. "If it does not kill you it will make a man out of you."[3]

Shortly after joining the mill, Klein was asked to play baseball for a nearby semipro team, and he competed after work and on weekends for the next several years. By then he had filled out his frame at six feet and slightly more than 185 pounds, his official baseball playing weight as a major leaguer.

It was not until 1927, when the fabled New York Yankees were running roughshod over the American League, that Klein was discovered for keeps. Prohibition was in play and an enforcement agent recommended him to the minor league Evansville Hubs. Things took off.

From there Klein joined the Central League's Fort Wayne Chiefs, earning weekly remuneration of $200, and he turned into a solid slugger. He was so good that the Philadelphia Phillies, recognizing his skills, bought out his contract following the team's 100-loss season, and Klein was heralded—although in whispered tones—as a possible savior for the struggling franchise.

"They tell me you can hit," forgettable manager Burt Shotton told Klein as the rookie reported for duty. "God knows we need hitters. We need everything."[4]

Although he couldn't offer the Phillies "everything," Klein could offer them a solid bat, which he did for most of 17 years.

The match—Philadelphia and Chuck Klein—seemed a good one from the start, although the City of Brotherly Love from the 1920s through the 1940s was not all that its name implied. Organized crime was vigorous during the period, with racketeers specializing in bootleg liquor, drugs, and prostitution; however, legitimate business also flourished—major corporations serving the area included Bethlehem Iron Company and the Philadelphia, Baltimore, and Washington Railroad.

Shotton inserted Klein into the starting lineup on the second day he was with the club, and during the 1928 season the young man responded by smacking 11 home runs, driving in 34 runs, and hitting .360 in fewer than 300 at-bats.

The following season Klein kept up the pace, hitting 43 home runs, driving in 145 runs, and batting .356. He followed that up by hitting .386 in 1930, .337 in 1931, .348 in 1932 (an MVP season), .368 in 1933 (winning a batting title and finishing second in the battle for MVP), and .301 in 1934 (earning his second and final All-Star Game appearance) before taking his foot off the pedal and hitting .293 in 1935—an average that most players would find more than satisfactory.

"One of the reasons I've been able to play baseball well is because it's fun for me," Klein said. "Many players find it work."[5]

Although Klein's best work was behind him, he had one more rabbit under his hat. On July 10, 1936, that rabbit would scurry around the bases after hitting baseballs out of the ballpark four times in one game for only the fourth time since major-league baseball began.

After six seasons in Philadelphia, the last two finishing first and second in National League MVP balloting, respectively, Klein was traded to the Chicago Cubs prior to the 1934 campaign, earning a place on the All-Star team despite suffering a pulled muscle that would hamper him throughout the next two seasons.

"When I joined the Cubs [in 1934] I started out doing good work," he said, continuing,

I thought I was set for one of my best years, but . . . while I was running the bases, I tore a muscle loose [on] the back of one of my legs. It bothered me, but I stayed on my feet for some time until I discovered that I was making a bad matter worse. Without any hesitation I'll say that my disappointing work in 1934 was mainly due to my leg. It hurt me in 1935, too.[6]

After leading the Cubs to the World Series in 1935 while suffering with the painful leg injury, his drinking became a problem and Klein was traded back to

Philadelphia on May 21, 1936. Before returning to the Phillies, however, he got married in Chicago, then continued on to his new baseball home.

Playing at Forbes Field in Pittsburgh, Klein's first at-bat in the game of his career came in the top of the opening inning with leadoff hitter Ernie Sulik and left fielder Johnny Moore on base. Klein greeted starting pitcher Jim Weaver with a blast that cleared the right-field fence for his first home run of the game. The Phillies added another run and just like that they led the Pirates, 4–0—an advantage they wouldn't relinquish until the ninth inning.

After that the offense largely rested on Klein's shoulders. In the second inning his second drive of the game sent right fielder Paul Waner to the wall as he reeled in the ball, the only time Weaver and relief pitchers Mace Brown and Bill Swift would get Klein out that day. Three innings later, in the top of the fifth, Klein greeted Weaver one last time by again drilling a pitch over Waner's head and into the right-field bleachers. His second solo blast of the game put the Phillies ahead 5–1 after five innings, but Klein was just starting to break a sweat.

Facing reliever Brown in the seventh inning, Klein again went deep to right, where he kept Waner busy throughout the game. His third homer of the contest put the Phillies up 6–4.

Through nine innings Klein had been almost perfect, belting three home runs and sending a long fly to right field that was caught for an out at the wall. But he had one more opportunity left to tie the single-game major-league home run record.

In the 10th inning Bill Swift, a right-hander whose lifetime earned run average was less than 4, was brought in to relieve Brown and try to keep the Phillies in check. He was met by leadoff hitter Klein, who smashed his fourth home of the game—where else?—over Waner's head and into the right-field stands. Although the Phillies scored two more runs before the dust had settled, Klein's home run proved to be the game winner. He finished the day with a three-run homer in addition to three solo home runs and a long fly ball that almost left the ballpark. Only the slightest of breezes blowing out toward right field might have put Klein in the record books alone with five home runs.

Klein's line score that day was ferocious: 5 at-bats, 4 home runs, 4 runs scored, and 6 runs batted in. He had entered the game with 10 home runs on the season, and by the time the game was finished Klein had increased that total by almost half. It was clearly one of his finest hours in a baseball career filled with many outstanding performances.

"The $100,000 folly of the Chicago Cubs, Charles [Chuck] Klein, today stole a bit of the spotlight that was his back in 1932 and '33 when he was the most feared batsman in the National League," wrote one scribe. "Smashing out four home runs against Pittsburgh, Chuck not only won a ballgame for the

Phillies yesterday, but he accomplished a feat that only one man in modern baseball has equaled"—Lou Gehrig.[7]

What made Klein's accomplishment all the more spectacular was that it occurred at Forbes Field, a spacious ballpark that had opened in 1909 with a distance to right field and deepest center field of 376 feet and 462 feet, respectively. It was hardly considered a home run hitters ballpark, and Klein's triumph that day laid to rest the notion that much of his success hitting home runs throughout the years had been due to the small ballpark the Phillies called home. National League Park, commonly known as Baker Bowl in honor of one-time Phillies owner William F. Baker, had a right-field fence that stood only 280 feet from home plate. In the down-and-dirty parlance of the day, hitters could almost spit from the batter's box to the bleachers.

At that point Klein's career was on the downslide. Although he played eight more seasons in the major leagues, all of them with the Phillies, he hit only 55 more home runs after 1936 compared with 245 during the first half of his career. He would hit above .300 just twice more and his biggest RBI season after the four-home run barrage of 1936 was 57 the following season.

Klein retired from baseball in 1944 with a laundry list of offensive accomplishments. In addition to his better-known achievements as a hitter, he had led the league in home runs during his first full season in the majors, won the Triple Crown in 1933, and still holds the modern major-league record for assists by a right fielder with 44. Perhaps most extraordinary, at almost 32 years of age Klein became the oldest player to hit four home runs in a major-league game.

After his retirement from baseball Klein operated a modest bar near Philadelphia. He began drinking heavily, which, in time, affected his overall health and sent him into a gradual tailspin. Eventually, a central nervous system disorder apparently exacerbated by alcohol overtook the slugger and left him partially incapacitated, and in 1947 he left the bar behind and returned to his hometown, Indianapolis, to live with relatives. Sadly, he never fully recovered, surviving 11 more years before succumbing to a brain hemorrhage in 1958.

Klein was laid to rest at St. Joseph's Cemetery in Indianapolis. His uniform was retired by the Phillies on August 6, 2001, 43 years after his passing. Wrote one correspondent,

> Funeral services will be held Tuesday for Charles H. [Chuck] Klein, who left his native Indianapolis 31 years ago to become one of baseball's greatest sluggers and returned home to die in virtual obscurity. Klein, 52, was found dead by his sister-in-law, Mrs. Edward Klein, Friday in the bathroom of her home, where he had lived since he returned to Indianapolis as a semiinvalid in 1947. Dr. E. F. Boggs

diagnosed the cause of death as leakage at the base of Klein's brain, possibly trace-able to heavy drinking.[8]

Despite overt career offensive numbers, Klein's election to the Hall of Fame was anything but certain. In 1948, his first year of eligibility, just 2.5 percent of sportswriters voted for his election, a number that climbed to 28 percent in 1964—not even close to the 75 percent required for induction. Then, the tide began to turn. After a Philadelphia school teacher began a letter-writing campaign aimed at members of the Hall of Fame's Veterans Committee, Klein's name appeared on an all-time baseball team selected by President Richard Nixon. The double whammy worked its charm. Letters continued pouring in, and on March 12, 1980—22 years after his death—Klein was elected to the Baseball Hall of Fame. One person who appreciated Klein for more than just his bat was Hall of Fame second baseman Billy Herman, himself a 10-time All-Star.

"Chuck was a real nice guy and strong—very, very strong," said Herman. "And, a hell of a competitor."[9]

5

PAT SEEREY

July 18, 1948

If excess pounds were home runs, Pat Seerey might have won election to the National Baseball Hall of Fame years ago.

Unfortunately, to a ballplayer excess pounds are excess baggage, while home runs are, well, home runs—a slugger's bread and butter. The two are mutually incompatible—unless, of course, Babe Ruth is in the room.

Seerey, nicknamed "Fat Pat," might disagree. In the six full seasons that he played in the major leagues, his home runs counted for a lot. In fact, while sparse in their totality, a handful did put him in the record book while ensuring his rightful place among some of the greatest home run hitters of all time.

Although Scooter Gennett has hit the fewest number of career home runs of any player in the Four Home Runs Club, Seerey's overall statistics are even less substantial. In fact, Seerey, who was anything but a household name during his short major-league career, may have been fortunate to last as long as he did in the big leagues, given his propensity to strike out and inability to hit for average. In the seasons that he played—a little more than five years with the Cleveland Indians and roughly a season with the Chicago White Sox—Seerey hit only 86 home runs, knocked in a meager 262 runs, and netted only 406 total hits en route to posting a lifetime batting average of just .224. The only category he ever led the league in was strikeouts, and to his discredit he accomplished that unenviable achievement four times during his six-plus-year career: between 1944 and 1946 and again in 1948, the year of his four-home run onslaught. If anything good could be said of his strikeouts, at least they didn't preclude Seerey from completing one of the great offensive gems in baseball history.

Despite his offensive shortcomings, Seerey's name is inscribed forever along-side those of baseball immortals Lou Gehrig, Willie Mays, Mike Schmidt, and the 14 other players who were good enough, or perhaps fortunate enough, to hit four home runs in a single game. In fact, the muscular parvenu almost accomplished the feat twice. Perhaps that's why at only 5-foot-9 Seerey, in one

Pat Seerey. *Courtesy of Dennis Seerey*

way, stands above most of the other players in the Four Home Runs Club. His minimal stature was certainly no handicap.

For Seerey, his first 15 minutes of fame occurred on July 13, 1945, just weeks before the end of World War II and as players were beginning to think about returning to the ball field from the battlefield. On that day he blasted three home runs—including a grand slam—and a triple, driving in eight runs in a 16–4 victory over the New York Yankees at Yankee Stadium. Then on July 18, 1948, almost three years to the day after that, Seerey again made headlines with four monumental clouts that cleared the fences at Shibe Park in Philadelphia. Seerey and Hall of Famer Willie Mays both collected 31 total bases in two combined ballgames.

That he made the major leagues at all and even had an opportunity to hit four home runs in a ballgame may have been due to a quirk of timing or perhaps even fate: Seerey rose through the minor-league ranks just as World War II was shifting into high gear, and as players continued drifting from the big leagues to the shores of distant lands, the likable Seerey, classified 4-F by his local draft board, remained behind to help fill the void created by major leaguers who were serving their country. His tenure in the majors lasted from 1943 to early 1949, just long enough to cover a good portion of the war and the few seasons that followed, a postwar period when the game was refilling its ranks. While devastating to much of the world, the war was good to at least one person: Pat Seerey of the Cleveland Indians and Chicago White Sox. In return Seerey was good for the game of baseball—unforgettably good, at least for two very high-octane games.

Born James Patrick Seerey in Wilburton, Oklahoma, Seerey entered the post–World War I universe, appropriately, on St. Patrick's Day, March 17, 1923, the son of James and Marie Seerey. The family—his father was a railroad baggage worker—eventually relocated to Arkansas, where the boy graduated from parochial high school following a high-visibility prep football career. Still, baseball for Seerey eclipsed the bruising pigskin game, and he pursued his newfound sporting love with commitment and passion.

"Sure, I played football," he once said. "For four years I was the big, crashing fullback . . . I wasn't a speed demon, but I'm not as slow as you might think."[1]

In the early 1940s, when Seerey was in high school, players with budding talent often found their way to the American Legion circuit, and the young man was no exception. It was there that a Cleveland Indians scout noticed his ability sometime after graduation from high school in 1941, and he eagerly signed the 5-foot-9, 220-pound bulldog to a minor-league contract.

Seerey was assigned to play for the Appleton Papermakers of the Wisconsin State League, where he hit an unanticipated .330 with 31 home runs. After earning a "look" during spring training with Cleveland in 1942, Seerey was sent to the Indians's Cedar Rapids team in the Three-I League, where he hit 33 more home runs and batted .303 for the Raiders. The following season he was rewarded when the Indians called him up to the big club from the Wilkes-Barre Barons, and he hit .222 with one home run in 26 games—an inauspicious start for the wide-eyed young man, someone who did not see a big-league ballpark until he signed with Cleveland. Even then, in his folksy manner, Seerey compared Cleveland Stadium's vast size with a southern cow pasture.

"I never saw a major-league park in my life until I joined the Indians," he said. "The stadium looked as big as a cow pasture in Arkansas."[2]

Seerey's sparse numbers and country metaphors aside, the 1943 season proved to be a stepping-stone to greater things. In 1944 he was thrust into Cleveland's starting lineup for the long term, playing various outfield positions, although left field became his preference—not only as a fielder, but also offensively: The home runs he hit often were sent flying in the general direction of the beckoning left-field bleachers.

As his athletic stock matured during the years that followed, Seerey earned a couple of nicknames from sportswriters and ballplayers, including "The People's Choice" and "Fat Pat," due to his ample girth.

"I like to eat when I'm hungry," he once explained. "I don't do much eating between meals. An average breakfast, a fair lunch, and a hell of a big dinner to keep me going."[3]

With his sturdy build, vast strength, and eagerness to swing for the fences, Seerey demonstrated significant potential to become a leading home run hitter for the Indians long into the future; however, he never fully realized that potential— except, perhaps, on one day in 1948 soon after after he was traded in midseason from Cleveland to the White Sox, when one-fifth of the home runs he would hit that year rained down during one stellar performance, a 12–11 extra-inning, nail-biting victory against the Connie Mack-managed Philadelphia Athletics.

At the time, with the war recently over, the trade seemed to favor the White Sox. The crosstown Cubs had not won a World Series since 1908, and for the Sox it had been almost as long: 31 seasons. During the trade year, 1948, the *Chicago Daily Sun and Times* sprang from a merger, forming what eventually would become the *Chicago Sun-Times*. With a little luck Seerey and his formidable bat swing might lead the White Sox to a world championship, and a fresh and sizable newspaper outlet would be eager to tell the story of which Chicago team was the better one: the Cubs or the Sox.

Shibe Park in Philadelphia, where Lou Gehrig had joined the Four Home Runs Club 16 years earlier, was vast and spacious, and anything but a hitters ballpark during the 61 years that it served Major League Baseball. On July 18, 1948, in the final months of his last full season, dimensions apparently meant little to the stocky, right-handed Seerey, who pummeled the double-deck left-field bleachers, as well as the roof that sat atop them, from game time until the last out was recorded 11 innings later.

His heroics began in the fourth inning when, with his team behind 5–1, and facing journeyman right-hander Carl Scheib, Seerey caught a curveball just right and sent it soaring onto the roof in left field for a solo shot that closed the gap to 5–2.

The following inning, with his team still trailing the Athletics, Seerey came to the plate against another right-hander, Bob Savage, with the same result: He lashed a fastball over the left-field fence for a two-run round-tripper, giving him a pair of home runs. He made it three home runs an inning later, lining a Charley Harris fastball onto the roof in left field for a three-run shot, marking the second time in his less-than-illustrious career that Seerey had connected for three home runs in a ballgame. He also became the first White Sox player since the well-traveled Carl Reynolds in 1930 to hit home runs in three consecutive innings.

Seerey's consecutive innings home run streak meant little by the 11th inning, when, with the teams tied 11–11, Seerey came to bat against left-hander Lou Brissie. Swinging from the heels as he always did, he drove another pitch into the left-field stands for his second solo shot and fourth home run of the game, giving his team a dramatic 12–11 extra-innings win. Ironically, Gehrig's four-home run game also occurred at Shibe Park. Watching Seerey circle the bases over and over that day from his seat in the grandstand was former pitcher George Earnshaw, who surrendered three of the four home runs Gehrig hit in his one-game offensive barrage 16 seasons earlier.

For Seerey, his four home runs were sufficient payment for a job well done; however, when the game ended a bonus awaited him: Weather King Batteries presented the slugger with $500 as remuneration for its promise that any player who hit four home runs during a ballgame at Shibe Park that season would be duly compensated. In those days $500 was more than adequate compensation for the best game of his life.

The following day, newspapers throughout the country had a field day with Seerey's rare on-field accomplishment. The *Altoona* (Pennsylvania) *Mirror* wrote in its irreverent coverage of the ballgame, "Pat Seerey, the guy nobody wanted because he got too fat, had his greatest day in baseball when he hit four homers in an 11-inning, 12 to 11 White Sox victory over the Athletics at Philadelphia, the final smash winning the game."[4]

The *Mansfield* (Ohio) *News Journal* was equally eloquent in its assessment of Major League Baseball's unequivocal player of the day, waxing poetic:

> The much-discussed and frequently cussed Pat Seerey, whose weight and batting average ride opposite ends of the fulcrum with the avoirdupois usually in the ascendency, was the toast of baseball today for hitting four homers in one game. That isn't a feat to be taken lightly, even when you consider the bulk of the spade-jawed Irishman currently toiling for the Chicago White Sox. Only Chuck Klein and Lou Gehrig were able to do it in the modern era of baseball.[5]

Joking aside, the line score from Seerey's memorable day in the spotlight spoke volumes more about his unusual accomplishment than any sportswriter with a flair for prose possibly could. On that day, Seerey, batting cleanup for the Sox, came to bat 6 times, stroked 4 home runs, drove in 7 runs, and scored 4 times. His performance easily overshadowed the five hits that teammate Don Kolloway accumulated as well as the four collected by another teammate, Cass Michaels. In all the White Sox pounded out 24 hits in pulling out the narrow victory over Connie Mack's Athletics.

Howie Judson, a teammate of Seerey, pitched 5 2/3 innings in relief that day—including two of the final three outs. He thought little of Seerey's performance at the time but said that in retrospect it was truly memorable.

"I really didn't think [at the time] it was a special game—there's been a lot of guys who hit four home runs," said the 92-year-old Judson. He added that looking back, "I suppose it was something special."

Seerey was special, too, Judson said. "He was a big guy. When he hit the ball it went a long way."

Sixty-eight years after Seerey's big game, Billy DeMars, a pinch-runner for the Athletics that day, recalled the havoc that Seerey wrought.

"Every time we'd go ahead, he'd come up and mash another home run, and we'd be behind again," said DeMars, now 92, who played as a rookie that year. "It was amazing, he had great power—when he hit the ball it went a long way."

After the game an iconic photo was snapped in the clubhouse showing Seerey, flanked by several teammates and an unidentified young admirer, kissing a bat while looking mischievously toward the photographer.

From that point onward the battle was all uphill for the likable Seerey, who oddly considered his home run trilogy against the Yankees three years earlier the best game of his career.

"He didn't consider [the four-home run game] to be his finest," said his son Dennis. "He thought his three-homer game against the Yankees was his best performance."

The 1948 season proved to be Seerey's best, at least from an RBI standpoint. On the strength of 19 home runs he drove in 70 runs, although he only hit .229—five points above his lifetime batting average. The four-home run game proved to be his last hurrah, however, as things quickly unwound when the next season began and Seerey reported to the team overweight.

The White Sox brought in former major leaguer Jack Onslow to manage the club in 1949, replacing Ted Lyons, and Seerey greeted his new skipper by reporting to spring training at a whopping 234 pounds. He later explained why he had trouble losing weight.

"I'm sort of a rock head," he said. "When somebody tells me something and I'm not sure it's right, I get stubborn and won't do it."[6]

Although the slugger managed to drop 16 pounds as the season progressed, Onslow was a no-nonsense manager who insisted that his players be as fit as possible to compete at the highest level, and the club optioned him to Los Angeles of the Pacific Coast League after just four official at-bats—his final at-bats in a highly consequential major-league career.

Seerey finished the season with zero hits in those four at-bats before bouncing around the minor leagues for a while, playing with four teams in 1949, two more in 1950, and three in 1951, then finally calling it quits. Wrote the St. Petersburg (Florida) Times in a less-than-complimentary explanatory quip, "Seerey, a heavy slugger, has been bothered with his weight. When he reported for spring practice he was a fat 234 pounds."[7]

Seerey's fall from grace had truly been meteoric, especially for a man who put on two huge offensive displays in a little more than six seasons of ball. After the four-home run game he hit just eight home runs in what remained of his faltering major-league career, a monumental downfall. For all intents and purposes 1948 would be his final season, and The Game—clearly his greatest achievement as a player and a defining moment for Pat Seerey—would mark both a high point and the beginning of his baseball demise. When the 1948 season ended with the White Sox in last place, so did Major League Baseball for Pat Seerey, the man whose four-home run performance earlier in the season defied logic.

"He was an all-or-nothing ballplayer," said Hall of Famer Lou Boudreau, an expert evaluator of baseball talent. "He never held anything back. He went up there swinging."[8]

Swinging but often missing was something the fans learned to live with and only held against him for the short term—until the next time he came to the plate, trying with all his might to reach the distant fences.

"He was the most fascinating, frustrating character ever to wear the Tribe uniform," wrote Ed McAuley of the *Cleveland News*. "He could hit a ball with more sheer line-drive force than anyone in the history of the game. His friends numbered in the thousands and his critics in the tens of thousands, but you couldn't stay mad at him."[9]

Like everything, Seerey took his final demotion in stride. After playing for minor-league clubs in Los Angeles, Kansas City, Newark, and San Antonio in 1949 he was again demoted, this time to the Colorado Springs Sky Sox in the Western Association. There he had a huge year in 1950, blasting 44 home runs and driving in 117 runners. With only 112 hits that season he managed to score 113 runs while walking an incomprehensible 135 times. His final season in baseball was 1951, when he played with three clubs: Memphis, Colorado Springs, and Tampa. Finally, after trying out for a team in Ontario, Canada, he left baseball for good in 1952 after hitting 28 home runs in his final minor-league season. In all he hit 86 home runs in the major leagues and 156 home runs in the minor leagues for a grand total of 242—not bad for a guy who was vilified during much of his career for being overweight.

Married to his wife Jeanne in 1946, Seerey moved to St. Louis after retiring from baseball and worked in the maintenance department for the St. Louis public school system. He and Jeanne raised four children, and the blessing of parenthood eased Seerey's transition from a high-profile player and sometimes-star to private citizen. After his kids were grown he took pleasure in watching his grandchildren flourish, spending as much time with them as he could. They participated in sports and, as might be expected, "He went to all of their games," son Dennis said.

When baseball was over, Pat Seerey lived a pleasant life for more than 30 years, fishing and watching sports on television. He played golf, often with his sons—and as he'd done with baseballs, Seerey hit golf balls a country mile.

"Even into his 50s dad could still pound the golf ball," Dennis said.

Life was good for Pat Seerey after baseball, although he admitted shortly before his death that he no longer followed the sport. He also conceded that hitting four home runs in a game required much more than skill and brute strength.

"Anybody that hits four home runs in a game just has to be lucky," he said modestly.[10]

With a loving, dedicated wife and four children, there was never a need for much of anything else. Seerey lived a full life until developing lung cancer, a condition that—like his weight—he was unable to conquer. He died at his home in Jennings, Missouri, on April 28, 1986, at the relatively young age of 63 and was interred at Calvary Cemetery and Mausoleum in nearby St. Louis—loved and admired by everyone who knew him. Even the sportswriters who so often poked fun at his girth thought highly of him, and they wrote as much after he left the game that he had faithfully served for so many years.

Wrote Franklin Lewis of the *Cleveland Press* in a fitting obituary published many years later, "I saw Seerey, and I wouldn't have missed him for anything in the world."[11]

6

GIL HODGES

August 31, 1950

To most fans the forename "Gil" represents only one player: Gil Hodges.
Same thing with "Hodges." In the minds of nearly everyone, there is and was only one baseball-playing Hodges, former major leaguers Ron and Trey Hodges notwithstanding: Gil Hodges of the Brooklyn/Los Angeles Dodgers and New York Mets, a man who played the game with heart and intensity for more than two decades.

More than 40 years after his premature death from natural causes, people still remember the quiet, dependable Gil Hodges of the 1940s and 1950s—especially in the Dodgers organization. To them Hodges was a proverbial Boy of Summer and one of the most feared and revered players in the club's long and storied history.

In a 2015 poll of *Los Angeles Times* readers, Hodges was named the 18th greatest Dodger in team history. The blurb that accompanied his selection makes a good case for placing him in the top 20 ahead of 300-game winner and Hall of Famer Don Sutton, as well as Kirk Gibson, whose walk-off home run against the Oakland Athletics in the 1988 World Series still elicits oohs and aahs in conversations in and around Los Angeles. Wrote the scribe,

> Why isn't Gil Hodges in the Hall of Fame? The man is an eight-time All-Star, hit
> 370 home runs, hit .273 with an on-base percentage of .359, is one of only 16
> people to hit four homers in one game, was an integral part of two World Series
> championships as a first baseman, and managed the Miracle Mets to the 1969
> World Series title.[1]

Revered by almost everyone, there remains a sense of sadness associated with Hodges, who died in 1972 at the young age of 47 less than a decade after retiring as a player from the game he loved. Before that, he had been taken in the expansion draft by the lowly Mets, who experienced one of the worst seasons in baseball history. The following season the team that had traded him away, the Dodgers, beat the New York Yankees in four games to sweep the 1963 World Series in dominating fashion, a championship Hodges missed cel-

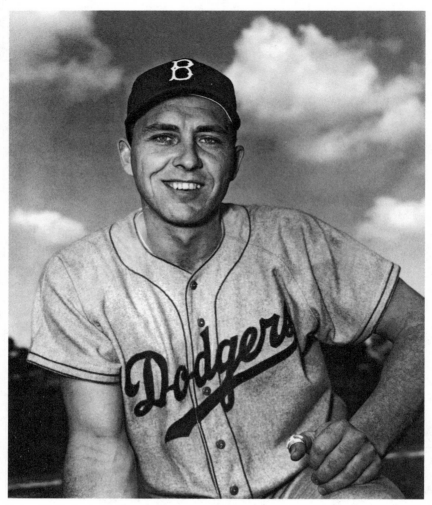

Gil Hodges. *National Baseball Hall of Fame*

ebrating by a mere season. Finally, he remains a Hall of Fame outsider despite statistics that many believe are good enough to warrant enshrinement in that coveted fraternity of stars.

Consider Yogi Berra, the venerable Yankee who died in 2015. A three-time MVP and member of the Baseball Hall of Fame, Berra's statistics are comparable to those of Hodges, although Hodges played one fewer season: Berra hit 358 home runs, 12 fewer than Hodges, while driving in 1,430 runs (Hodges's total was just shy of 1,300) and posting a lifetime batting average of .285—just 12 points higher than Hodges. Hodges hit 20 or more home runs in 11 consecutive seasons, a streak that surpasses Berra's 10 straight. The two were virtually tied in career triples, with Berra hitting one more than Hodges, and the Yankee also had an edge in doubles—358 to 295. What may have tipped the scales in Berra's favor were the three MVP Awards he earned and 10 world championship teams he played on, compared with two World Series titles for Hodges; however, based on sheer statistics and his standing alongside Berra, many believe Hodges belongs in the Hall.

A book written by Mort Zachter and published in 2015 makes a case in its title: *Gil Hodges: A Hall of Fame Life.* Statistics and other data confirm his worthiness. After his initial "season" in 1943, when he batted just twice, Hodges joined the military and missed two full seasons, returning to baseball in 1946 to play for the Class B Newport News Dodgers of the Piedmont League. With his two-year absence and the rustiness that resulted, after he returned to the major leagues Hodges was effectively starting over as, in effect, a virtual first-year player, garnering only 77 at-bats in 1947. He did not become an experienced big-league baseball player until 1948, when he hit 11 home runs and drove in a respectable 70 RBI. After that his success accelerated, and he continued on to hit 22 or more homers in 11 consecutive seasons. Not even Ted Williams, who many consider the greatest home run hitter of all time, accomplished that.

Throughout his career, Hodges, nicknamed the "Miracle Man," posted brilliant numbers before retiring in 1963 with a lifetime batting average of .273. He also recorded 1,921 hits, including almost 300 doubles and 48 triples. The native Indianan was an All-Star eight times, earned two Gold Glove Awards as a first baseman, and finished seventh in the Most Valuable Player balloting in 1957 and eighth in 1950. His best season was 1954 when he hit 42 home runs, drove in 130 runners, and batted .304, still finishing a distant 10th in the MVP balloting.

Hodges was an All-Star for the 1955 Brooklyn Dodgers, which won the first World Series title in the organization's history by beating the Yankees in seven games, and he helped lead the team to a championship against the Chicago White Sox in 1959. Not to be overlooked, on August 31, 1950, during one of his best seasons as a player, Hodges slugged four home runs in a game against the Boston Braves in front of a home crowd at Ebbets Field in Brooklyn. With that performance he became just the sixth player ever and the fourth in the then-half-century-old modern era to join the Four Home Runs Club.

Of course, not all of his numbers shimmered. In the 1952 World Series, which the Yankees won in seven games, Hodges failed to get a hit in 21 at-bats, prompting Father Herbert Redmond of St. Francis Roman Catholic Church in Brooklyn to implore, "Pray for Gil Hodges!" It must have worked, because the next season Hodges returned to his usual fine hitting form, belting 31 home runs and driving in 122 runners. You couldn't keep Gil Hodges down for long.

"I won't forget the hundreds of people who sent me letters, telegrams, and postcards during that World Series," Hodges exclaimed later. "There wasn't a single nasty message. Everybody tried to say something nice. It had a tremendous effect on my morale, if not my batting average."[2]

Many believe Hodges's career accomplishments are easily good enough to have landed him in the Hall of Fame. Not so. Instead, he remains an enigma—perhaps the most beloved and overall accomplished player never to make it into the Hall of Fame. He was doubtless a dominant on-field performer who was instrumental in building the Dodgers organization into one of the greatest franchises in modern-day baseball. He also was quiet and unpretentious, qualities that may have helped keep him out of the Hall. Despite his greatness he simply preferred to let others hype themselves.

"Shouting on a ball field never helped anyone, except where it was one player calling to another to take the catch," he said shortly before retiring.[3]

His "absence from baseball's Hall of Fame remains absurd," wrote author Thomas Oliphant in 2005.[4]

Gilbert Ray Hodges was born on April 4, 1924, to Charlie and Irene Hodges of Princeton, Indiana, a community that was devastated the year after his birth when a tornado killed 70 people. The son of a coal miner, he had two siblings: a sister, Marjorie, and a brother, Robert. As a young boy growing up in the eastern Indiana town of Petersburg, Hodges's father inculcated in his young son a passion for sports in an effort to help him go further in life than himself. That effort may have been slightly misplaced.

"Many children work hard to please their parents, but what I truly longed for was good times that were about us, not about me," Hodges said. "That is the real hole the Dodgers filled in my life."[5]

Nonetheless, his father's effort paid off, at least where sports were concerned. Young Gil became a basketball, track, and baseball standout and soon invited the delighted interest of professional sports teams that recognized his obvious star potential.

At the age of 17 Hodges enrolled at St. Joseph's College in Rensselaer, Indiana, after receiving a scholarship and studied—appropriately—physical education. While enrolled at St. Joseph's he played baseball during his freshman and sophomore seasons—1942 and 1943—and soon caught the eye of a Brooklyn Dodgers scout. The man signed Hodges to a baseball contract in 1943 and the team elevated him to the big club almost immediately. As a rookie during the war years, when the absence of players who had left for battle created a glaring hole, he played in just one game at third base, going 0-for-2 with a walk and a stolen base in three times to the plate; however, his career path was established.

As far as baseball was concerned, for Hodges, like other players who entered the service, that brief appearance would be it for the next two years. While at St. Joseph's he had served in the ROTC program, and as World War II was building steam, Hodges joined the marines, eventually fighting at Okinawa. Among the awards he received before his discharge from the service in 1946 was the Bronze Star for bravery.

Hodges returned from the war to a world of uncertainty. President Roosevelt was dead, the nuclear age had been ushered in at potentially great peril to the world, and the United States, led by a boom in housing, was poised to begin a decade of hope, prosperity, and rock 'n' roll. Nothing had changed much for the Dodgers, however, and with Hodges's return the Brooklyn team, the only one ever named after a neighborhood, still hadn't won a world championship.

After Hodges rejoined the team in 1947 his life once again took a turn, this time for the better. Then a part-time catcher, he was switched from third base to first, gained confidence as a reliable infielder, and in turn was able to corroborate his worthiness to everyone who saw him play, including fans and teammates. From a baseball perspective he continued to improve, and by the late 1940s Hodges was considered one of the finest first basemen in the National League, if not all of baseball.

"I put a first baseman's glove on . . . Hodges and told him to have some fun," former Dodgers skipper Leo Durocher, who last managed the team in 1948, once said. "Three days later I looked up and—wow—I was looking at the best first baseman I'd seen since Dolph Camilli."[6]

Unlike others in the Four Home Runs Club, Hodges's big moment came early in his career during his third season as a starter. Perhaps he was buoyed by the home-field advantage he enjoyed that day, although any benefit had to be offset by the slight attendance: Only about 14,000 fans showed up to watch his historic batsmanship.

To put the game in perspective is to examine legendary Ebbets Field itself. Built at a cost of $750,000, the stadium opened for business on April 9, 1913. When the doors swung wide and the turnstiles began whirling, the ballpark seated just 23,000 people; however, a series of expansions that added out-field bleachers in 1926 and extended the double-deck grandstand down the third-base line and on into center field in 1931 greatly increased that capacity. Hodges was a right-hander, and the left-field fence, the slugger's preferred destination for home runs, was a fair distance from home plate: 348 feet, to be exact.[7] On August 31, 1950, home run distance mattered little to Gil Hodges. Everything he hit that day seemed destined to fly over the fence.

Starting on the mound against the Dodgers that day was a future legend, Warren Spahn, who would win 21 games that season and 363 in his long career. Hodges greeted Spahn, who would go on to earn election to the Hall of Fame, with a two-run shot over the left-field wall in the second inning.

After surrendering five runs, Spahn was replaced two innings into the game by Normie Roy, a big right-hander whose only season in the major leagues would be 1950. Hodges faced him in the third inning and promptly hit a three-run home run, again into the left-field stands. The shot effectively sent Roy to the showers after only one-third of an inning pitched.

Hodges grounded out to third baseman Bob Elliott in the fourth inning and failed to match Pat Seerey's mark of hitting home runs in three consecutive innings. But he came to bat again in the sixth inning against reliever Bob Hall, a 6-foot-2, 195-pound right-hander who would win just three games in a brief, three-year career, and hit his second two-run home run of the game over the left-field fence. He then singled off the Braves' fifth pitcher, Johnny Antonelli, in the seventh inning, leaving himself one more chance to enter the record books with a fourth blast. Facing Antonelli again in the eighth inning, he drilled another home run, his third two-run shot of the game.

The line score for Hodges, who batted in the seventh spot that day: 5 hits in 6 at-bats, 5 runs scored, 9 RBI, and a record-tying 17 total bases. Interestingly, each home run occurred with Carl Furillo on base, and Hodges's nine RBI accounted for 8 percent of the runners he would drive in that season. He had become only the second person in modern major-league history and the first from the National League to accomplish the four-home run feat during a nine-inning game, something he achieved in only his third full major-league season.

"There were only 14,226 cash customers present to see Hodges's almost unprecedented feat—certainly unprecedented for a Dodger—but they enjoyed every minute of the entire performance," wrote Roscoe McGowen in the *New York Times Book of Sports Legends*. He added, "As the third player on the team to hit three or more homers in one game this season [Duke Snider and Roy Campanella were the others], Hodges also helped the Dodgers establish another major-league record."[8]

Although Hodges's four-homer accomplishment was every bit as important as that of the Yankees' Lou Gehrig almost two decades earlier, that's where the comparison between he and the fabled "Iron Horse" stops, Hodges said.

"[Gehrig] was a better ballplayer,"[9] said the ever-modest Hodges, matter-of-factly.

After the game Hodges received some high compliments from sportswriters who covered the game:

> Gil Hodges, called by many the strongest man in the National League, has just about proved it. The husky Brooklyn first baseman hit four home runs last night to record a feat performed only five times before in Major League Baseball. Hodges's walloping of four separate Boston Brave pitchers temporarily shared attention with the hot American League pennant race.[10]

The starting pitcher for Brooklyn that day was Carl Erskine, who threw a complete game and had a front-row seat to one of the greatest hitting performances in Dodgers history. Of the seven no-hitters thrown in the National League that decade, Erskine owned two.

"Three home runs is rare—four, of course, is exceptional," said the 91-year-old Erskine, who also accomplished something exceptional that day: He popped four singles in the 21-hit slugfest, an unheard-of performance for a pitcher. "Gil hit his third [home run], then of course he came up again and hit a fourth." Erskine then tittered, "[As a pitcher] I was more interested in our 19 runs."

Added Erskine, who is one of only a handful of players who played in the game still living, "We celebrated [Hodges's achievement] in the clubhouse, naturally . . . I don't want to say it was just another game—four home runs was special. To see that happen and be a part of it, especially to be in the lineup . . ." His voice trailed.

Hodges finished the 1950 season in grand style, and he kept up the pace during each of the nine years that followed. Starting in 1950 he hit 30 or more home runs in five successive seasons, twice hitting 40 or more. He drove in more runners during the 1950s than any other National League player—including the great Stan Musial.

The Dodgers moved to Los Angeles prior to the 1958 season, and the aging Hodges continued on with his career at Los Angeles Memorial Coliseum, site of the 1932 Olympic Games and the team's temporary headquarters before Dodger Stadium was opened in 1962. Hodges's first two seasons in Los Angeles were solid ones, but he was getting along in baseball years and his knees would soon hamper his mobility. Finally, the year after beating the White Sox in the 1959 World Series, the big first baseman's power fell off dramatically. After hitting 25 home runs in 1959 he hit just eight in each of the next two seasons and nine in 1962. His high for driving in runs during that three-year span was just 31.

With those conspicuous numbers Hodges was drafted by the expansion Mets in 1962, belting nine home runs but driving in only 17 runners during his second-to-last season as a player. His final season was in 1963 when he failed to homer. Hodges retired after the 1963 season with his head held high, knowing that even when he failed to hit or catch a ball he had always tried his hardest. He expected nothing less from his teammates.

"It's not whether . . . a teammate caught the ball, it's, 'Did he give it a try?'" he said. "That's very important, because from Little League to the major leagues, that 'try' is the one thing that each player owes to his teammates."[11]

Less than two months after the season was over the Washington Senators hired Hodges to manage their ball club, and he stayed on through the 1967 season despite losing 100 games in 1964—a benchmark for futility.

"There are only two kinds of managers," he said, perhaps anticipating the worst. "Winning managers and ex-managers."[12]

Hodges soon became an ex-manager, at least for the Senators, joining the Mets as manager in 1968. Not unlike his early years as a Dodger, it didn't take Hodges long to leave his mark in New York.

The 1968 season, Hodges's first with the team, was the Mets' seventh since their inception, and although they were vastly improved compared to earlier campaigns they nonetheless finished in ninth place in the National League. Not that there wasn't potential for significant improvement. While the team's hitting was modest and they finished the season with an anemic cumulative batting average (.228), the pitching staff had star potential. With a roster that included Jerry Koosman (19–12, 2.08 ERA), Tom Seaver (16–12, 2.20), and a future star named Nolan Ryan (6–9, 3.09), who during a 27-year career would throw seven no-hitters, there was reason for hope in 1969. Under Hodges, who as a player knew how to win ballgames, that hope wasn't wasted. Despite their maturing pitching staff, the Mets had to be considered a long shot to win the National League pennant, let alone the World Series.

In 1969 it wasn't only the pitching staff that came of age, although that certainly was the case. Seaver went 25–7 with a 2.21 ERA, followed by Koosman at 17–9, and Gary Gentry at 13–12. On the offensive side Cleon Jones hit .340 with 12 home runs and 75 RBI while Tommy Agee slugged 26 round-trippers and drove in 76 runs.

While the offensive numbers weren't overwhelming, Hodges somehow managed to make things click for the club, and the Mets finished in first place—eight games ahead of the second-place Cubs. After winning a title during the first season of divisional play, the Mets went on to beat the Atlanta Braves 3–0 in the National League Division Series, then faced Baltimore in the World Series.

The Orioles entered the series with a formidable pitching staff that included two 20-game winners: Mike Cuellar (23–11) and Dave McNally (20–7). They also had an imposing offensive lineup of long-ball hitters led by Boog Powell (37 home runs, 121 RBI) and Hall of Famer Frank Robinson (32 HR, 100 RBI). While pitching generally trumps power, and pitching *and* power trump everything, the Orioles' spirit-breaking lineup didn't seem to matter. The Hodges-led Mets won the series four games to one, and when the final out was recorded Shea Stadium erupted in pandemonium. In only their eighth season of frequently mediocre play, the once-lowly Mets, who in 1962 were considered the laughingstock of the league, had won a world championship. They owed everything to one man: the "Miracle Worker," manager Gil Hodges, who later explained his success.

"You look into the mirror after something doesn't work out," Hodges said, "and you ask yourself. 'Would I do the same thing again?' If you can say *yes*, that's fine. But when you start getting *no* back from the mirror, then you're in trouble."[13]

That season almost everything worked out. In the movie *Oh, God*, with the title character played by George Burns, the nonagenarian actor puts the 1969 Mets in perspective. "The last miracle I did was the 1969 Mets," God said. "Before that, I think you have to go back to the Red Sea."[14]

Clearly the Miracle Mets of 1969 were a monumental achievement. Sadly, for Hodges the championship would be his last one as either a player or manager. In 1970 the team finished third in the Eastern Division and out of the money, and in 1971 the Mets were fourth. As a consolation, however, in three out of four seasons with the team, Hodges led the once-lowly Mets to winning records.

In April 1972, Hodges was in Florida to play golf with three of his Mets coaches, former ballplayers Joe Pignatano, Rube Walker, and Eddie Yost. As he walked back to his motel room after completing 18 holes on the course, Hodges suddenly collapsed onto the ground, striking his head as he fell. He was driven to a local hospital but died within half an hour of arriving. He would have turned 48 years old two days later.

Unbeknownst to many, Hodges's heart attack was his second. In September 1968, just one year before leading his Mets to their miraculous World Series championship, he suffered a minor heart attack that forced him to miss the final weeks of a disappointing season. Although the Mets skipper recovered nicely, the infarction was a prelude to something much bigger, a catastrophic medical event that would claim his life. One account following Hodges's untimely death read as follows:

> Gil Hodges, the one-time star of the old Brooklyn Dodgers who managed the Miracle Mets of New York to baseball's world championship in 1969, collapsed and died Sunday. Hodges had just finished a golf match at the Ramada Inn and was strolling back to his motel room with companions when he slumped to the ground. He was rushed to Good Samaritan Hospital, where was admitted at 4:25 p.m. CST. He died 20 minutes later, the hospital said.[15]

Reached for comment following Hodges' death, Hall of Famer Jackie Robinson expressed shock at his former teammate's departure, saying,

> With this and what's happened to Campy [former Dodgers great Roy Campanella, who at that time lay critically ill in a New York hospital] and a lot of other guys we played with, it scares you. I've been somewhat shocked by it all. I have tremendous feelings for Gil's family and kids.[16]

As did everyone else, especially those in Brooklyn where Hodges continued to reside after his playing days were through. His funeral, attended by a who's who of current and former teammates, was held at his Brooklyn parish, Our Lady Help of Christians. He was interred at nearby Holy Cross Cemetery.

"Gil Hodges was beloved in Brooklyn, the person parents wanted their kids to emulate," author Thomas Oliphant wrote. "He was not just quiet and well-mannered; he also worked ceaselessly, hustled like a rookie, and never complained." He added, "Hodges really was all he seemed."[17]

As a fitting memorial to a man who bridged the gap between good and great, a span that crosses the White River's east fork in Indiana was later renamed the Gil Hodges Memorial Bridge. Near the bottom of a stone monument a space was left where the words on Gil Hodges's hoped-for Hall of Fame plaque might someday be inscribed. The space has been empty for many years—too many years, his adoring fans believe. More than 50 years after his playing days ended, Gil Hodges remains a stranger to the Baseball Hall of Fame.

7

JOE ADCOCK

July 31, 1954

On a sizzling summer day in 1954, with Dwight Eisenhower now firmly at the nation's helm and Don Larson's perfect World Series game still two seasons in the future, Joe Adcock donned his scratchy flannel uniform and put on what may have been one of the greatest hitting displays in major-league history. On that day, in five plate appearances against the Brooklyn Dodgers at Ebbets Field, Adcock collected four home runs and a double that came within inches of clearing the fence for what would have been an unprecedented fifth home run. In the history of Major League Baseball, no player—not Babe Ruth, nor Lou Gehrig nor anyone else—had ever accumulated 18 total bases in a single game, although Josh Hamilton later tied the mark and Shawn Green broke it. Adcock's searing performance was, many believe, the greatest display of offensive might in the history of Major League Baseball.

Adcock's success that day against the Dodgers was his finest hour in a season—and eventually a career—full of fine hours, a campaign in which he hit 23 home runs and drove in 87 runners, the latter mark a career high. The game also defined Adcock as not only a fearsome home run hitter, but also a player who could come through in the clutch. He was, at age 27, a cynosure, a man of vast talent whose future as a member of the feared Milwaukee Braves was a bright one.

The following day, after Adcock doubled against those same Dodgers, Clem Labine struck him in the head with a pitched ball and put him in his place: flat on the ground. The slugger, who had floated above the ground since his offensive display just 24 hours earlier, was down for the count and had to be carried off the field. Fortunately, he recovered nicely and continued on as one of the most formidable power hitters of the 1950s.

Adcock's major-league debut occurred in 1950, the year that Gil Hodges homered four times in a game at Ebbets Field. Coincidentally, several Dodgers in the starting lineup during Hodges's big day were also in the game when

Joe Adcock. *National Baseball Hall of Fame*

Adcock hit his four home runs against them, including Pee Wee Reese, Duke Snider, Jackie Robinson, Carl Furillo, and, of course, Hodges.

As a strapping 6-foot-4, 210-pound rookie on a Cincinnati team that included such home run luminaries as veteran Ted Kluszewski, Adcock was described by one reporter as an "intimidating presence even without a bat."[1] The 23-year-old, who made his big-league debut on April 23, less than a month after the 1950 season began, made a rippled splash that year, slugging 8 home runs, driving in 55 runners, and hitting a respectable .293 for the Reds during his first year of action. During the next 16 seasons playing with four different clubs, he would not fail to hit at least 10 home runs even once. Adcock followed up his 1950 success with 10 home runs in 1951 followed by 13 in 1952, but with his RBI count leveling off he was traded to the Milwaukee Braves prior to the 1953 season. It was there that Adcock truly showed his stuff.

To many people, baseball came of age during the 1950s. Gone were the likes of Ruth and Gehrig, baseball's slugging forefathers, replaced instead by a new generation of players, men like Hank Aaron, Willie Mays, and Sandy Koufax. Milwaukee also was coming-of-age. Toward the end of the decade its population would peak at more than 740,000 as the city grew in size and stature. As a reward perhaps for good performance it was granted hosting duties for the 1955 All-Star Game, held on July 12, 1955, featuring a player who would figure prominently in Adcock's future: pitcher Harvey Haddix.

The nation too was in flux. The Korean conflict had run its course, cars with fins were all the rage, and Rosemary Clooney and Eddie Fisher were dominating the pop charts with a series of hits.

In his first season with the Braves, Adcock offered up his own series of hits while proving beyond a doubt that the team had made a correct decision in acquiring him from the Reds, as he slammed 18 home runs, drove in 80 runners, and hit .285—at the time his best season in the big leagues. For good measure he also hit six triples and 33 doubles while leading the league in one unenviable category: hitting into double plays. No one was too concerned about the double plays—at his formidable size Joe Adcock was hardly expected to be a speedster on the basepaths. The youthful slugger was well on his way to becoming a star as the Braves' regular first baseman, a position he would share for the next six seasons.

Often platooned or injured, Adcock managed to put up strong numbers and become a feared hitter despite enduring a limited number of plate appearances. In 13 of his 17 seasons he recorded fewer than 400 at-bats, and in four of those seasons he came to the plate 300 times or fewer. His production was steady however, as in 1955 he walloped 15 home runs in just 288 at-bats and two years later he belted 12 home runs in only 209 at-bats. Finally, coming off a 29-homer binge in 1962, the Braves traded him to Cleveland the following season. A year later the Indians traded Adcock to the expansion Los Angeles Angels, where he finished his career in 1966. As an Angel, Adcock averaged 18 home runs in three seasons before retiring at the age of 38 with 17 major-league seasons to his credit. The most unforgettable one had to be the 1954 season, the year he leapt into headlines in the midst of his best season hitting for average. His day in the spotlight notwithstanding, it also was a good home run year for Adcock, helped along by his four-dinger game on July 31.

Joseph Wilbur Adcock was born on October 30, 1927, in Coushatta, Louisiana, near the banks of the Red River, a tributary of the Mississippi also referred to as the Red River of the South. His father Ray was a man of many talents, working variously as a businessman, farmer, and county sheriff, while his mother Helen taught school. As a boy, Adcock and his sister Mary Ann learned the meaning of hard work early on, pitching in to help out on the family farm in Red River County. The work ethic he developed as a boy would serve him well, not so much on the farmlands of rural Louisiana as on the ball fields of Cincinnati, Milwaukee, Cleveland, and Los Angeles, the baseball municipalities where most of his games ultimately would be played.

Always a physically striking man, Adcock's early athletic interests centered on basketball, partly because baseball was a secondary sport in Depression-era Louisiana. Although there was little opportunity to play much other than basketball, his success on the court was the augury of a bright athletic future.

"There was no town team, no school team, not even a diamond," Adcock would later say. "I'd hit a rock with a stick out by the roadside down home, and I'd knocked corn cobs up on the barn roof with a broomstick. But as for playing baseball, that was just something I heard my dad talk about."[2]

Adcock never had much of a chance to develop a serious interest in baseball until 1944, when he enrolled at Louisiana State University on a basketball scholarship. Also a baseball star at LSU through his junior season, the scouts soon came calling, and Adcock left school in 1947 to sign a contract with the Cincinnati Reds, joining a minor-league affiliate at the Single-A level.

Adcock's first professional assignment was with the Columbia Fireflies of the South Atlantic League, and with his substantial height he was naturally assigned to play first base. He started off slowly and in two seasons with Columbia popped a total of 13 home runs. Those numbers apparently suited the Reds fine, and he was elevated to the Double-A Tulsa Oilers in 1949. There he came of age as a ballplayer, hitting 19 home runs while batting just under .300.

That one season in Tulsa was all the Reds needed to see, and the following year—1950—Adcock was promoted to the major-league club. Despite another slow start, it didn't take long for him to become a respected major-league hitter.

Unfortunately, when Adcock arrived in Cincinnati there was no room for him at first base. That position was already occupied by the great Ted Kluszewski, who would hit 25 home runs and drive in 111 runners during Adcock's rookie season. Adcock clearly had potential, however, and soon the two began platooning, with Kluszewski starting against right-handed pitchers and Adcock against lefties. Thus began a longer-than-anticipated—and most likely unsatisfactory—history of sharing first base duties for Adcock, who was disappointed at not securing the position outright.

Probably hoping for more playing time, Adcock agreed to play in the out-field during his sophomore season of 1951, ensuring that the Reds would have at least two solid home run hitters in the lineup at the same time: him and Kluszewski. At least for Kluszewski, the succor of relative stability at first base paid off. Two years later he began a string of three seasons hitting 40, 49, and 47 home runs, respectively, while driving in 108, 141, and 113 runners. In contrast, Adcock averaged fewer than 19 home runs, taking a back seat to the big, dependable slugger in the power department. Still, the platooning, both at first base and in the outfield, continued. Even as Kluszewski's numbers began slipping in 1957, while Adcock's were rising, the Reds continued their shared duties at first base.

That despite the game of his career.

In 1954, Adcock almost single-handedly demolished the Dodgers, tying an all-time major-league mark with nine home runs against the team at Ebbets Field, where Gil Hodges had become the sixth player to hit four home runs in a game just four years earlier. Adcock's own four-homer game did much to pad that total, although he clearly had the Dodgers' number throughout the 1954 campaign.

His big game may have been influenced by his outstanding performance the day before, when Adcock homered, doubled, and singled in a Braves victory on July 30. At that point in the season he was seeing the ball as well as ever and hoping his success would carry over to the following day.

Starting for the Dodgers that day was Don Newcombe, one of the team's premier pitchers and a man who would win 27 games just two years later in an MVP and Cy Young Award–winning season. Newcombe, the first black player to win MVP, Cy Young, and Rookie of the Year honors, was a durable pitcher who once threw 272 innings in a season, and he figured to be around in the game for a while. Adcock had something else in mind, not only for Newcombe but also for the cadre of relievers who would follow him.

Batting in the second inning, Adcock hit a Newcombe fastball over the fence for a solo shot and his first home run of the game, and by the time the third out had been recorded the Braves led the seemingly perennial National League pennant-winners, who were playing under first-year manager Walt Alston, 4–1. Both Newcombe and his mound successor, Clem Labine, would be gone by the end of two innings, but not before Adcock came up again in the second and slapped a double.

After Erv Palica replaced Labine on the mound in the third inning, Adcock returned to the plate two innings later and hit a three-run shot that put the Braves up 9–1, his second home run coming off a slider. To those watching, the Braves were, sadly, dismantling the Dodgers' prized pitching staff.

Adcock batted again in the seventh inning, with right-hander Pete Wojey on the mound. Wojey, who would win only one game in a short three-year career, threw a curveball that Adcock waited patiently for and hit for his third home run of the game, a two-run blast. Wojey failed to make it out of the seventh inning and was promptly replaced by a second-year left-hander named Johnny Podres, who the following season would earn World Series MVP honors as Brooklyn won its only Fall Classic. The relatively inexperienced Podres served up a fast-ball that Adcock hit over the left-field fence for his second solo shot and fourth round-tripper of the game. The final score: Milwaukee 15 Brooklyn 7.

"I hit a fastball for the first homer, a slider for the second, a curve for the third, and a fastball for the fourth," Adcock proudly told a reporter after the game.[3]

Batting fifth in the lineup, Adcock's numbers that day were eye-catching: 5 hits in 5 at-bats, 4 home runs, 7 RBI, and 5 runs scored. Eddie Matthews added two home runs for the Braves and, not surprisingly, Four Home Runs Club member Hodges homered for the Dodgers.

"Strictly luck," Adcock said of his performance, probably with tongue in cheek.[4]

Watching from the bench that day was Dodgers pitcher Carl Erskine, who had also witnessed Gil Hodges's four-home run game. Erskine recalled the game with clarity many years later.

"I saw a player (almost) hit five," Erskine said, referring to Adcock. He continued,

> Joe Adcock, in Ebbets Field, hit four home runs, came up a fifth time, and the ball he hit then was the hardest hit of the four that went for home runs. It was hit to deep left-center, about 380 (feet), but it hit the rail and came back onto the field for a double. Six inches higher and he would have had five home runs.

The self-satisfaction that Adcock must have felt was tempered the following day when Labine plunked him on the head. Six weeks later, again in Brooklyn, Newcombe came after him once more. After Adcock homered on September

10 to set a record for home runs hit by a visiting player, the big right-hander popped him on the thumb, breaking the digit and putting an end to his prodigious season just as the Braves seemed poised to make a late-season pennant run. Adcock put up big numbers against the Dodgers that season, but in the end Brooklyn had the final say in a heated 1954 rivalry.

"When they throw at me high and tight, I can duck," said Adcock. "But when they throw behind your head, they mean business."[5]

The four-homer game, which put him in the books as the seventh member of that elite coterie, was a gratifying one for Adcock, and a well-traveled United Press wire photo shows the smiling first baseman holding up four fingers after the contest had ended. In the photograph the slugger appears fatigued but nonetheless gratified at his achievement.

Speaking to reporters after the game, Adcock noted that he broke his regular bat the previous night and was forced to use one belonging to a teammate. It was, he said, the heaviest bat on the team—and one he could barely lift.

Adcock's showmanship was chronicled by a sportswriter later that day:

> Joe Adcock, Milwaukee Braves first baseman, slugged four home runs against the Brooklyn Dodgers today, tieing (*sic*) the major-league record for round-trippers in a game and leading the red-hot Braves to their ninth-straight victory in a 15–7 romp. Adcock, only the fifth batter in the long history of the major leagues to hit four out of the park in a nine-inning game, also belted a double, and the combination of long hits also gave him a record of 18 bases in one game.[6]

Adcock finished the season injured, but he returned in 1955 to hit 15 home runs—most of them as a first baseman. The following season was his best ever: He belted 38 home runs, drove in 103 runners, and hit .291, still finishing a distant 11th in the MVP balloting.

Following the four-homer landslide, Adcock still had two big games left in him. On May 26, 1959, after Pittsburgh's Harvey Haddix had pitched 12 perfect innings against the Braves, Adcock came up in the 13th frame with two runners on base and promptly blasted a Haddix pitch out of the park to break up the no-hitter and end the marathon. Because he had inadvertently passed teammate Hank Aaron on the bases, Adcock was credited with a one-run double and the Braves won the game 1–0 instead of 3–0.

Adcock wasn't through yet. On June 8, 1961, Eddie Matthews, Aaron, Adcock, and Frank Thomas combined to hit four consecutive home runs against Cincinnati, becoming the first players to achieve the feat. Players on two American League and one National League team have since hit four consecutive home runs, matching the rare accomplishment.

Adcock continued putting up strong numbers until his retirement five years later. After his playing days were over he was hired to manage the Cleveland Indians in 1967. Despite a lineup that included another member of the Four Home Runs Club, Rocky Colavito, the Indians finished in eighth place in the American League at 75–87. The season was a disappointment, one of Cleveland's worst in many years, and Adcock was replaced as manager by fiery Alvin Dark, who reversed things and led the team to a third-place finish in 1968. As a player and a manager, Joe Adcock was at long last out of baseball.

Following his retirement from the sport he had spent the better part of his life trying to master, Adcock and his wife Joan moved back home to Louisiana, where they owned some farms and had often spent their winters; in their spare time they also bred thoroughbred horses. The couple, who were married in 1956, had raised four children, and they enjoyed their life away from baseball. As a result Adcock drifted away from the sport he loved. In 1975, at the age of 48, the Louisiana Sports Hall of Fame inducted him into that elite athletic body.[7]

His later years were not so kind to the slugger. Adcock eventually developed Alzheimer's disease, and on May 3, 1999, he passed away at the age of 71. Adcock was buried at Holly Springs Cemetery in Marin, Louisiana. He was remembered in a thoughtful obituary:

> Joe Adcock, the Milwaukee Braves' strapping first baseman who put on some of baseball's most remarkable displays of power hitting and broke up the longest no-hit game in major-league history, died yesterday at his home in Coushatta, La. He was 71. He had Alzheimer's disease, his family said. Teaming up with Hank Aaron and Eddie Mathews in a fearsome lineup of the 1950s, the right-handed-batting, 6-foot-4-inch, 220-pound Adcock achieved a host of long-ball feats on the way to 336 career home runs.[8]

During his 17 years as a player, Adcock came to bat roughly half the number of times that teammate and former major-league career home run and RBI king Hank Aaron did, recording just less than half the number of home runs and RBI. Had he not platooned and instead batted an equivalent number of times, it's reasonable to expect that Adcock might have hit more than 600 home runs while driving in 2,000 runners. Without a doubt, in the history of Major League Baseball few players have developed the reputation for big games and long-ball hitting that Adcock did. He hit the ball often, he hit it with vigor, and he often hit it at just the right moment. And although he failed to post Hall of Fame numbers like Aaron and others did, he is fondly remembered by many as one of the great home run hitters, at-bat for at-bat, of all time.

8

ROCKY COLAVITO

June 10, 1959

The name oozes with power: Rocky . . . Colavito. Nickname? "The Rock." Now the oldest living member of the Four Home Runs Club, Colavito was a powerful hitter in his day. His career statistics reiterate that authority.

Colavito demonstrated his power in a mighty way on June 10, 1959, when as a 25-year-old outfielder for the Cleveland Indians, he swatted four home runs against Baltimore on the Orioles' home field. In all, he hit 42 balls over various American League fences that season, leading the league in that category but finishing a disappointing fourth in the MVP balloting. With 3 1/2 dozen homers and the 111 RBI they helped to produce, Colavito might easily have walked away with an MVP Award, something the six-time All-Star never managed to do in 14 seasons as a big-league player. Despite that disappointment, he remains one of the most highly respected power hitters in Cleveland or Detroit history.

That respect was magnified when, after Colavito hit .257 for the Indians in 1959, they abruptly traded him away for that season's American League batting champion, Harvey Kuenn, who had hit almost 100 points higher than Colavito and also led the league in hits and doubles. Not since Rogers Hornsby won the National League batting crown in 1928, then was whisked away to the Cubs, had a reigning batting champ been effectively told that his services were no longer required.[1] In the case of Colavito, one team's .257 was another team's .353, or something like that. Detroit obviously needed his home run power more than it needed Kuenn's ability to hit for average, and vice versa.

Rocky Colavito. *National Baseball Hall of Fame*

"The Cleveland Indians have had many star players on their roster during the past decade," wrote David Zingler in 2002, citing Albert Belle, Manny Ramirez, and Roberto Alomar. "None of them has approached the popularity of Rocky Colavito, the most beloved Indian of all time."

Zingler added, "A strong case can be made for a Veteran's Committee induction into the Hall of Fame."[2]

Induction or not, Colavito remains a baseball favorite in both Cleveland and Detroit, a man who broke into the majors in 1955 and promptly hit .444, albeit a batting average computed on four hits—two of them doubles—in nine at-bats. With that limited success, the Indians *had* to bring him back for a longer look in 1956, and he quickly affirmed the team's wisdom in inviting him to return rather than sending him down to the minors for more preparation.

After that abridged season Colavito did everything *but* hit for average during the 13 campaigns that followed. He hit 372 home runs, including 40 or more in three of four seasons and 20 or more in 11 consecutive seasons. He led the league in home runs once, although his 45 in 1961 might have earned him more notice had Roger Maris and Mickey Mantle not hit 115 between them in their high-profile, high-intensity intrasquad battle that resulted in Maris setting a new single-season home run mark. Colavito also led the league in RBI once, in 1965. And at various times he was tops in the American League in slugging percentage, games played, walks, and plate appearances, coming to bat almost 700 times in 1963. He even hit .300 once—.303 to be exact, in 1958.

Colavito was, by all standards, a dangerous offensive and defensive ballplayer, someone who simply made the teams he played for better by his presence. Unfortunately, the teams he played for never made it to a World Series, and because of that Colavito was not able to put his arsenal of skills on display in the highest profile of all baseball arenas, although he did hit a double and a single in six All-Star Game appearances.

Curiously, Colavito also pitched three innings for the Indians in 1958, striking out one batter, allowing no runs, and finishing his season with a 0–0 record. A decade later he pitched another 2 2/3 innings, this time for the Yankees, again notching a single strikeout and finishing the season 1–0 with a .000 earned run average. Colavito it seems could do it all.

"It's hard for younger fans to understand the popularity of Colavito and the loss felt when he was traded," wrote Terry Pluto, author of *The Curse of Rocky Colavito*. "In the next five seasons Colavito hit 173 homers for the Tigers. He finished with 374 and played again for the Indians in (1965)-67."[3]

Colavito's final season in Cleveland, when he hit five home runs, gave him 190 career homers with the Indians compared to 139 playing for the Tigers.

Rocco Domenico Colavito was born on August 10, 1933, in the Bronx, New York, the youngest of five children produced by parents Rocco and Angelina Colavito. His father drove an ice truck while Rocco, now Rocky, grew to a formidable size and eventually enrolled at Theodore Roosevelt High School, quitting after his second year to pursue a career in baseball. Although he later lamented the example he set for others by not finishing school, Colavito's ambition of becoming a professional baseball player was realized at the young age of 17 when he signed a bonus contract with the Cleveland organization following a tryout at Yankee Stadium. The contract, it was later revealed, was offered largely because of his arm strength and provided him with $3,000 in up-front remuneration.

"I saw Rocky make a throw from the outfield," scout Mike McNally said. "That was enough for me. I don't think I have ever seen a stronger arm."[4]

Statistics bear out his ability to play solid defense. In 1965 Colavito started all 162 games for the Indians, making zero errors. In 14 seasons playing mostly right field and left field he made just 70 errors, an average of five per year.

In 1951, the year after he signed, Colavito entered the Indians's minor-league system with the Class D Daytona Beach Islanders of the Florida State League and immediately made an impression. During his first season of professional baseball he slugged 23 home runs, hit .275, and earned a promotion to the Class B Spartanburg Peaches of the Tri-State League and later the Cedar Rapids Indians of the Three-I League, where he again impressed the powers that be by hitting 30 home runs. While he demonstrated real power, Colavito had settled into a trend that must have confounded managers throughout his career: He didn't hit for average, something that may explain why he remained in the minor leagues for half a decade.

After a year with the Class B Reading Indians, where he hit 28 home runs, his last two minor-league seasons, 1954 and 1955, were spent with the Triple-A Indianapolis Indians of the American Association, where he hit 68 homers. Based on his proven offensive capabilities the Indians decided it was time that Colavito try his luck in the major leagues.

Before that happened he met and married his wife Carmen in 1954, and the two would spend their offseasons working in the team's offices. Living and working together, the couple demonstrated that theirs clearly was a marriage made in heaven—well, Cleveland anyway.

The 1950s were a rich time for the world and the world of baseball. The entertainment industry was changing rapidly, and a new outlet called television was about to visually propel the sport into people's homes. A singer named Elvis Presley would make a splash of unprecedented importance before entering military service. Ballpark attendance was on the rise, especially in such large markets as New York and Chicago. And by 1958, Major League Baseball would settle in the West in faraway places such as Los Angeles and San Francisco. Baseball would soon be a "national" pastime in every sense of the word, and Colavito got in on the ground floor.

After he racked up 41 home runs the previous season, the Indians expected big things from Rocky Colavito in 1959. On June 10 those expectations were met, even though things started off poorly at Baltimore's Memorial Stadium, a double-deck ballpark that had opened in 1954.[5]

Colavito entered the game with just three hits in his previous 28 at-bats, and his home run production totaled only three from late May through game time. He was admittedly in a mild slump; however, it was one that wouldn't last for long. When a sportswriter asked him before the game when he believed he might kick the slump, Colavito replied, perhaps prophetically, "Tonight might be the night. You never know."[6]

While rumors that the slumping Colavito might be traded had begun to heat up, that's not the only thing that was hot on June 10. Temperatures that day rose to 93°F, an extreme that was not necessarily conducive to good hitting from the standpoint of sweaty hands: During hot weather the hands perspire more than usual, rendering the bat more difficult to grip and making hitting for power without a glove a greater challenge. For the sparse crowd in attendance that day, the only challenge as the game wore on was which Baltimore pitcher might be able to stop the otherworldly Colavito, who broke from his slump wholeheartedly.

That challenge was magnified by the Orioles team itself. Colavito would be facing a club that was tied for first place in the American League, although Baltimore would eventually slip to sixth place. The starting pitcher that day was Jerry Walker, who would finish the season 11–10 with an ERA under 3.00—the big right-hander's best season in an eight-year major-league career.

Walker promptly walked Colavito in the first inning and the big right fielder came around to score on Minnie Minoso's three-run home run. Three innings later a fan would abruptly toss a libation on Colavito after he made a fine running catch on a line drive to right field hit by Albie Pearson.

"He threw a beer right in my face," Colavito said. "I was livid. The nerve of somebody doing that [when] I'm only doing my job."

Pearson, Rookie of the Year for the Washington Senators in 1958 and an All-Star for the Los Angeles Angels five years later, confirmed that Colavito's recollection was correct. "I do remember that (Rocky) made the play and (someone) dumped a beer on him," he said. "That's a true story."

For the rest of the game Colavito would be hot, sweaty, and sticky, not to mention understandably irritated, at least early on. It didn't matter, as Colavito picked himself up, dried himself off, and managed to wallop every pitch thrown to him.

In the third inning, with his team up 4–3 and Vic Power standing on first base, Colavito came to bat again against Walker and hit a changeup down the short, 309-foot left-field line for his first home run of the game. After three innings Cleveland had broken out to a 6–3 lead.

Following the brew-tossing incident and facing right-hander Arnie Portocarrero in the fifth inning with no one on base, Colavito next drew a slider and drilled it over the 390-foot mark in left field, receiving a loud round of cheers from the 15,883 fans in attendance. Cleveland led the Orioles, 7–3, and Colavito's slump was fast becoming ancient history.

He made it three consecutive home runs in the sixth inning. With Cleveland leading 8–3, Portocarrero, apparently having learned little from his previous encounter with Colavito, came at him again with a slider and the big outfielder was waiting for it. He sent the ball sailing over the left-center-field fence again for a 410-foot blast that drove in teammate Tito Francona and put the Indians ahead 10–3. At that moment the fan who had doused Colavito suddenly switched gears.

"By the time I hit the third one and I came out to the field he was giving me a standing ovation along with everyone in the bleachers," Colavito said. "He was definitely one of [those who were applauding]."

Cleveland was ahead 10–8 in the ninth inning when Colavito came to bat for what figured to be his final shot at a record-tying fourth home run. Until that day no player had ever hit more than two homers in a game at Memorial Stadium, but Colavito had changed all that with his third blast. About to face Ernie Johnson, a right-hander in his final major-league season, Colavito got some needed encouragement from roommate Herb Score, a former Rookie of the Year who would remain a lifelong friend until Score's death in 2008.

"OK, roomie," he said. "Don't fool around. Go up there and hit that fourth home run."[7]

At that moment Colavito, who never imagined he would enjoy the kind of game that was unfolding, may have been skeptical that a fourth home run was possible. Certainly any hit giving him a 4-for-4 day would have satisfied the slugger.

"I don't think anybody could imagine [hitting four home runs in a game]," he said.

Pitcher Johnson wanted to keep him skeptical and he brushed Colavito back with a high and tight fastball at the chin. Although brushback pitches were an accepted part of the game in 1959, Colavito wasn't thrilled about being intimidated by a man who threw 90-mile-per-hour heat.

Back came Johnson with an inside fastball and this time Colavito was ready. With a smooth swing he sent the ball soaring, again to left-center field where it landed some 415 feet away. As he glanced up into the bleachers, Colavito could see the man who had saturated him with brew—waving admiringly in support.

"Rocky was a very strong guy," Pearson said. "He was a high fastball mistake power hitter. If you threw a ball above his waist, either a breaking ball, slider, or fastball, forget about it."

After Colavito's final homer a disappointed Jerry Walker, who had started the game, said, "Those last three would've gone out of Yellowstone."[8]

In a footnote to his historic blasts, Colavito had become just the third player in history to achieve the four-home run delight in four straight at-bats during a game that did not go into extra innings. He had not failed to homer in any at-bats after his first-inning walk, and unlike others in the Four Home Runs Club he only required the prescribed nine innings to punch his name into the record books. Colavito had achieved one of the purest four-home run games on record in leading his team to a narrow 11–8 win against the first-place Orioles. His numbers that day? A neat, clean 4-for-4, with six RBI and five runs scored.

In retrospect the beer-throwing incident may have motivated Colavito. Each time he homered the crowd cheered him on, and by the end of the game even the disgruntled fan was in Colavito's corner. As the home runs mounted, the fan's anger about his catch on Pearson abated. Colavito never saw the man again.

"I wouldn't know him if I saw him on the street," he said.

Colavito's final home run of the day was his 18th on the season, a season in which he would hit 24 more and 42 in all. To top off the day, the 16 total bases he rang up tied an all-time American League mark. Without a doubt, Colavito's 3-for-28 slump had come to a dramatic conclusion.

"Oh my gosh, four homers?" Pearson asked, rhetorically. "I look back and I think, 'Wow—I remember it, but did I really play in that game?' I watched history."

He added, "It's really much bigger to me today than it was back then. At the time I think I remembered the beer [incident] more than I remembered the four homers."

According to Colavito, the game held huge significance for not only him, but also others. Even fans who were not in attendance that day claimed years later that they were on hand to watch him clear the fences four times in succession.

"People who were there say they saw [the game], people like to say they were there when they weren't—it goes with the territory," he said.

After 1959, Colavito's career remained on track. Six seasons later and back with Cleveland after stints in Detroit and Kansas City, he was still a highly regarded hitter, knocking in more than 100 runs per season with 20 or 30 home runs. Perhaps being in Cleveland again made a difference.

"I'm glad to be going home—and I do mean home," said Colavito at the time. "Every year when I went into Cleveland with the Tigers or Athletics, I would say to myself, 'Wouldn't it be nice to be playing here again?'"[9]

The niceness wouldn't last forever. In 1966, still playing for Cleveland, things started going south: he posted seventy-two RBI that year and fifty the following season, when the Indians cut his salary and manager Joe Adcock, a fellow member of the Four Home Runs Club, began platooning him.

"I'm not happy about the cut," Colavito said at the time. "No conscientious player ever is . . . I hope to have a big year and win the cut back."[10]

He didn't. After a mediocre season in 1968, playing for two different teams, Colavito retired as a player, although he remained connected to baseball for several years. For the next five seasons he worked intermittently as a television color analyst for WJW-TV in Cleveland, taking time off in 1973 to join the coaching staff of the Indians—a position he also held from 1976 to 1978. After leaving the Cleveland organization he returned to baseball and joined the Kansas City coaching staff for the 1982 and 1983 seasons. In 2001, many years after leaving baseball altogether, the Indians named Colavito one of the team's top 100 players of all time. A half-century after dropping out of high school to pursue his dream of becoming a Major League Baseball player, Colavito had become one of the greatest players in Cleveland Indians history.

Today the Pennsylvania resident is a survivor, not only of baseball wars but also various serious health issues. During the past couple of decades he has survived prostate cancer and heart bypass surgery. More recently, in 2012, his right leg was amputated after circulation problems arose. Colavito gracefully overcame each challenge to throw out a first ball in 2013 on the occasion of his 80th birthday. At least to those in Cleveland it appears there will always be a Rocky Colavito.

"It's just life," he said of his health misfortunes. "None of us should ever take all the good things for granted."[11]

For Colavito, high on the list of "good things" are baseball and the Cleveland Indians.

9

WILLIE MAYS

April 30, 1961

Since professional baseball emerged as an American institution, few players have been immortalized in song as often as Willie Mays, known to everyone as the "Say Hey Kid." It's a well-deserved honor, as few players enjoyed careers as harmonious and melodic as his was.

For starters, there's "Willie Mays Is Up at Bat," "Sometimes I Dream of Willie Mays," "Say Hey, the Willie Mays Song," and, of course, "Talkin' Baseball," otherwise known as "Willie, Mickey, and the Duke."

Willie Mays is a baseball icon, unofficially established as such on September 29, 1954, during Game 1 of the World Series, played between the New York Giants and Cleveland Indians. With the score tied in the top of the eighth inning, Cleveland outfielder Vic Wertz hit a towering smash to the deepest part of center field in New York's capacious Polo Grounds, where Mays, with his back to home plate, made a running, over-the-head catch near the wall to the delight of Giants fans. The play, which was captured on film, is indelibly etched on the minds of almost every baseball fan alive today.

"I turned my back and ran, looked over my shoulder once to gauge the flight of the ball, then kept running," Mays said. "I caught it the way a football end catches a long leading pass. Then, I spun and threw."[1]

Added Mays, of his ability to chase down difficult drives, "When I made a great catch it was just routine. I don't compare 'em, I just catch 'em."[2]

It wasn't the first great catch of Mays's long career, nor would it be the last; however, that play more than any other went a long way toward symbolizing the 1954 season for the eventual 11-time Gold Glove Award–winning center

Willie Mays. © 2017 S. F. Giants

fielder, who hit 41 home runs and batted .345 en route to winning the National League batting crown. After the World Series ended with the Giants sweeping one of the all-time great American League teams, Mays was named MVP. It was truly a dream season for the future Hall of Famer, one of many that the 5-foot-10, 170-pound Alabama native would enjoy. Before he was through there would be 22 seasons in all, almost every one of them exceptional from both an offensive and a defensive standpoint.

The Polo Grounds catch aside, and perhaps even the 30 home runs per season that he averaged between 1951 and 1973, Mays is best remembered for a single game that occurred shortly after the season began in 1961. On April 30 he became only the ninth player in baseball history to hit four home runs in a major-league game, a mighty deed that one aging witness rightfully marveled at.

"I just watched them go into the stands," reflected 83-year-old former Milwaukee Braves outfielder Mel Roach, who played in the outfield that day.

Mays orbited the bases four times that day against the always-tough Milwaukee Braves, whose lineup included former home run king Hank Aaron, Hall of Fame third baseman Eddie Matthews, and Joe Adcock, who had completed his own four-home run game less than seven seasons earlier, in 1954—the year of Mays's famous World Series catch. Pitching for the Braves was Lew Burdette, a tall, sinewy right-hander who would win 200 games during his major-league career.

In his legendary career it took more than an exceptional pitcher like Burdette to prevent a great player like Mays from doing anything he wanted at the plate. His military service managed to ground him for the 1953 season, but other than that the negatives on his baseball resume were few, far between, and for the most part inconsequential. He achieved almost everything he attempted to do on the field with improbable consistency and success.

In 22 seasons Mays failed to hit 10 or more home runs only three times: during his abbreviated second season (1952), when he hit just four balls over various major-league fences in a sparse 127 at-bats, and during his final two campaigns—1972 and 1973—when his skills were diminished, retirement was within sight, and he struggled to hit eight and six home runs, respectively. In contrast, he hit more than 40 round-trippers six times in his career and more than 50 twice, the last time in 1965 when his 52 blasts were good enough to earn him a second MVP Award. Mays's 660 career home runs rank him fifth on the all-time list behind Barry Bonds, Hank Aaron, Babe Ruth, and Alex Rodriguez—elite company to be certain.

Mays recorded 1,903 RBI, placing him 11th all time behind such notable names as Aaron, Ruth, Lou Gehrig, Cap Anson, Stan Musial, Ty Cobb, and Jimmie Foxx. He and Gehrig are the only members of the Four Home Runs

Club to make the career top 25 RBI list, and Mays is the only member of the club listed on the all-time top 15 home run list.

Mays also led the National League in home runs four times, triples three times, hits once, runs twice, and stolen bases four times. And he led the league in slugging percentage a handful of times. Mays was, without a doubt, one of the greatest ballplayers ever to wear a uniform.

"If you can . . . run, hit, run the bases, hit with power, field, throw, and do all the other things that are part of the game, then you're a good ballplayer," he once said.[3] Years later he added, with that boyish Mays twinkle in his eye, "I think I was the best ballplayer I ever saw."[4]

Willie Howard Mays was born on May 6, 1931, in Westfield, a north-central Alabama community that was razed in 1963 to accommodate the expansion of a U.S. Steel plant. His father, Willie Howard Mays Sr., was a steelworker who played pro ball for the Birmingham Black Barons of the Negro League, and young Willie had an obvious pedigree.

Much like his dad, the boy demonstrated exemplary baseball skills. As his ability to play the game matured, everyone recognized how good he had become, thanks largely to his dad's tutelage—especially the local scouts, who followed Mays with great interest during his teen years. Although he starred in several sports early on at Fairfax Industrial High School near Birmingham, baseball was tops on Willie's short list of things he enjoyed doing. Credit for that goes to his father, who worked with the boy until he became more proficient with the bat and glove than most of the other youths and even many adults.

After playing with the Black Barons beginning in his mid-teens and leading the team to the 1948 Negro League World Series, Mays once again became the center of attention as he signed a contract with the New York Giants in 1950, receiving a $4,000 bonus before he was assigned to the team's Class B Trenton Giants of the International League. While in Trenton, where he reportedly earned $250 per week, the young man wasted little time making himself known among the various minor-league teams.

Mays hit only four home runs that first season but batted a lofty .353. The following year he was elevated to the Double-A Minneapolis Millers of the American Association, where he hit an astronomical .477 with eight home runs and 30 RBI. With those numbers in his wallet and the huge potential that Giants management saw in him, Mays was promoted to the big club midway through his 1951 season with Minneapolis, eventually turning up the heat and hitting 20 home runs through the end of his abbreviated first campaign in the majors—

success he indirectly attributed to Hall of Famer Jackie Robinson's struggle to break the color barrier.

"Every time I look at my pocketbook I see Jackie Robinson," he once said.[5]

Mays came along at just the right time—for baseball, for African Americans, and for himself. After Robinson entered the major leagues in 1947, a trickle, then a flood, of African Americans followed after him; Mays was the seventh. He, Hank Aaron, and Ernie Banks were among the first great black home run hitters, and they underscored the truth that they belonged in—and were good for—the game of baseball. A decade later, vindication of sorts would come when the Civil Rights Act of 1964 was passed, ending segregation in public places— segregation that many black players suffered under during the 1950s.

After his debut with the Giants, Mays never looked back—he didn't have do. With his great strength at the plate, his speed on the basepaths, and an uncanny ability to play the outfield, there were few players better than Willie Mays. And, he knew his role.

"They throw the ball and I hit it. They hit the ball and I catch it," he said.[6]

His greatness came into sharp focus during the 1950s when, as a "youngster" in his 20s, he hit 250 home runs. During the 1960s, a decade that began when he was already 30 years old, Mays hit 350 more homers. Even in the 1970s, when he played just four seasons before announcing his retirement following the 1973 season, Mays hit another 60 home runs. He also finished in the top 10 for MVP balloting a remarkable 12 times. The former Rookie of the Year made the All-Star Team 20 times, the last time in 1973 when he batted just .211. Despite disappointing numbers during his final season with the Mets, fans wanted to see him play in one more Midsummer Classic. Unfortunately he disappointed those in attendance, going 0-for-1 with a strikeout, in his final All-Star Game appearance.

Smack dab in the middle of his career was the four-home run game, played at Milwaukee County Stadium on April 30, 1961, and roughly coinciding with several other monumental events that year, including the first manned space flight, John F. Kennedy's inauguration, and the construction of the Berlin Wall. A hitter's ballpark, County Stadium opened for business on April 6, 1953, with field dimensions measuring 320 feet down the left-field line, 315 feet to right, and 402 feet in dead center field. The stadium's seating capacity was 43,394,[7] and on that particular Sunday there were just 13,114 fans in attendance. Those on hand would be treated to a classic slugging confrontation.

Hitting in the third spot and suffering from the ill effects of a meal he had enjoyed late the previous night, Mays came to bat in the first inning against

CHAPTER 9

Lew Burdette, a control pitcher who was MVP for the 1957 World Series. Hitless in the first two games of the series, Mays wasn't impressed with either Burdette's past accolades or his imposing stature: The pitcher was 6-foot-2. Using a bat borrowed from a teammate, he promptly lashed Burdette's first pitch over the center-field fence for his first home run of the game, a solo shot that gave the Giants an early 1–0 lead.

Mays faced Burdette again in the third inning and hit a sinker over the 392-foot mark in left-center field for his second home run of the afternoon, this time a two-run shot that drove in Jim Davenport, who had walked. The Giants added another run on Jose Pagan's first career home run and led Milwaukee 4–3 at the end of three innings.

The struggling Burdette was replaced in the top of the fourth inning after giving up another home run, and when Mays came to bat in the top of the fifth he faced Moe Drabowsky, a journeyman right-hander who, at 6-foot-3, had won just 32 games in five seasons with the White Sox and Braves. Mays greeted him by hitting a fly ball that was caught in the outfield, the only out he would make during the game.

The next inning was a different story. Opposed this time by lefty Seth Morehead, Mays hit a hard slider that sailed over the head of left fielder Roach and cleared the fence, a three-run blast that increased the Giants' lead over the Braves to an insurmountable 11–3 after six innings. The home run was Mays's third of the game.

By then the meager crowd was fully aware that they were witnessing something potentially historic. Balls were flying out of the park in all directions—in addition to Mays's three homers, Hank Aaron and Pagan had hit two each and Orlando Cepeda and Felipe Alou had each hit one.

As the top of the eighth inning rolled around, Morehead was long gone, replaced by Ken Mackenzie who, in turn, was supplanted by Don McMahon, the fifth relief pitcher used by Milwaukee that afternoon. With Davenport on third and McMahon having acceded to Adcock's admonition to not serve up anything appealing to Mays, the center fielder strode to the plate and hit a pitch that Roach watched soar 430 feet over the left-field fence for his fourth home run of the game. The Giants would not score again after the eighth inning, although Mays was on deck with a chance to hit his fifth home run when his team's final out was recorded in the top of the ninth. The final score: San Francisco 14, Milwaukee 4. Willie Mays had done the improbable.

His line score that day was an extraordinary one: 5 at-bats, 4 home runs, 8 RBI, and 4 runs scored.

"I should've had five [home runs]," Mays said. "Aaron caught one ball that was going over the center-field fence."[8]

With that performance the Four Home Runs Club added its only member of the 1960s and the only new one it would welcome for the next 15 years. On that day Mays underscored that he was a both an All-Star and a superstar.

"He could do the five things you have to do to be a superstar: hit, hit with power, run, throw, and field," said Leo Durocher, Mays's first manager with the Giants.[9] Added Ted Williams, who knew something about hitting home runs, "They invented the All-Star Game for Willie Mays."[10]

One media account of the game seemed to echo that sentiment:

> Willie Mays, the San Francisco Giants' great center fielder, found the sure way to break out of a minor slump. The cure: the most explosive hitting performance of his nine-year career. The former "Say, Hey" kid, now a poised veteran of nearly 29, became the ninth player in major-league history to hit four homers in a game as the Giants buried the Milwaukee Braves 14–4 Sunday with a spectacular display of power.[11]

Fifty-five years later, Braves left fielder Roach, who in 1961 was playing in his second-to-last season in the major leagues, recalled the center fielder's great performance.

"I was playing left field," he said. "We were all aware of [what was going on as Mays hit his second and then his third home run]." He added that even as Mays came to bat in the eighth inning with three home runs in the books, he did not believe the slugger would hit a fourth.

"We were just saying, 'Get him out, get him out.'"

All day long the Braves failed to get Mays out, and no one knew that better than Roach. "He hit a couple over my head," recalled the bespectacled left fielder, who as a starter that day singled in four at-bats, including the final shot to left field, which completed a landmark performance.

"It really [was] a great achievement," he said.

Frank Bolling, the Braves' second baseman, also recalled Mays's hitting that day with admiration. "It was pretty fantastic," said Bolling, who went hitless in four at-bats. "It's not like it was unexpected, though. If anybody were to do it, it would have been Mays. You have to take your hat off to him, it was quite a feat."

No one should have been surprised at Mays's performance that day. He went on to hit 40 home runs during the 1961 season, knocking in 123 runners, hitting .308, and winning a fifth Gold Glove Award for fielding excellence. He finished sixth in the MVP balloting behind Frank Robinson, Orlando Cepeda, Vada Pinson, Roberto Clemente, and Joey Jay; Cepeda and Clemente would eventually go on to win MVP Awards in their own right.

"It isn't hard to be good from time to time in sports," Mays later said. "What's tough is being good every day."[12]

Obviously, Mays wasn't through. He hit 341 more home runs in the next 12 seasons before finally calling it quits in 1973. With that, an era spanning the Giants' final seven years in New York and their first 15 seasons in San Francisco had come to an inglorious end, with the Say Hey Kid barely hitting above .200 for the New York Mets at the end. His last hit drove in a game-winning run for the Mets in a 1973 World Series game against the Oakland Athletics, a series that Oakland won, 4–3. With that, Willie Mays officially retired.

"It's like crying for your mother after she's gone," he said of his departure. "You cry because you love her. I cried, I guess, because I loved baseball and I knew I had to leave her."[13]

After he retired, Mays worked as a coach for the New York Mets, assisting younger players; he also spent 12 years working for a multinational consumer products company, primarily in public relations, and did time as a representative for Bally's Casino in Atlantic City, New Jersey. As a result of that position and the association Bally's had with gambling, baseball eventually cut its ties with Mays; however, he was later welcomed back in good standing when a new baseball commissioner took the helm.

Mays was elected to the Baseball Hall of Fame in 1979 and he returned to coaching with the Giants in 1986. Seven years after that, he was given a lifetime contract to remain part of the organization he loved and had served so faithfully for more than 40 years. Now 86 and widowered since 2013, Mays remains a baseball legend, someone the *Sporting News* named the number-two player on its All-Century Team. Who was number one? Babe Ruth.

"Maybe I was born to play ball," Mays once said in a statement that would elicit few arguments from those who saw him play. "Maybe I truly was."[14]

🔟

MIKE SCHMIDT

April 17, 1976

If players could script their dream season, Mike Schmidt's would be 1980. That was the year he led the National League in home runs and RBI, guiding his team to a World Series championship against the Kansas City Royals. Schmidt, who was chosen National League Most Valuable Player when the season ended, also was named World Series MVP after hitting 2 home runs, collecting 8 hits, and batting .381 in the six-game series, which the Phillies won, 4–2. Without a doubt, the hard work Schmidt put in from March through October was incrementally reflected in the daily box scores and ultimately catapulted his team to triumph in the Fall Classic.

"If you could equate the amount of time and effort put in mentally and physically into succeeding on the baseball field and measure it by the dirt on your uniform, mine would have been black," Mike Schmidt once said, perhaps explaining his remarkable success that year.[1]

Unfortunately, the postseason didn't always proceed rhythmically for Schmidt. In playoffs spanning six seasons, including two World Series—one that would see him hit only .050 with one hit in 20 at-bats—Schmidt batted a cumulative .236. In four of eight postseason series he batted .208 or less, twice hitting below .100. Still, season to season he was one of the most consistent home run hitters the game has known.

While still-active Scooter Gennett holds down the bottom rung of the career home runs ladder among members of the Four Home Runs Club, Schmidt stands near the top. His 548 home runs in 18 big-league seasons, all of them playing for the Philadelphia Phillies, rank second on the leaderboard to Willie

Mike Schmidt. *National Baseball Hall of Fame*

Mays and well above the next man, Lou Gehrig, who hit 493. Even more striking is his standing among the all-time major-league career home runs hierarchy, where Schmidt, nicknamed "Schmitty," ranks 16th, ahead of legendary Hall of Famers Mickey Mantle and Jimmie Foxx. Also trailing the native Ohioan are Hall of Famers Ted Williams, Ernie Banks, Mel Ott, Stan Musial, and Carl Yastrzemski.

"Mike was one of the best I ever played with," said 1967 Cy Young Award winner Jim Lonborg, who closed out Schmidt's momentous four-home run game just minutes after the slugger's 10th-inning blast. "He was a hard worker. He was given a gift by God, and he worked and used it and was able to enter the Hall of Fame."

Only two members of the crowned Four Home Runs Club hit 500 or more career home runs, and Schmidt is one of them. He, like Mays, is an anomaly, remembered as much for hitting home runs in an entire career as he is for slugging them during one very special game in 1976. That game was played on April 17 at Wrigley Field in Chicago.

As a power hitter Mike Schmidt could do it all. He led the National League in home runs for the first time in only his third season of ball, knocking 36 over the fences and driving in 116 runs in 1974. After that he would lead the league in round-trippers for seven more seasons, the last time in 1986 when he was an aging 37-year-old. That year, during a season of life when most players are beginning to think about retirement, he also managed to drive in 119 runs and flirt with a .300 batting average, something he would achieve only once in his career. His most productive home run season was 48 in 1980, the year he earned his first MVP Award; he also was named league MVP in 1981 and 1986. In all, Schmidt ranked among the top 10 in MVP balloting nine times during his career.

He also made the All-Star Team a dozen times, something that shouldn't come as a surprise. His high-profile offensive numbers aside (Schmidt led the National League in RBI 4 times, slugging percentage 5 times, and total bases 3 times), he also led the league in numerous lower-profile but offensively important categories, one of which was sacrifice flies—twice. While the mark of a great player is his ability to do the little things well for the team's overall betterment, Schmidt is best known for doing the big things well: His 1,595 career RBI rank him 37th on the all-time list—two ahead of seven-time batting champion and two-time home run leader Rogers Hornsby.

On the down side, Schmidt also led the league in strikeouts four times, something he once joked about. "A guy who strikes out as much as I do had better lead [the league] in *something*," he said in 1976 after leading the league in home runs.[2]

His endless offensive capabilities aside, Schmidt was an exceptional third baseman as evidenced by his nine Gold Glove Awards (not to be confused with his six Silver Slugger Awards). In 1986 he made just six errors in 124 games at third base, cementing his stature as perhaps the greatest offensive and defensive third basemen of all time.

To underscore his career accomplishments, in 2008 the website PhilliesNation.com unveiled its top 100 Phillies of all time. Heading the list was Schmidt, leading such luminaries as fellow Four Home Runs Club members Ed Delahanty (ranked fourth) and Chuck Klein (eighth) as well as Hall of Famers Grover Cleveland Alexander (fifth) and Nap Lajoie (36th). *Sports Illustrated* also named him the sixth-best native Ohio athlete of the twentieth century. The bottom line: With thirteen 30-homer seasons, eight 100-RBI seasons, and 2,234 career hits to his credit, the likable Schmidt is forever embedded in the hearts of Phillies fans across several generations.

Billy DeMars, a pinch-runner in Pat Seerey's 1948 four-home run game, was the Phillies' hitting coach and a witness to history when Schmidt duplicated the feat. He described his teammate as a consummate home run hitter.

"He had a great swing and great power, and when he made contact the ball was gone," DeMars said.

Michael Jack Schmidt was born on September 27, 1949, in Dayton, Ohio, the state's sixth-largest city and the administrative center for Montgomery County. In his early years, young Mike spent considerable time around sports, as his parents, Jack and Louise, managed a Dayton-area restaurant that was situated within a swimming complex. While the club was dedicated to water activities, other sports also were offered. Young Mike wasted little time testing the waters, so to speak.

Later on, Schmidt attended Fairview High School in his hometown, where he played baseball and quickly became accomplished in the sport. He was so good and demonstrated such power at the plate that major-league scouts began coming around more and more frequently, and it wasn't long before the young man's future began to crystallize. That future would be baseball.

"My dreams started on a small playground near my home, where I first learned how to hold a bat," Schmidt once said.[3] He never let go of it.

At the age of 18, Schmidt enrolled at Ohio University on a baseball scholarship, playing every infield position except first base during his freshman, sophomore, and junior seasons. It was during his final year of college, however, when he really came into his own.

That year, Schmidt set a school record for home runs, walloping an amazing 45 and once again attracting the attention of eager scouts. One of them convinced the Philadelphia Phillies to give Schmidt a shot with the organization, and the team selected him in the second round of the 1971 amateur draft. Mike Schmidt was on his way.

That "way" meandered, however. In 1971, shortly after signing with the Phillies, Schmidt was sent to the organization's Reading, Pennsylvania, club— the Reading Phillies, a Double-A team that played in the Eastern League. While there he performed below his capabilities, hitting eight home runs and batting only .211. His slow start didn't discourage the Phillies' front office, as they advanced him to the Triple-A Eugene (Oregon) Emeralds of the Pacific Coast League in 1972. The less-than-distinguished start that he'd experienced in 1971 was soon forgotten, as Schmidt blasted 26 home runs and drove in 91 runs for the Emeralds. Before the season was over the Phillies had seen enough, and they brought him up to the major-league club. Thereafter, he wore his Phillies uniform proudly until the day he retired.

"To me, everyone who wears a uniform carries the responsibility of becoming a positive role model," he would say many years later. "When I think about it, this is more important than any home run, any play, or any statistic. All these fade with time. But, being a positive role model both on and off the field helps others become better human beings."[4]

When Schmidt joined the big club he did so at the right time. The tumultuous 1960s had left an aftertaste, the Watergate era was careening to a head, and the Space Age was picking up steam following the tragic deaths of three American astronauts in a 1967 ground test for Apollo 1. The country was ready for some carefree baseball featuring the likes of the likable third baseman.

Schmidt saw little action during the remainder of 1972, playing in just 13 games. He did manage to hit one home run, although he drove in only three runs and hit an anemic .206. With numbers like those, members of the front office may have been rethinking their decision to bring him up.

The following season Schmidt began to show signs of the greatness that would be his trademark. Although he batted only .196 as the Phillies' regular third baseman, he did hit 18 home runs. That year would mark the last time that Schmidt would ever look over his shoulder. In 1974 he broke strong and stayed that way throughout the season, slugging 36 home runs and driving in 116 runs. His home run total that season would lead the National League;

he also would lead the league in homers in 1975 and again in 1976, although one game would overshadow the entire 1976 season. That game was against the Cubs.

Originally named Weeghman Field and later Cubs Park, Wrigley Field, nicknamed "The Friendly Confines," is a baseball and cultural landmark. Opened in 1914 on the North Side of Chicago, its ivy-covered walls and hand-turned scoreboard are true icons. On August 8, 1988, Wrigley became the last ballpark in either league to add lights for night baseball, belatedly ushering the stadium into the twentieth century.

Wrigley is a veritable time machine, with an antiquated marquee reading "Wrigley Field, Home of Chicago Cubs" situated like a beacon at the home plate entrance and reflecting its rich heritage. That heritage is an important one. The stadium was built for only $250,000 back when automobile sightings were rare occurrences on Lake Shore Drive, and it opened with odd dimensions: a paltry 310 feet in left field, a more robust 356 feet to right, and an ample 440 feet in straightaway center. Today, Wrigley's field dimensions are much more moderate than they were during earlier days, measuring 355 feet in left field, 353 feet in right, and 400 feet to dead center[5]—just the sort of dimensions that a long-ball hitter like Mike Schmidt could capitalize on. Capitalize he did.

Baseball aside, the year 1976 was significant on several fronts. The nation's 200th birthday was celebrated on a broad scale, the United Nations Security Council voted 11–1 to seat the Palestine Liberation Organization, and an earthquake in China killed 655,000 people. In baseball, Ted Turner became CEO of the Braves and Cubs outfielder Rick Monday prevented two fans from setting an American flag on fire at Dodger Stadium.

It also was significant for the Phillies, who began the 1976 season, a campaign in which they would win 101 games and capture the National League East Division title, slowly, winning just one of their first four games. The fifth game, however, was a barn burner and for most of the game Mike Schmidt held the match.

As is often the case in Chicago, the wind was blowing formidably that Saturday when Schmidt, batting sixth in the lineup, led off the second inning against Cubs ace Rick Reuschel, a 215-pound right-hander who usually had good control. He flied out routinely to center fielder Rick Monday; however, the Phillies would score a run to take an early 1–0 lead.

The Cubs came back with seven runs in the bottom of the second, knocking Phillies ace Steve Carlton out of the game and threatening to make the contest a rout before most fans had even warmed their seats. Schmidt did manage a hit when he came to bat again in the fourth, singling off Reuschel to lead off, but he was not able to score. After four innings the Cubs still held a sizable lead over the Phillies, 7–2. Then Schmidt went to work.

With his team down 13–2 in the top of the fifth inning, Schmidt came to bat against Reuschel for a third time and greeted him with a two-run shot that cleared the fences. At the end of five innings Chicago held a hefty lead, 13–4.

Back came the Phillies again in the seventh inning. With Reuschel still in the game, Schmidt, facing him for the fourth time, blasted a solo shot that, combined with two more Phillies runs that inning, brought the team to within six runs of the Cubs, 13–7. Schmidt and his teammates had managed to trim the Cubs' lead almost in half with two innings yet to play in regulation.

Schmidt batted again in the eighth inning and, with Mike Garman pitching, hit his third home run of the game, a three-run shot that helped cut the Cubs lead to 13–12. The Phillies had managed to claw their way back from a 13–2 deficit and now trailed the Cubs by just a run.

They completed their comeback in the ninth, scoring three runs to pull ahead, 15–13. But the Cubs scored two of their own in the bottom half of the frame to send the game into extra innings. Fortunately for the Phillies, the red-hot Schmidt was due up again in the 10th. Facing Paul Reuschel, a 6-foot-4, 225-pound bear of a man and the brother of starting pitcher Rick Reuschel, Schmidt put the game away with his fourth home run of the contest, a towering drive over the 368-foot mark in left-center field that knocked in Dick Allen. After trailing most of the game the Phillies won the donnybrook, 18–16, thanks to 24 hits—and Mike Schmidt's four home runs. On the day, Schmidt went 5-for-6 with eight RBI and four runs scored.

The game took three hours, 42 minutes to complete. There were 43 hits by both teams combined and 9 home runs (including two by the Cubs' Rick Monday), and 13 pitchers were used. The game may have marked the first time in major-league history that a batter—Schmidt—had hit home runs off two brothers during the same game, two off Rick Reuschel and one off Paul.

Phillies hitting coach DeMars, witness to Pat Seerey's four-home run game, was stationed in the coach's box at third base that day as Schmidt rounded the bases with precision.

"I was the hitting coach and the day before, we hit off the batting tee," De-Mars said. "The next day he hit the four home runs."

DeMars implied that the stationary nature of the tee may have worked some magic for his prize third baseman. If it did, it also enabled DeMars to be among the first to congratulate Schmidt all four times that he cleared the fences.

"Every time he came around third base he shook my hand," he laughed.

Lonborg, the eighth pitcher used by Philadelphia that day, compared Schmidt's accomplishment to a hole in one. "The chances of something like that happening are a million to one," he said. "For a professional baseball player hitting against professional pitching to make contact four times and hit home runs each time, it's like hitting a hole in one."

Lonborg added that 40 years later, having played in the game that day remains a highlight for him. "It's historic," he said. "It happens so seldom."

Schmidt's tear continued during the month of April, as he hit 12 home runs in his first 15 games. The four dingers against the Cubs didn't hurt his cause, and Schmidt would prove throughout his career that the blasts in Chicago were far from a fluke: He would hit 50 home runs in Wrigley Field before calling it quits as a consummate home run hitter.

"I stopped thinking as though every trip to the plate was a life-or-death proposition," he said in 2006, explaining his maturity as a hitter. "Instead of thinking I had to hit every pitch with every ounce of strength, I tried to pick out a good pitch and swing naturally."[6]

In his coverage of The Game, one reporter officially added an 11th member to what he dubbed the "Elite Club," otherwise known as the Four Home Runs Club:

Mike Schmidt said he "was only trying to get a single" when he belted his fourth-consecutive home run of the game to set a modern-day National League record and lead the Philadelphia Phillies back from an 11-run deficit to an 18–16, 10-inning triumph over the Chicago Cubs Saturday.[7]

Schmidt entered the game hitting just .167 and he finished the contest with four balls worthy of display in the Hall of Fame, assuming anyone ever identified the recipients. He explained his slow start, one that would accelerate resoundingly until it culminated with a third-place finish in the National League MVP balloting, to reporters after the game.

"I have been off to a very slow start, if you can call less than 20 times at bat a slow start," he said. "The team has been in somewhat of a slump and I have been trying to figure out what I've been doing wrong."[8]

Obviously, he figured it out against the Cubs.

"When you get behind 13–2 like we did, most guys would have quit and thought about tomorrow, but it made me more relaxed and I started swinging away. I hear I set a modern-day [National League] record and it's kind of nice, but I'm one guy who doesn't think about records."[9]

After 40 years, perhaps Schmidt should give the record more consideration, although he did hit 34 more during the course of the season. He finished the 1976 season with 107 RBI, winning a Gold Glove Award to boot.

There were many more successful seasons for Schmidt after that. On that day in 1976 Schmidt was at the peak of his game, and the peak would last another 11 years—until he retired following a disappointing 1989 season. Nonetheless, he is remembered as a hard worker and a tireless on-field performer.

Schmidt's eventual departure from the game was a difficult one. Rather than drift away quietly as many ballplayers do, he held an emotional news conference to reveal that he was quitting. His final game was on May 28, and even though he was gone from baseball, fans voted him onto the All-Star Team one last time. Perhaps fittingly, he wouldn't appear, leaving a hole on the 1989 squad that only Mike Schmidt could truly fill.

The following year, Schmidt stood by his decision to retire despite skills that were still formidable. "I have no desire to play baseball anymore," he said. "I'm totally finished with it."[10]

In 1990 Schmidt's number 20 jersey was retired by the Phillies, the team's highest compliment. After that the accolades poured in. He was inducted into the Peter J. McGovern Little League Museum Hall of Excellence in 1991, and in 1995 Schmidt was voted into the Baseball Hall of Fame—the ultimate mark of recognition for a ballplayer. Eventually a statue of Schmidt was erected at Citizens Bank Park in Philadelphia, where the team now plays.

Since retiring, Schmidt's involvement with baseball has been varied. He has worked as a color analyst for the Phillies, assisted as the team's spring training guest instructor, and in 2004 managed the Clearwater Threshers, the Phillies' Single-A Florida State League team. Under Schmidt, the Threshers finished the season 55–81, well down in the standings.

In 2014, the slugger stunned everyone by revealing that during the previous year doctors had discovered a melanoma on his back. They removed 33 lymph nodes as a precaution against metastases and initiated interferon and radiation treatment, but by 2014 the cancer had spread to his lungs and brain. Then, things turned around—as of 2017 he was free of cancer.

Despite that serious health challenge, Schmidt has remained optimistic in interviews. He continues to follow his doctor's orders and has put his health—and life—in the hands of God and his squadron of doctors. What does the future hold for Mike Schmidt? Apparently, quite a lot.

"I'm planning on living to be 100," he said.[11]

11

BOB HORNER

July 6, 1986

Noticeably missing from Bob Horner's major-league career vitae is the year 1987, when the burly, curly, blonde-haired slugger departed the United States to play baseball in Japan. While performing his craft in the Land of the Rising Sun, Horner did what he always did: He hit home runs. And he earned a special nickname: Aka-oni, meaning "red devil."[1] Horner always *was* a devil with the bat.

Playing ball for the Yakult Swallows of the Japanese Central League, Horner picked up where he had left off with the Atlanta Braves, hitting 31 home runs. Then, as quickly as he had arrived to the approbation of admiring fans, Horner disappeared from the league, joining the St. Louis Cardinals in 1988 for his 10th and final season in the big leagues. To the many faithful fans who had followed Horner in the United States and welcomed his return home, Aka-oni was once again just plain Bob.

The timing of Horner's return stateside was propitious. After hitting four home runs on July 6, 1986, he had taken a well-deserved interlude from the pressures of American baseball and headed for Japan after the season ended. The fans who had celebrated him while he played nine seasons with the Braves barely had time to bring their collective applause to a crescendo after his record-tying game. Three months later Horner was packing his grip and headed for the nearest airport—and a paycheck scrawled in Japanese script.

Although he returned to U.S. soil the following season and joined a different club than the one he had left behind, Horner was nonetheless back in the National League where he always belonged. And Braves fans could either cheer him or not every time he returned to Atlanta, albeit wearing a St. Louis Cardinals uniform.

"I don't want to be forced to go halfway around the world to play something that isn't baseball," Horner proffered to those scrutinizing his return to American baseball, explaining his reason for leaving Japan. "There is little

Bob Horner. *Copyright Jerry Coli/Dreamstime.com*

semblance between baseball games in Japan and the game I loved and grew up with in the States."[2]

The comment came after Horner had declared early on in his Japanese experience: "I think I'm going to like this."[3] Apparently, he didn't.

As it turned out, Horner's time in St. Louis wouldn't last long either. He retired from baseball after one season in the Gateway City. His legacy as a slugger, however, was by that time cemented, largely because of the four-home run game—the 11th in major-league history.

During his tenure as a major leaguer, Horner was an unexceptional star, one whose light never shone as brightly as others in the Four Home Runs Club. Players such as Lou Gehrig. Or Willie Mays. Or Chuck Klein. But he did put up respectable numbers for a respectable number of years and was highly regarded during his years as a member of the Braves organization.

Although he played solidly for a full decade, Horner never led the National League in any notable offensive category. He did earn Rookie of the Year honors in 1978 when he hit 23 home runs and knocked in 63 runners. And he was named to the National League All-Star Team once, in 1982—arguably his statistics were good enough that he should have been selected more than once.

Horner hit 30 or more home runs three times and belted them out in double figures in nine of his 10 seasons as a pro. His best season was his second one, 1979, when the slugger hit 33 home runs and collected 98 RBI while hitting .314, the first of only two seasons in which he would hit over .300; however, his 1979 statistics were only good enough to earn him a disappointing 28th place in the MVP balloting.

Despite the absence of award recognition, Horner kept swinging away. He hit 35 homers in 1980, finishing ninth in the MVP balloting. There were 32 homers in 1982, his only All-Star year. In three of his last four big-league seasons he hit 20, 27, and 27 home runs, respectively. Then he was off to Japan, then back again to St. Louis and a string of injuries. Still, at least one memory stuck: the memory of swatting four home runs in an 11–8 loss to the Montreal Expos at Atlanta's Fulton County Stadium. No one can take *that* away from him.

James Robert Horner was born in Junction City, Kansas, on August 6, 1957, but he was reared in California after his father moved the family to the Los Angeles area in 1971 before eventually settling in Arizona. Even as a boy baseball was important to Horner, and he left a legacy of greatness at Apollo High School in Glendale, Arizona, and later at baseball powerhouse Arizona State University. It was at ASU where Horner earned College World Series MVP

honors in leading the Sun Devils to the 1977 national championship—the
school's fourth title—against the University of South Carolina. That season
Horner was tops in the nation in home runs, with 22, and RBI, with 81, and
he batted a sterling .444 in the World Series, drilling two home runs and collecting nine RBI. Not bad for a guy hoping to springboard his way to the major
leagues. Springboard he did.

After having been chosen out of high school in the 15th round of baseball's
amateur draft by the Oakland A's, but electing to turn the team down, Horner's
stock continued to rise and he was selected first in the 1978 draft. So grand a
prospect was he that he never spent a minute in the minor leagues. Instead the
Atlanta Braves immediately elevated him to the big club, where he homered
during his first professional game. Bob Horner was on a fast track to stardom.

His immediate success should not have been a surprise. While a teen he
graced the cover of *Arizona Prep* magazine after advancing to become one of
the finest high school ballplayers in the state's history, a legacy brought home
in 2009 when Horner was initiated into the *Arizona Republic*'s Arizona High
School Sports Hall of Fame. From there it was on to Arizona State, consistently
one of the finest baseball programs in the country at that time.

While at ASU, Horner was one of the nation's top ballplayers, twice an All-
American, and the only Sun Devil up until then to bat over .400 (.412), hit 25
home runs, and knock in 100 runners in one season; his 56 homers during a
superb collegiate career set a school record, while his whopping .720 slugging
percentage was second best in the school's history. As the 1977 College World
Series rolled around, all eyes were understandably on Horner, who at that point
led everyone anywhere in home runs, RBI, hits, and total bases.

His velocious ascendance to the big leagues was a dream come true for the
formidable Horner, whose playing height and weight are listed at a healthy
6-foot-1 and 195 pounds, although he fluctuated and at one point weighed as
much as 215. "I accomplished a dream," he said. "My father always wanted
to play in the big leagues, and I kind of lived his dream out for him. And, I
wouldn't trade a minute of it."[4]

After homering in his first game, Horner continued strong throughout his
rookie season. When his name was announced as Rookie of the Year, the ac-
colade culminated a lifetime of hard work and sweat. Then came a flurry of
injuries, including a shoulder surgery after the 1978 season and an ankle injury
the following year.

After that his time on the field was limited. In 1981 he tallied only 300 at-bats
and his numbers descended to 15 home runs and 42 RBI. He had 386 at-bats in
1983, just 113 in 1984, and 206 in 1988, his final season as a major leaguer. In

10 seasons he averaged only 102 games played and 378 at-bats per season, not enough to secure his legacy as an all-time great.

Still, as 1986 rolled around, Horner had one more great performance left in him, and he saved the best for his final season with the Braves. On July 6 Horner had his finest hour as a major-league player. Thirty years later it hasn't been forgotten.

In 1986 the United States needed a happy milestone. The country had largely put behind it the attempted assassination of President Ronald Reagan five years earlier; however, two years after that a deadly disease with the curious acronym AIDS was recognized by the Centers for Disease Control and Prevention. If that weren't enough, the Space Shuttle Challenger exploded just months before the 1986 baseball season began, killing all seven crew members. A landmark baseball event would surely boost the nation's spirits.

There would be several that season. The Giants' Willie McCovey became the 16th player unanimously elected to the National Baseball Hall of Fame, Roger Clemens became the first pitcher to strike out 20 batters in a nine-inning game, and Barry Bonds hit his first major-league home run. Finally, there was Horner of the Braves.

When the Braves moved from Milwaukee to Atlanta in 1966, their first home was Atlanta Fulton County Stadium. Sharing the grounds with them were the Atlanta Falcons, making Fulton County Stadium a dual-purpose (football and baseball) stadium.[5]

The most memorable moment during the stadium's first decade occurred on April 8, 1974, when Hank Aaron hit his 715th homer to break Babe Ruth's all-time career home run mark. Twelve years later, Horner would challenge that accomplishment for memorability when he sprang into the record books in his own baronial style.

In 1977, 11 years after it opened and 19 years before it would close, Fulton County Stadium received some plastic surgery: Colorful plastic seats replaced aging wooden ones and a modern scoreboard was erected just below the roof and above the center-field bleachers. Through it all one thing remained constant: the stadium's highly reachable 330-foot left-field wall.[6] On a summer day in 1986 Horner applauded its reachability.

Facing him for the Montreal Expos that day was Andy McGaffigan, a six-year veteran who, at 6-foot-3 and 185 pounds, was enjoying his best season in the big leagues. Hoping to help his team avoid a three-game sweep by the Expos, Horner, hitting cleanup and playing first base, came to bat in the first inning with 13 homers and 49 RBI to his credit midway through the season. With

18,000 fans looking on he hit a fastball off the right-hander toward the left-field foul line and just over the 10-foot-high mesh fence to give the Braves a 1–0 lead.

Montreal came back with a run of its own in the third and three more in the fourth to take a 4–1 lead; however, down 2–0 in the three-game series, Horner was up to the challenge of leading his team back from defeat. Once again facing McGaffigan, this time in the fourth inning, he drilled a pitch toward the same spot in left field where he'd homered earlier, clearing the fence again and cutting the Expos lead to 4–2. The blast gave him his second multi-home run game of the season.

By the bottom of the fifth inning, with the Expos holding a 10–2 advantage, McGaffigan had wearied of Bob Horner. In two at-bats the hefty first baseman had hit two home runs to the same location. Facing Horner in the bottom of the fifth, McGaffigan was searching for a solution.

Once again Horner confounded him. He caught another McGaffigan fast-ball solidly and sent it soaring 10 rows deep into the left-field bleachers for a three-run homer. In three at-bats he had connected for three home runs and five runs batted in off the right-hander, who left the game after giving up seven runs—four of them earned. McGaffigan also earned the distinction of being one of the few pitchers in major-league history to give up three home runs to the same player in the same game, something that required only four-plus innings of work.

"It was exciting," McGaffigan said. "There are days you'd like to forget, but for the most part those are few and far between."

In acknowledging that he is now the answer to a trivia question—name a pitcher who gave up three home runs to a player who hit four home runs in a game—McGaffigan chuckled. "Much of my career is the answer to a trivia question." He added, "I'd rather be known for pitching a perfect game in the World Series like Don Larson did. I guess that wasn't my lot in life, so I'm all right with it."

McGaffigan—the start would be his final one with Montreal before the Expos turned him into a relief pitcher—was replaced in the fifth inning by right-hander Tim Burke, who two innings later would have the pitching staff's only success against Horner that day. After Burke forced Horner to pop out to first base-man Wayne Krenchicki in the seventh inning, Montreal led the Braves by what would prove to be an insurmountable score, 11–7.

"I never liked facing Bob Horner, because he stood right on top of the plate like nobody I've ever seen before," said Burke, who pitched 2 2/3 scoreless innings that day. "I remember the pressure that was on me because he had hit three [home runs] by the time I came in. The last thing I wanted to do was to give up a history-making home run—I knew it would be on the highlight films for a long, long time."

Instead, Burke rose to the occasion—"It was a huge relief," he said—and today he considers it a memorable accomplishment to have pitched in the game without giving up either a home run to Horner or a run to the Braves.

"It was a huge thrill to be the only guy not to give up a home run to him," said Burke, who posted a career ERA of 2.72 in eight seasons. "I thought that was really, really cool. And, I thought it was really cool to watch someone achieve something incredible like that."

Although Burke plugged the levy, the flood wasn't over yet. Jeff Reardon came in to replace Burke with one out in the eighth inning, and by the time Horner came to bat in the ninth the challenge was on again. Could Reardon, as Burke had done, stop Bob Horner from doing the unthinkable? The answer was a resounding *no*.

With two outs in the ninth inning and his team still trailing the Expos, 11–7, Horner was down to perhaps his last shot at the record. Once again he powered a solo blast over the left-field fence that dropped in front of the blue bleachers. With the crowd roaring excitedly, Horner pumped his fist as he rounded first base and proceeded to enjoy his trot around the bases, tipping his cap and waving to the crowd after he touched home plate and stepped down into the Braves' dugout.

"It was crazy to watch someone hit four home runs in a game," Burke said. "It's just unbelievable."

While the Braves would go on to lose the game, 11–8, Horner would enter the record book with four home runs in a single contest—three of them solo shots.

"The ball was jumping that day, because *I* even got a hit," McGaffigan said. "And I was one of the worst hitters in the game. For me to get a hit I just figured the ball was jumping.

"I threw well. I just couldn't get that guy out. Historically, I don't know what he hit against me, but I'm sure it was well into the .300s and maybe higher. He was just one of those guys who I had a difficult time getting out."

McGaffigan added, "I had a lot of family members at that game, which was a little embarrassing. But, you take the good with the bad."

With his final homer, Horner became a rarity, hitting four home runs in a losing cause. And while the loss stung, his personal accomplishment that day went a long way toward helping to ease the pain.

"I was fortunate to do it," Horner said of his performance. "It's a great personal accomplishment and great for the team."[7]

The only lament that Horner might have had was his failure to come to bat with runners on base. As a result, his statistic line for the game is light on RBI: He ended the day going 4-for-5, with 4 home runs, 4 runs scored, and 5 RBI.

"I don't think any of the home runs I hit even tied (the game), much less put us ahead," Horner once recollected. He added, "It was a wonderful feeling. But it's a team game in a team sport, and there wasn't much to celebrate about because we lost."[8]

Still, the game was one for the record books and one that the media raved about the following morning. One account of Horner's accomplishment was as follows: "Bob Horner did the right thing on the wrong day. Horner became the 11th player in major-league history to hit four home runs in a game but did it on a day when Mitch Webster went 5-for-6 to lead the Montreal Expos to an 11–8 victory over Horner's Atlanta Braves."[9]

Midway through the season, Horner had increased his home run total by almost a third in just one game—from 13 to 17. Little did he know that time was running out for him at Fulton County Stadium.

Horner would hit 10 more home runs during the second half of the season and 13 in his career, eventually playing out his option with the Braves and leaving the country. While playing with Yakult the following season he would earn his keep, leading the league in homers before declaring his residency there finished as well.

After signing the deal with the Cardinals, it quickly became evident that Busch Stadium, whose left-field fence was deeper than the one at Fulton County Stadium, would be a challenge. In the end, it and other things were challenges that Horner simply could not overcome.

Once again injuries became a problem, and Horner retired following a season of disappointment. Playing in only 60 games with the Cardinals, he swatted just 53 hits, hit 3 home runs, and drove in 33 runs. At the age of 30 and just two years removed from his fabulous four-home run game, Bob Horner retired from baseball. But not from life.

"I couldn't focus on making the club because I was always worried about the shoulder so much," Horner said of a final tryout with Baltimore before he retired. "One thing I didn't want to do was go out and do something major to it and have a broken-down arm the rest of my life. I've got children I want to raise and teach sports to. The last thing they need is a crippled father."[10]

In the 30 years since his heroic game, Horner has had considerable time to reflect on the accomplishment. He described the day as a perfect storm of baseball good fortune.

CHAPTER 11

"It was a Sunday getaway day, and we were playing at home," he said, continuing,

> Right after the game [we were] getting on the plane and flying to Philadelphia. The whole game, [we were] behind. Every time I came up to bat, [we were] behind, so the pitchers, luckily for me, [were] trying to come after me because they had nothing to lose.
>
> The stars aligned. [They were] throwing at me and trying to get me out, and [we were] behind every time [we were] at bat. It happened, and my only regret is we didn't win.[11]

After retiring, Horner found many ways to keep himself busy. He settled in Irving, Texas, where his children were raised. He played some golf and even spent several years volunteering for an Irving-area human services agency called Irving Cares. One of the organization's charges was to provide food for the needy, and Horner worked as a volunteer in its food bank. In 2006, almost 30 years after graduating from ASU, he was finally inducted into the College Baseball Hall of Fame.

Through it all, the good and the not so good, baseball has remained a big part of Horner's life, and he continues to follow the fortunes of the Braves, for whom he labored for so many years. Baseball has been good to Bob Horner, and as age 60 approached he had few regrets.

"I had a great time," he said. "I lived a dream. I wouldn't trade it for anything in the world."[12]

MARK WHITEN
September 7, 1993

If the destination stickers on his luggage are any indication, Mark Whiten may be the most widely traveled player in the history of the Four Home Runs Club. Oddly, Whiten's team-trotting didn't stop with his "amazing" offensive performance, as one player put it, on September 7, 1993, which also produced a record-tying 12 RBI. Instead, the franchise hopping that already had begun seemed only to escalate during the years that followed.

"It was just amazing," Reds pitcher Chris Bushing, who had a front-row seat for Whiten's historic performance, said of the four-home run game.

Whiten was an unlikely hero that day, a player already competing for his third team in just four seasons as a major leaguer. His movement from team to team was likely due to his tendency to disappoint management from an offensive perspective during mostly shared seasons with two other teams early on in his career (his composite batting average prior to 1993 was .251). Not that he had much of an opportunity to prove himself as a young ballplayer.

Whiten broke in with the Toronto Blue Jays, coming to bat only 88 times during his first season and 149 times in 1991. He was traded to Cleveland in mid-year 1991 and played with the Indians through the remainder of that season and the next, hitting .243 and .254, respectively. Then, in a twist of fate, he ended up with the St. Louis Cardinals organization in 1993. There would be six more major-league employers before Whiten retired in 2000 with only 105 career home runs, an inauspicious total for a guy largely remembered for homering.

It's fair to say that The Game, which Whiten modestly put in context by saying, "It was just my turn," might never have occurred if destiny hadn't played

Mark Whiten. *National Baseball Hall of Fame*

a role. Whiten owes his fame, in part, to a pair of Cleveland Indians pitchers who were killed in a freak boating accident on a lake not far from where he was reared. That twist of fate occurred on March 22, 1993, when Steve Olin and Tim Crews perished after the boat they were riding in struck a dock on Little Lake Nellie near Cleremont, Florida. Both were pitchers, and the tragedy left the Indians reeling.

Desperate to replace the two tragic victims and at the same time hedge their bets on pitcher Bob Ojeda, who suffered a serious head injury in the accident, Cleveland turned to the St. Louis Cardinals, who were willing to give up pitcher Mark Clark and another player in exchange for a position player with potential. That player was Whiten, who was stunned by the deal.

"It was a shock for me," he said at the time. While admitting his shock, he also conceded he was still a little green. "I'm still learning," the surprised Whiten said.[1] Learn he did.

After joining the Cardinals, Whiten hit slightly below what would become his career average of .259; however, he managed to put away 25 home runs and knock in 99 runs. Based on his first season with the club, the Cardinals were more than satisfied with the acquisition they had made.

On the other end of the deal, Clark went 7–5 with a 4.28 ERA for the Indians. And although he would continue on to average 10 wins per season before his career would end in 2000, at least during that first season in St. Louis Whiten appeared to enjoy the better end of the deal.

Just a six-hour drive from where Olin and Crews were killed, Mark Anthony Whiten was born on November 25, 1966, in Pensacola, Florida. His athletic skills became apparent later in high school than others in the Four Home Runs Club, and he was recruited for the Pensacola High School football team his junior year.

Whiten eventually became a star on both the football and baseball fields, so much so that Pensacola Junior College considered it a coup when the school was able to sign him on in 1984. By then baseball was the young man's preferred athletic preoccupation.

Known affectionately as "Hard Hittin'" Whiten, he excelled during his tenure in college, earning team MVP honors as a rifle-armed outfielder. As a result, after he completed his education the Blue Jays selected him in the fifth round of the 1986 amateur draft. Whiten signed with the team three months later, on April 28, 1986. That was the easy part.

Like most ballplayers, Whiten began his career in a rookie league, in his case with the Medicine Hat Blue Jays in the Pioneer League. While there he played superbly, hitting an even .300 with 10 home runs and earning a promotion to Single-A ball at Myrtle Beach in the South Atlantic League in 1987. At Myrtle Beach he hit 5 home runs, collected 64 RBI, and hit .253. The potential was there—all he needed was some discipline at the plate.

After two successful minor-league seasons the promotions came swiftly. Whiten spent 1988 with the Dunedin and Knoxville Blue Jays in Single-A and Double-A, belting a combined total of nine home runs. He returned to Knox-ville the following season, where his numbers improved again—although not obviously. He earned another promotion to the next minor-league level.

Whiten began the 1990 season with the Syracuse Chiefs of the International League, a Triple-A club managed by former Blue Jay Bob Bailor. Once again, his production was noteworthy—he had 14 home runs to go along with an ex-cellent .290 batting average, and once again the Blue Jays promoted him—this time to the big club for the remainder of 1990. Unbeknownst to Whiten, the roller-coaster ride that would imprint his career had just begun.

During that first partial season with Toronto, Whiten hit a respectable .273, but with only two home runs, and the following season his average dropped 30 points. After apparently becoming impatient with his slow progress, Toronto traded him to Cleveland just 149 at-bats into the 1991 season, one that was blemished by a well-publicized brawl involving pitcher Jack McDowell of the White Sox.

"It was something I had to do," said Whiten, who was ejected and later suspended after charging the mound and striking the pitcher on the jaw with a roundhouse punch following an alleged brushback pitch.[2]

After Toronto traded him, the change of scenery must have helped the strug-gling Whiten. That year he upped his home run total to nine from only two in his rookie season 1990, and he drove in 45 runners. The following season he hit nine more home runs and drove in 43 runs. Despite those successes, when the 1992 season ended he was once again gone, this time sent to the Cardinals. While there, he would flourish—at least for one season and part of a second.

At 6-foot-3 and 235 pounds, Whiten was an up-again, down-again anomaly. He could throw with the best and hit from either side of the plate, and when hitting in his groove the baseball would travel. In 1993, his best season hitting for power, the ball traveled often and far—frequently over the fence. That was the case when the Cardinals traveled to Cincinnati for a game against the Reds toward the end of that season.

On September 7, 1993, Whiten found his groove more than ever before—in fact, he grooved the ball more than almost any other ballplayer in major-league history had ever done on a given day. Good thing, because the following season he would once again find himself playing in the minor leagues at the Triple-A level. After that, Mark Whiten would never quite replicate his former hitting success.

"I just anticipate getting every at-bat I possibly can," Whiten once said, explaining his hitting philosophy in the simplest of terms.[3] That day, he needed just five.

Built to replace historic Crosley Field, Riverfront Stadium opened in 1970 on the Ohio River near downtown Cincinnati. Its genesis can be traced to the 1940s, when talk of constructing a new stadium first surfaced. The conversation continued off and on through the 1960s, when the Cincinnati Bengals were awarded a National Football League franchise. After that the eventual decision became an easy one: build a multipurpose stadium that would accommodate both teams.

Once completed, the four-level stadium was large by 1970s standards, having a capacity of almost 60,000 fans for football and 53,000 for baseball. Riverfront Stadium's expansive capacity was due in large part to an unusual wheeled configuration: To accommodate football, the lower-level field box seats running from home plate to the left-field fence during baseball season were shifted using wheels to create a football gridiron.[4]

Until 1993 the stadium's pedigree meant little to Whiten, who simply wanted to hit baseballs. His timing couldn't have been better.

Just months earlier the World Trade Center had been bombed, presenting an early indication that terrorism had arrived in the United States. Two months later a siege on a religious compound in Waco, Texas, ended in a conflagration that killed 80 people. At the country's helm was Bill Clinton, a personable man who had carried into office his own baggage of alleged infidelity. America needed a diversion, if only an athletic one.

The baseball world also would see change. Bob Horner's teammate, Dale Murphy, would retire that year just two home runs shy of 400, Carlos Baerga would become the first ballplayer ever to belt home runs both right- and left-handed during the same inning, and fire would break out in the press box at the Braves' stadium.

Somewhere in the mix would be Mark Whiten, and standing in his way on September 7 was Cincinnati right-hander Larry Luebbers, a rookie who, following the 1993 season, would spend five years out of Major League Baseball as he bounced around the minor leagues before briefly returning in, perhaps ironically, a Cardinals uniform.

Batting sixth in the lineup and playing center field in the second game of a doubleheader, Whiten came to bat in the first inning with the bases loaded and drilled a fastball over the left-center-field fence for a grand slam. The Cardinals took an early 4–0 lead after half an inning of play, and Whiten put four RBI in his pocket.

The Reds came back with two runs of their own in the bottom of the first, cutting the Cardinals' lead to 4–2 with the only runs they would score in the game. It remained that way when Whiten led off the fourth inning and unceremoniously fouled weakly to third baseman Chris Sabo to start a one–two–three inning for Luebbers. The at-bat marked the only time that Reds pitchers would get Whiten out.

"You always like to be on the good side of a historic game, but just to have been a part of that one is a good feeling," said Luebbers, the losing pitcher that day.

Luebbers was replaced after five innings by Mike Anderson, a 6-foot-3, 200-pound right-hander who would appear in only three games during a short major-league career—all of them in 1993. Batting in the sixth inning with two men on base, Whiten took Anderson deep, blasting a pitch over the 375-foot mark in right-center field for a three-run home run. In three at-bats, the big center fielder had hit two home runs and driven in seven runs.

The following inning, Whiten duplicated his sixth-inning shot against Anderson. With two men on base he hit another service over the right-center-field fence, driving in three more runners with his second three-run homer of the game and boosting his RBI total to 10. After seven innings Whiten had hit three home runs and the Cardinals were pummeling the Reds, 12–2.

"To tell you the truth I was more excited about hitting the third one than I was the fourth," he said. "That was the first time I'd hit three."

At one point before his fifth and final at-bat the Cardinals batboy asked Whiten if he planned to try to hit a fourth homer. Whiten calmly shrugged.

"I told him that I didn't try to hit the first three, so why should I?" he laughed.

Whiten's final at-bat in what had become a lopsided ballgame occurred in the ninth inning. With one out and Gerald Perry on first base following a single, Whiten sent a 2–0 Rob Dibble fastball sailing over the right-center-field fence for a two-run home run, his fourth blast of the game. With that, Whiten's totals on the day were mind-boggling: 4-for-5 with a grand slam, two 3-run home runs, a 2-run home run, 12 RBI, and 4 runs scored. His hitting accounted for all but three of the Cardinals' 15 runs in a game that marked one of the greatest hitting performances in major-league history.

"I didn't do anything different that day," said Whiten, who never hit three home runs in a game either before or after that. "I'm a firm believer that you play the hand you're dealt. That particular day was just one of those days."

Whiten added that much like Shawn Green when the Dodgers slugger hit four over the fences in a game, he had gone about a month without hitting a home run.

The following day, Whiten's homerfest was described by one sportswriter in belletristic terms:

> In one game, Mark Whiten hit 1,634 feet of home runs—four drives that traveled more than a quarter of a mile. . . . With four swings he became the first player in 69 years to knock in 12 runs in a game. . . . Four homers. Twelve RBIs—13 overall in the doubleheader. It was one of the greatest offensive nights in major-league history.[5]

"If you're an everyday player and you keep going out there, everybody has a chance to have that kind of day," said Whiten, who does not consider himself a home run hitter. "If you go out and play hard, it could happen."

The only Reds pitcher to not give up a home run or even a run that day was Chris Bushing, a 25-year-old right-hander who pitched just a fraction of one season—1993—in the big leagues. That day he would pitch one-third of an inning, and he would appear in only six games in the major leagues before arm trouble ended his career. Bushing recalled his involvement in Whiten's performance as a raw rookie.

"I had just been called up [from the minors]," he said. "I wanted the opportunity to face [Whiten] to see if I could stop him and to get as much exposure as I could. I knew who he was. Our game plan would have included how to pitch him, but some hitters have those days—very seldom do they have those days."

Bushing added an afterthought: "Honestly, I wish he would have hit the fourth home run off of me. That way, I would have been remembered for *something* in baseball. I guess I'm remembered as the only pitcher he didn't hit a home run off that day."

Luebbers, the losing pitcher, owns the distinction of enabling Whiten's first home run by virtue of the first-inning grand slam he gave up.

"I started the game bad and with two outs had a chance to get out of the inning," said Luebbers, who left the game with three strikeouts and four walks in five innings pitched. "The grand slam changed the inning, changed the game—changed everything. I knew he was a great hitter."

He added, "[The game is] always a good conversation piece."

Unlike some who accomplished the four-home run feat deeper into the twilight of their careers, Whiten was just 26 years old and would spend seven more seasons in the big leagues. The best, he figured, was yet to come. He was wrong. As the 1993 season came to a close, the best, as it turned out, was about to end.

After hitting 25 homers and driving in almost 100 runs, Whiten's numbers would begin a long, slow slog. He would slam 14 home runs the following season while hitting a respectable .293. In 1995 things would decline even further, down to 12 homers before Whiten recovered briefly to hit 22 homers in 1996; however, as his statistics took a temporary leap, a worrisome trend was beginning to develop. The trend, a series of trades that sent Whiten packing, was not one that a player with proven ability likes to experience.

Whiten played for two clubs in 1995, three more in 1996, and another one in 1997 before returning to the Indians in 1998, where he would play out the final seasons of his at-times inglorious big-league career. Along the way there were stops in such minor-league towns as Pawtucket and Buffalo (both Triple-A), then Las Vegas (Triple-A) toward the end. Finally, at age 33, Whiten quietly exited the minor- and major-league continuum. Following the 2002 season in Las Vegas the end came at last.

After retiring from baseball, Whiten changed tacks. With more free time on his hands he ramped up participation in his children's upbringing and eventually started a gardening business. "Just me, keeping myself busy, basically," he said.[6] To keep even busier, he began working as an administrator with the Reviving Baseball in Inner Cities (RBI) program, which is sponsored by Major League Baseball and promotes the sport to girls and boys who reside in disadvantaged areas of the country.

"Hopefully, they get that fire lit in them to where they want to play a lot more baseball," Whiten said. "When they're young they play all the time. As kids get older they tend to fade away a little bit."[7]

And what about the fire that was lit under Mark Whiten on September 7, 1993. Did The Game change his life at all?

"Not really," he said. "At that point in my career I was still learning the game, still learning to hit, still learning a lot of things. I don't think it changed anything."

Still, the performance is one that will long be remembered. In fact, Whiten has the four home run balls to prove it, retrieved after the game by the Cardinals grounds crew and presented to him as a keepsake. It's a keepsake he appreciates more and more as the game settles into his long-term memory.

"I got 12 RBIs, that's a shared record [with Jim Bottomly, also of the Cardinals, 1924]. I got four home runs, that's a shared record [with 17 other players]. But to get the four home runs *and* the 12 RBIs in one game, that's not shared with anybody. That's my claim to fame."

⓭

MIKE CAMERON

May 2, 2002

To those who saw him play, Mike Cameron was a star: He hit 278 home runs, knocked in almost 1,000 RBI, won 3 Gold Glove Awards, and appeared in the 2001 All-Star Game, doubling in 3 at-bats. On top of those offensive accomplishments, Cameron was considered one of the finest center fielders in the game, committing only 71 errors during his long major-league career.

Still, there's a disconnect. After completing almost two decades in the major leagues, the 6-foot-2, 210-pound Cameron remains underrated.

For one day, however, Cameron was the biggest star in baseball, hitting four home runs against his former team, the Chicago White Sox, at Chicago's Comiskey Park. The four blasts were among 25 he would hit that season, shots that unfortunately were offset, at least in part, by his league-leading 176 strikeouts and a .239 batting average. For all that he accomplished during a highly productive major-league career, Mike Cameron was an up-and-down ballplayer, although a popular fellow in the clubhouse.

The "ups" in his career included the record-tying 4-home run game, the 110 RBI he recorded in 2001, 11 consecutive seasons hitting 10 home runs or more, 8 seasons with 20 or more homers, and the 30 home runs he hit in 2004, which again were partially offset by a proclivity to strike out: He whiffed 143 times that season and batted only .231. The "downs" included more than 1,900 career strikeouts and a significant drop in offensive production midway through his career, from 24 home runs and 70 RBI in 2009 to only 13 home runs and 42 RBI combined in 2010 and 2011, his final year in baseball. There also was a bone-chilling injury.

By some accounts, Cameron suffered one of the worst injuries in baseball history when he collided with New York Mets teammate Carlos Beltran while the two were chasing a fly ball at full speed early in the 2005 season. In the collision, described as "horrifying" in a *Washington Post* headline, Cameron broke both cheekbones, fractured his nose, suffered a mild concussion, and was removed from the field on a stretcher.[1] At least one teammate admitted he turned

Mike Cameron. *Copyright Jerry Coli/Dreamstime.com*

away after seeing the extent of the player's injury and the significant amount of blood it produced.

"I feel like I got hit by a train," Cameron said after the collision, adding, "I don't remember anything of what happened."[2]

Although teammates feared that their talented outfielder might miss the remainder of the season, Cameron returned to hit a respectable 12 home runs for the Mets that year, respectable considering the physical and emotional trauma he had endured. You could knock Mike Cameron down, but he loved the game too much not to get back up. He got back up a lot.

Along the way the likable center fielder even wrote a book titled *It Takes a Team: Mike Cameron*. In his motivational biography, Cameron discusses how teamwork, self-confidence, and open-mindedness can be the keys to success in any life endeavor. Who better than Cameron to broach the topic of success than a guy who also overcame the threatened loss of his sight when a fly ball fractured his eye socket during a minor-league game?

In the dozen and a half seasons that Cameron wore major-league uniforms he played for seemingly every team. The Chicago White Sox, Cincinnati Reds, Seattle Mariners, New York Mets, San Diego Padres, Milwaukee Brewers, Boston Red Sox, and Florida Marlins all posted his name on their roster at one time or another. In the minors he plied his trade for the Gulf Coast League White Sox, Utica Blue Sox, South Bend White Sox, Prince William Cannons, Birmingham Barons, Nashville Sounds, St. Lucie Mets, Norfolk Tides, Lake Elsinore Storm, Portland Sea Dogs, and Pawtucket Red Sox. It's a testament to his greatness, his persistence, and his likable persona that new teams always seemed willing, if not eager, to welcome him aboard. After all, reflecting a range from a low of .194 to a high of .268 his lifetime batting average was a shade under .250. Indisputably, Cameron was doing some things right, not the least of which was his ability to hit home runs season after season.

Michael Terrance Cameron was born on January 8, 1973, in LaGrange, Georgia, a working-class community that claims West Point Lake, a 26,000-acre reservoir offering bass fishing and antebellum gardens, as one of its top attractions. As a youth growing up on Render Street, Cameron attended LaGrange High School, where he quickly made his mark in baseball not far from where the Mike Cameron Indoor Hitting Facility, funded through a $45,000 grant that he graciously provided, now stands.

Cameron was so talented as a prep athlete that he was chosen straight out of high school in the 18th round of baseball's 1991 amateur draft by the Chicago

White Sox, who signed him on June 12 of that year and immediately sent him down to the low minor leagues for some preparatory work.

The young man made his professional debut later that year with the Gulf Coast League White Sox and he had little success, at least in the home run department. Playing regularly, he hit zero home runs, not the production one would expect from a future home run hitter. During the next three years he played with three different Class A clubs, experiencing the most success with the Prince William Cannons, slugging six home runs and knocking in 48 runs. With those numbers the White Sox elevated Cameron to the Double-A Birmingham Barons of the Southern League in 1995, where he hit 11 home runs and drove in 60 runners.

People in the front office must have seen what they had hoped for, and Cameron was again promoted, this time to the major-league White Sox toward the end of the 1995 season. Thus began an up-and-down period that would see him dropped back down to Birmingham after hitting under .200 for the Sox, then elevated later in 1996 before being sent down to the Triple-A Nashville Sounds. He finally settled in the big leagues for good with the White Sox in 1997. Or so he thought.

After hitting 14 home runs in 1997 followed by eight in 1998, the Sox traded him to Cincinnati, who sent him on to the Seattle Mariners where his hitting, which had begun to accelerate in Cincinnati, continued to progress. After hitting 21 homers with the Reds in 1992 he hit 87 with the Mariners between 2000 and 2003, including a remarkable four on May 2, 2002, against the White Sox. Mike Cameron was earning his keep in the Emerald City.

By the date of Cameron's landmark game few ballparks had cultivated more history than old Comiskey Park. Opened in 1910 at the corner of Shields Avenue and Thirty-Fifth Street, the park expanded its seating capacity with regularity until 1953 when it peaked at almost 53,000. The first night game played there was in 1939, and the smallest attendance ever recorded at Comiskey was 511 fans on May 6, 1971.

After Comiskey's closure the year before Cameron's selection in the draft and its subsequent demolition during his first season in the minors, a newer version of Comiskey Park opened across the street from the old stadium, becoming U.S. Cellular Field in 2003 and later Guaranteed Rate Field. Field dimensions remain 377 feet to left field, 335 feet to right, and 400 feet to dead center field.[3]

On the mound against the Mariners that day was rookie Jon Rauch, who at 6-foot-11 and 290 pounds was a Pantagruelian figure. On paper, however, Rauch would prove to be less imposing than his physical stature, posting a 2–1 record and a 6.59 ERA that season and winning only 41 more games during the next decade. Cameron took charge of the rookie early.

Having played for the White Sox from 1995 through 1998, the third-year Mariner said he always tried to perform particularly well against his former team, and that day was no exception. "I wanted them to understand what they were missing," Cameron said of the team that had drafted him and then traded him away. "I felt I needed to show [them] something." Adding incentive for the slugger was a side bet that Bret Boone, batting second in the lineup, had with the man who on that day followed him: Cameron.

"It was something like $100 for an RBI and $50 for a hit," Cameron said. "He got up and hit a two-run homer in the first inning."

Cameron, who had been slumping, came to bat next and was not to be out-done, drilling a fastball over the 400-foot mark in dead center field. He could not recall the exact sum that home runs paid in his competition with Boone, but at that moment and in that game he and his second baseman, a 10-year veteran, were tied in that department, although not for long.

The Mariners continued to rally, and after Boone's second two-run shot of the inning Cameron once again came to the plate, this time facing Jim Parque, who at 5-foot-11 was a foot shorter than the pitcher he had replaced. Cameron welcomed Parque the same way he had Rauch, knocking another booming solo shot to the identical spot over the center-field fence. The blast marked a first in major-league history.

"We hit back-to-back homers twice in the inning, something [that had] never been done," said Boone, who would tie Cameron's RBI production in the game with four.

That big first inning was a warmup for Cameron, who declared, as if it weren't transpicuous, "I was starting to feel pretty good at the plate." With the game appearing to be an early fait accompli, there was no need for White Sox hurlers to pitch around him or bear down. Instead, they would serve up exactly what he wanted all game long: fastballs or sliders and even a changeup, which he hit for a homer.

In the top of the third, with two outs and his team still leading, 10–0, Cameron once again faced Parque. This time the left-hander dished up a slider that Cameron hit for distance, swatting it several rows deep into the left-field bleachers. In just three innings of play Cameron had hit three solo home runs.

"Anything else was gravy," Cameron said. There was gravy yet to come.

By the fifth inning Seattle had increased its lead to 12–1, but with Cameron coming up again that margin would grow. With Parque still in the game, Cameron slammed a 3–2 changeup over the fence in straightaway center field for his fourth solo home run of the game and his third one drilled to that same spot. With his team now ahead 13–1, and four innings still to play, the slugger would have two opportunities to become the first major leaguer in history to hit five home runs in the same contest.

"That was just one of those days when I was able to get the ball in the air," Cameron said.

When he came to bat in the seventh inning Cameron got the ball in the air again, although the record was not to be his, not then. The White Sox had brought in Mike Porzio, a 6-foot-3, 190-pound left-hander who may have had a dubious mission in mind: to thank Cameron for embarrassing his teammates, pitchers Rauch and Parque, by hitting three home runs against them. Whether it was intentional or not, Porzio plunked Cameron with a pitch and postponed any hope he might have of hitting a fifth home run.

Cameron would have one more at-bat, however. Batting against Porzio with two on and no one out in the ninth inning he hit a long fly that Jeff Liefer caught at the top of the right-field fence on the warning track—just short of a fifth home run.

"He almost hit five," Boone said, adding that never in his wildest dreams would he have guessed that Cameron might hit four home runs in a single game. "No—heck," he said. "How many times has it been done? What are the odds—one in a billion?"

The three-time All-Star added, "If a player hits two home runs in a game, that's considered great. Three home runs and it's unbelievable. Four? Who would pitch to someone after he has hit three home runs?"

Porzio did, and Cameron's fly ball to right marked his final plate appearance in a wild game, one that the Mariners won, 15–4, in front of only 12,891 fans. Despite the cool weather (it was 54°F at game time), moderate wind (17 miles per hour), and having to wait interminably in the cool weather between his two first-inning at-bats, Cameron had achieved greatness: He had hit four solo round-trippers in a game, and he'd needed only five innings to do it.

"It was really fun to watch," said John Halama, a 6-foot-5, 215-pound left-hander who watched Cameron hit all four home runs from his seat in the bullpen before pitching the final two innings in relief of starter James Baldwin. "At that time I was in the bullpen and I was watching from a different angle. But it was still fun to watch."

Halama described Cameron as a hard worker who up until then probably didn't figure to hit four home runs in a game. After all, those home runs aside he only hit 14 other homers that entire season.

"He just kept his focus and was able to go out and get some pitches that he could drive," Halama said. "He was plenty strong and could hit to the opposite field, to straightaway center, and he could pull the ball. At that time I didn't consider him in the category of players who could hit four home runs in a game, but he has to be in that category now because he's done it."

Compared with Mark Whiten's 12 RBI during his memorable game, Cameron's statistics looked modest. Still, they could not escape the history books: 4 home runs in 5 at-bats, 4 RBI, and 4 runs scored.

"It was special," Cameron said. "For me, the joy was being able to enjoy it in Chicago, because I was getting booed. I remember going around the bases, looking up and thinking, 'Man—I just hit four homers.' Everyone gave me a standing ovation."

He added, "I was a *bad* man that day. It was a good day, a good solid day."

Cameron's record-tying game came just eight months after terrorists had leveled the World Trade Center towers and the same year that England mourned the death of Queen Elizabeth, the Queen Mother. In sports, baseball, perhaps suspicious after Barry Bonds hit 73 home runs in 2001, was gearing up to begin testing players for banned substances. For at least a moment, the country could put both the shadow of international terrorism and the specter of player drug use behind it as it watched Cameron circle the bases four times under the watchful eye of an ever-expanding and still-fledgling internet. He received his pleasant due in newspapers the following morning:

Mike Cameron was always known as the guy who took away home runs. Not anymore. Cameron hit four homers and came close to a record-setting fifth Thursday night, leading the Seattle Mariners over the Chicago White Sox, 15–4. Cameron, until now recognized for his Gold Glove and being part of the trade for Ken Griffey Jr., became only the 13th player in major-league history to homer four times in a game and the first since Mark Whiten in 1993.[4]

After the game Cameron tried to explain the inexplicable to reporters: "I just felt like I was the king of the hill today," he said. "It's a thing of beauty."

He added, with a touch of modesty, "I'm just putting a good swing on the ball."[5]

On the flip side, after the game White Sox starter Rauch and his reliever, Parque, were both optioned to the minor leagues.[6] Only the Sox' final pitcher, Porzio, who gave up one run in 2.2 innings of relief, was left standing when the dust of that memorable game had cleared.

At only 29, Cameron was still a young man with a great future ahead of him. He hit 18 home runs in 2003 before the Mariners sent him over to the Mets. He spent 2004 and 2005 there, averaging 21 homers per season; 2006 and 2007 with the Padres, again averaging 21 blasts; and 2008 and 2009 with Milwaukee, hitting 24 home runs during his final season with the Brewers. Unbeknownst to Cameron, at that point the ride was coming to a conclusion.

After hitting four home runs with Boston in 2010 and nine with Boston and Florida in 2011, the end finally came. Mike Cameron retired.

"Mike Cameron Retires: A Look at an Underrated Legacy," read one headline.[7] Wrote one scribe,

> Few baseball players have a legacy as diversified as Cameron. Some will remember him as one of the finest defensive outfielders of his generation. . . . Others will remember him as a journeyman with strikeout issues who suffered one of the scariest injuries of the past decade. . . . Still others will remember him as one of the classiest players of his generation. . . . Few, however, will remember him for what he really was: a player whose contributions were never properly appreciated until he was on another club.[8]

Toward the end he truly was unappreciated, and within a few years after his brilliant 2002 game the luggage stickers began to accumulate. He spent bits of the 2005 season in Single-A and Triple-A ball before returning to the Mets. Then it was on to Lake Elsinore, the San Diego Padres, Nashville, the Brewers, Portland, Pawtucket, the Red Sox, and finally the Florida Marlins. When the Washington Nationals offered him a minor-league contract, Cameron finally, and ever so respectfully, said no.

"I get a thrill out of going to [the] ballpark every day and trying to create excitement," he once said. "Not everyone can say that. Not everybody can say that he goes to the ballpark to work and has fun."[9]

Cameron was through, but not before having given teammate Boone a thrill on that special day in 2002. "We knew [at the time] how special it was," Boone said. "Mike couldn't even believe it. There are certain things you do on a given day and you just kind of look up and wonder how you're even doing it. It was really cool to be a part of."

After baseball, the excitement Cameron experienced was different. He couldn't have been prouder when son Dazmon, a 6-foot-2, 185-pound outfielder/designated hitter from Eagle's Landing High in McDonough, Georgia, was chosen by the Houston Astros in the first round of the 2015 June amateur draft. Daz, who is 21 and a Mike Cameron look-alike, has played two seasons in Single-A ball after spending a year in the rookie league; in 2017, he slugged 14 home runs.

"I'm having fun, because I know how much it means to him," the elder Cameron said of his son. "And the hard work he put in—it just makes it that much more gratifying."[10]

Cameron, founder of the Mike Cameron Baseball Academy in Stockbridge, Georgia, knows something about hard work and the gratification—fun—it can produce. On May 2, 2002, the years of hard work that he put into baseball paid off big time when he slugged four home runs in a single ballgame. On that day Cameron was anything but underrated. He was, unequivocally, the greatest baseball player in the world.

14

SHAWN GREEN
May 23, 2002

At 6-foot-4, Shawn Green was one of the tallest men ever to hit four home runs in a single game. Weighing in at a lean 190 pounds he was also one of the lightest players. It goes to show that neither excessive height nor massive bulk are necessarily determinants of a ballplayer's power or capability to hit for distance.

While an able hitter throughout his career, Green's quiet demeanor and refusal to use steroids in an era of performance-enhancing drugs often left him on the fringe of stardom. As a result, few are aware of his many significant offensive achievements. For starters, he holds the Dodgers franchise record for most home runs hit in a season with 49 in 2001, his second year with the club. Neither Gil Hodges, the only other Dodger in the Four Home Runs Club, nor home run hitting Dodgers Hall of Famers Roy Campanella and Duke Snider came close to hitting 49 homers in a season.

Franchise records aside and the big-league mark for home runs hit in a game notwithstanding, Green broke or tied a surfeit of major-league marks before his career ended with a final solid season in 2007. Those include a record for most home runs hit in three consecutive games (7) and most total bases collected in a single game (19), as well as shared records for most extra-base hits in a single ballgame (5), most runs scored in a game (6), and most home runs hit in consecutive games (5). He also hit 10 home runs in a seven-game span and 22 in 34 contests during a 42-homer season in 2002.

In all probability, Green's offensive performance on May 23, 2002, was the greatest in major-league history. That he did it in the midst of a slump—he had

Shawn Green. *Copyright Jerry Coli/Dreamstime.com*

recently gone a month without hitting a home run, encompassing more than 100 plate appearances—and three weeks after Mike Cameron hit four out in a game makes the accomplishment all the more remarkable.

"I was struggling really bad," Green said. "I had only three home runs and we were a quarter of the way through the season. At one point in the recent homestand I was 0-for-18."

In an interview at the time, Green said the baseball "had been looking like a Ping-Pong ball."[1] On the day of his brilliant offensive showing it must have looked like a beach ball. To the Milwaukee Brewers, the Dodgers' opposition that day, Green looked like a wrecking ball by the time the game was in the bank.

"It's not often that a player goes 6-for-6 with four home runs," said Mike Buddie, who pitched two scoreless innings for the Brewers that day and was an unlikely bright spot for the team as a middle reliever. "Hitting four home runs is achievement enough, but to get hits in your other two at-bats against an array of left-handers and right-handers, power pitchers, and slow pitchers. . . . He was obviously seeing the ball very well that day."

Others in the elite cadre of home run hitters may have driven in more runs during their moment of fame, for example, Mark Whiten with 12 and Scooter Gennett with 10, but Green's run of the table that day helped him to a piece, if not all, of just about every other significant one-, two-, or three-game offensive record on the books during his 15-year career. He did it all while declining to play on the Jewish holiday Yom Kippur. Add up the Yom Kippur games he sat out during his career and Green, who popped 328 home runs, might have topped the great Hank Greenburg (331) as the most prolific Jewish home run hitter of all time.

"It's something I feel is an important thing to do," Green said in 2004 of his departure from playing in games on Yom Kippur, "partly as a representative of the Jewish community, and as far as my being a role model in sports for Jewish kids to basically say that baseball, or anything, isn't bigger than your religion and your roots."

He added, "I'm committed to my religion and what I stood for in the past."[2]

Today, many consider Green the greatest Jewish player since Sandy Koufax, high praise for a man whose baseball skills were cultivated on the ball fields of little-known Tustin, not far from the beaches of Southern California.

Shawn David Green was born in Des Plaines, Illinois, on November 10, 1972. His family moved to Santa Ana, California, when Shawn was just a boy, and he attended Tustin High School in Orange County, where the youth quickly became a standout and set school records in hits and stolen bases. Green was so good that in 1991 he was selected by *USA Today* to its All-USA high school baseball team, and he was named a high school All-American by the American Baseball Coaches Association. Despite the distractions inflicted on him by baseball, Green earned a perfect 4.0 grade point average in the classroom, completing his studies near the top of his class.

After finishing his prep career with a .430 batting average and 147 hits, the latter mark tying a California Interscholastic Federation record, the left-hander signed to play baseball at Stanford University; however, a college baseball career was not in the cards. Having been selected in the first round (16th pick) of the 1991 amateur draft by the Toronto Blue Jays, like so many high school ballplayers he chose to continue competing in the sport he loved rather than immediately enroll in college. In foregoing a college education, at least for the time being, and accepting a $700,000 signing bonus from Toronto, Green did convince the Blue Jays to let him attend Stanford in the fall and spring, which necessitated him reporting to spring training late.

Once Green signed with the Blue Jays the team sent him to their Single-A Dunedin, Florida, affiliate in 1992, where he played in the outfield. Although his .273 batting average that first year was more than acceptable and his 49 RBI nothing to shrug at, he only hit one home run. The next year, playing for the Double-A Knoxville Smokies, Green's batting average bumped up slightly to .283 and he hit four home runs. A hint of the delitescent home run power that he possessed was beginning to emerge.

Although Green was elevated straight from Double-A to the Blue Jays toward the end of the 1993 season, he saw limited action that year and failed to get a base hit. As a result he started the 1994 season with the Blue Jays' Triple-A affiliate, the Syracuse Chiefs, and tore the cover off the ball. In 109 games he hit .344 with 13 home runs and 61 RBI. Toronto brought him up again at the end of the 1994 season and he went 3-for-33. But the team saw greater potential that time around than before and Green was in the major leagues for keeps.

During the 1995 season, Green's first full campaign in the majors, he performed capably, hitting .288 with 15 home runs. His numbers would level off in the 1996 and 1997 seasons when he hit 11 and 16 home runs, respectively. Then came 1998.

Playing mostly in left and right field, with a couple dozen games in center field, Green came alive at the plate. By the time the season was over he had belted 35 home runs and knocked in 100 runners. He also stole 35 bases, a career high. Perhaps more important, players on teams throughout the American League were beginning to recognize the significant skills of Shawn Green. The best awaited them.

After 1998 there was no looking back. Between 1999 and 2002 Green averaged almost 40 home runs and 115 RBI per season. He was rewarded for his offensive production by making the 1999 All-Star Team and earning Gold Glove and Silver Slugger awards at the end of the season, finishing ninth in the MVP balloting.

The year 2002, when he hit 42 home runs and again made the All-Star Team, was also Green's last exceedingly significant offensive season (not defensively, however, as he went the entire 2005 season without making a single error), buoyed, in part, by the four-home run game on May 23. By all accounts the victory against Milwaukee that day was a game for the ages.

Plans to construct a ballpark that would replace historic County Stadium began in earnest in the 1980s and culminated when Miller Park opened in 2001, a year later than anticipated due to a tragic construction accident that killed several workers and seriously damaged part of the stadium. As seems appropriate in a brewing town, the stadium was named for the Miller Brewing Company.

Featuring a red brick façade and clock tower near the main entrance, the ballpark displays statues of its most famous alumni, one of whom is one-time home run king Henry Aaron. Perhaps more dazzling, however, is the 12,000-ton roof, which can open and close within minutes. These and other features make Miller Park, with the capability to seat about 42,000 fans, one of the most unique stadiums in baseball.[3]

On May 23, Green didn't care about the retracting roof or the statues that adorned the stadium. His immediate concern was Glendon Rusch, a left-hander who had won just 31 games while losing 48 during five seasons in the big leagues. Still, he was a big man at 6-foot-2. The bigger they come, the harder they throw and the farther the ball travels, Green may have reasoned. That reasoning would have been correct: Despite a career won–loss record that was under water, Rusch did manage to average approximately 100 strikeouts per big-league season.

Following a single by leadoff batter Cesar Izturis and a groundout by Adrian Beltre, Green came to bat with one out in the first inning and a runner on second base and drilled a two-strikes curveball over first base and down the line for a double that scored Izturis. Just like that . . . 1-for-1.

The Dodgers scored two more runs and led the Brewers, 3–1, after an inning of play. Then they broke the game open in the second inning, largely due to Green's timely hitting. With runners on first and second and two out, Green broke his bat on a 1–1 inside pitch and sent a Rusch fastball sailing into the right-field stands, increasing the Dodgers' lead to 6–1. A Brian Jordan home run following a double by Eric Karros made it 8–1 in favor of the Dodgers after two innings.

"From that point on I felt I was pretty locked in and really relaxed," Green said.

With the Dodgers still leading 8–1, Green led off the top of the fourth inning against a new pitcher, Brian Mallette, a 6-foot right-hander playing in his only major-league season. Mallette would pitch two innings that day and only five in his entire career. Green didn't help the rookie's prospects any.

With the count 1–1 he sent a Mallette slider over the fence and onto a landing in right-center field, giving the Dodgers a 9–1 lead and Green his second home run. Following a single, two walks, and a wild pitch Mallette was mercifully out of the inning—and soon out of the ballgame.

His exit would come an inning later. In the top of the fifth with the Dodgers still leading 9–1, Green came to bat again against Mallette with two out and went the other direction, hitting a two-seam fastball deep to left that cleared the fence and landed well back in the bleachers. With Green's big swing and third home run of the game the Dodgers led the Brewers 10–1. After retiring the next batter to end the inning, Mallette never pitched in the major leagues again.[4]

Milwaukee scored a run in its own half of the fifth, cutting the lead to 10–2. Facing the Dodgers next was Mike Buddie, a 6-foot-3 right-hander in his fifth and final major-league season.

Buddie set the team down in order in the sixth and put them away easily in the seventh before Jose Cabrera, also pitching in his final major-league season, came on in the eighth inning. Green again led off and drilled a single to center field on a 1–0 fastball, giving him a 5-for-5 afternoon—so far. A home run by Hiram Bocachica two batters later made the score 12–2.

At that point Dodgers manager Jim Tracy wanted to pull Green from the game, giving him some well-earned rest before the team flew out of Milwaukee that evening; however, Green, by then thinking four home runs was a possibility, asked to stay in the lineup. Tracy agreed.

"You don't think about hitting four home runs until an opportunity is presented," Green said. "Then, obviously, you do think about it."

Perhaps the most significant drama of the game occurred in the ninth inning with a runner on second base and two out. Beltre greeted pitcher Cabrera by hitting a shot over the left-center-field fence for a home run, giving Green one more chance to hit his record-tying fourth homer. He would later write that he believed almost every player and fan watching that day wanted him to tie the home run record.

Green took advantage of the opportunity, blasting a 1–1 fastball from Cabrera deep onto the landing in right-center field to become the sport's newest head turner.

"Four home runs for Shawn Green to tie the major-league record," Dodgers announcer Ross Porter told his excited listeners as Green ran around the bases. "The Milwaukee fans are on their feet, giving a standing ovation as he circles third. What a day."

To rub salt in the many wounds inflicted by Green that day, Dave Hansen, the next batter up, also homered to give the Dodgers three-consecutive home runs. The team went on to win the game by a lopsided 16–3 margin—and Green finished the contest physically exhausted.

On the day Green single-handedly demolished the Brewers' pitching staff, going 6-for-6 with 4 home runs, 1 double, 6 runs scored, and 7 RBI. His 19 total bases is a major-league record that still stands.

"Everything does have to come together" for a player to hit four home runs in a game, Green said. "The fact that we were blowing them out meant they were going to continue pitching to me—there was no reason to walk me. I never got up with runners on second and third and a base open," where Milwaukee could intentionally walk Green to prevent him from driving in runners.

In fact, Green, who had hit three home runs in a game in 2001, led off in two innings and came to bat with the bases empty in the ninth. In four of six at-bats he came to the plate with the bases empty, ensuring that pitchers would give him an opportunity to hit.

"It definitely hasn't sunk in yet," the formerly slumping Green, who later that season hit four-consecutive home runs in two games against the Angels, said after the game. "I wish I had a few days off so I could enjoy it. It's something I'll never forget."

He added, "When [Mike] Cameron [hit his four homers] I thought, 'Man, that's a great couple of weeks right there.' No one in this game needed this more than I did, because I was getting pretty down."[5]

The following morning a local writer put Green's productive afternoon down on newsprint:

> Shawn Green came to the land of beer and bratwurst mired in the worst slump of his eight-year career, a season-long slide that punctured his reputation as one of the game's premier power hitters, shattered his confidence, and prompted fans in Dodger Stadium to boo him during the last homestand. The Dodger right-fielder left Milwaukee on Thursday with his name etched alongside Hall of Famers such as Lou Gehrig, Willie Mays, and Mike Schmidt, and plastered all over baseball's record books.[6]

A less-conspicuous success story that day was Buddie, a 31-year-old journeyman reliever who would retire at season's end with a career 5–4 record and a lifetime 4.67 ERA. While his fellow pitchers were struggling, giving up 16 runs on eight home runs, Buddie pitched two scoreless innings in the middle of the onslaught.

According to Buddie, Green was on deck when he completed his stint on the mound by getting the final out in the seventh inning. The last thing Buddie wanted was to face the even-tempered slugger.

"I faced seven hitters that day, and Shawn was one of the few that I didn't," he said. "That didn't break my heart at all." He added, "It was a magical day for him."

Buddie continued, "I don't know that I considered it a thrill [to have played in the game] at that time. The longer I'm removed from my baseball career, the more I appreciate seeing these achievements. He was a heckuva ballplayer."

Brewers catcher Paul Bako always took great satisfaction in helping his pitchers not allow runs, but on that day both he and the pitching staff had limited success. He recalls the blowout as dispiriting.

"I took pride in trying to get my pitcher through games as effectively as possible," he said. "That was obviously one of the worst days we could have had."

Bako added a caveat: "We were a very bad team."

"Shawn was and is an underrated player considering the era he played in—if he had played either before then or now, he would have been an absolute superstar because he had terrific offensive ability and was a clean player from a performance-enhancing standpoint."

The four-home run game turned the season around for Green, who hit a home run in his first at-bat the following day and went on to hit 42 on the season, finishing fifth in the MVP balloting; however, after 2002 it was a short glide from greatness to retirement. Green would average fewer than 19 home runs during the following five seasons compared to almost 40 the previous five. The Dodgers traded him after the 2004 season, sending him to the Arizona Diamondbacks, who sent him on to the New York Mets after that. His final season, 2007, would be a decent one: He hit 10 home runs, drove in 46 runs, and posted a .291 batting average. Nonetheless, despite declaring free agency after the 2007 season, Green, who was 35, chose to retire from the grind of baseball to spend more time with his wife and two young daughters. His decision was announced just days before spring training began in 2008.

With Green gone, a breath of fresh air had disappeared from the game. While a Dodger, Green was reported to have given batting gloves to young fans following each home run he hit in Dodger Stadium. He also donated $250,000 to the Dodgers Dream Foundation each season that he played for the team, a total of some $1.5 million in six seasons. The money was used to help develop ball fields throughout the Los Angeles area and buy books for local grade schools and community programs that assisted children.[7]

Since his career as a player ended Green has kept busy. In 2012 he represented Israel's national team in the World Baseball Classic, held in Florida. At age 39 he collected three hits in nine at-bats playing alongside athletes half his age. One of them was Joc Pederson, who now plies his trade with Green's former team, the Dodgers. Then, in 2016, Green announced his involvement in something different: a tech company called Greenfly.

Already a member of the National Jewish Sports Hall of Fame, Green was named to the International Jewish Sports Hall of Fame in 2014. He has been involved with a number of high-profile charities, including the United Jewish

Federation, the Special Olympics, the Juvenile Diabetes Research Foundation, and the Parkinson's Foundation. Finally, he has assisted the Jewish Federation of Greater Los Angeles as a spokesman for literacy.[8]

Despite all the good work he has done, Green's performance swinging a piece of wood on May 23, 2002, remains his overpowering legacy. As the epic game wore on, Green said the baseball kept looking bigger and bigger, resembling a softball toward the end. Green, too, loomed bigger and bigger each and every time he came to the plate, in the estimation of Jerry Royster, the Brewers' manager that day.

"I've never witnessed anything like it," he said.[9]

Dodgers then-manager Tracy agreed, saying his right fielder had a career day—even a historic one.

Said Tracy, who hit fewer home runs in his two-year major-league career than Green hit on May 23, 2002, "He had a day . . . that goes down as one of the greatest in the history of the game."[10]

15

CARLOS DELGADO

September 25, 2003

Loosely translated, "Delgado" in English means "thin" or "delicate." Perhaps Carlos Delgado, a 6-foot-3, 215-pound image of baseball hulk, was switched at birth.

Delgado was anything but thin or delicate when he played in the major leagues. Instead he was big and strong, a sturdy study who hit booming home runs more often than almost anyone else in professional baseball at that time. In a highly visible 17-year career he popped almost 500 of them out of various ballparks of the American and National leagues. Four of those were blasts for the ages.

The four shots, all of them hit in a single game played on September 25, 2003, came during a 10–8 Toronto Blue Jays nail-biter against the Tampa Bay Devil Rays in the fourth-to-last game of the season.

"I took a little nap before the game," Delgado said in a dubious attempt to explain his success that day, adding, "You can't predict what's going to happen in a baseball game. It's definitely the best day in my baseball career."[1]

The achievement marked the 15th time that a player had hit four home runs in a ballgame and the third time it had been done in a 16-month period. Unlike Delgado, no other player had accomplished—or has since accomplished—the feat in only four plate appearances, an exploit that awed at least one player on the opposing team that day.

"If you put a ball on a tee at second base, I still don't think I'd hit four out in a game," said muscular, hard-hitting Devil Rays designated hitter Aubrey Huff, who on that day tripled and hit his 34th homer of the season in a rousing 2-for-4 performance that nonetheless paled in comparison to that of his Toronto counterpart.

Carlos Delgado. *Rafael Amado Deras*

Delgado, who went 4-for-4, made his own triumph look easy. Why wouldn't he? Although it took him a couple of seasons to find steady employment in the major leagues, once he did so it was smooth sailing. For 13 consecutive seasons Delgado hit 20 or more homers. He hit 30 or more home runs 11 times. He hit 40 or more three times—twice in succession. He retired from the game with a grand total of 473 round-trippers to his credit, an average of almost 30 per season not counting his first season as a Blue Jay, when he came to bat only once. Carlos Delgado was truly a Hall of Fame–caliber player.

Caliber maybe, but he's not there. In the minds of many baseball observers he may never gain enshrinement in baseball's esteemed Hall of Fame.

To be sure, Delgado was a top home run–hitting first baseman for more than a decade. His 473 career homers rank 32nd on the all-time list while his 1,512 RBI rank 52nd, the latter mark positioning him higher than Hall of Famers Mickey Mantle and Eddie Matthews and fellow Four Home Runs Club member Ed Delahanty. Although he never won an MVP Award, Delgado did finish ninth or higher in the Player of the Year balloting four times; in 2003 he was second, racking up 42 home runs, 145 RBI, and a .301 batting average. He also made the All-Star Team that season and earned a Silver Slugger Award.

"You create your own momentum," Delgado said in 2006, explaining his hitting success. "You just have to approach every game like it's the last game you're going to play."[2]

So, eight years after his retirement, why isn't Delgado in the Hall of Fame? Perhaps it's his dearth of All-Star Game appearances—unbelievably for such a great slugger he only made that elite team twice. And his home run production falls 27 shy of the coveted 500 figure, a recognized benchmark for true greatness. As one writer put it, 500 is the new 400 (making 600 the new 500?). Carlos Delgado may just be the greatest baseball player to fall off the ballot following his first year of Hall of Fame eligibility, having failed to receive the required minimum 5 percent of votes from sportswriters.

Consider that his 145 RBI led the American League in 2003, three years after his 57 doubles and 378 total bases led the league in 2000. He led the National League with 10 sacrifice flies in 2006. And the 15 times he was hit by pitches in the year 2000 unquestionably demonstrates his aggressiveness and determination as a hitter, not to mention the dread he instilled in opposing pitchers.

There's one more important statistic. In two consecutive seasons, 2000 and 2001, Delgado played in all 162 regular-season games for the Blue Jays, a mark of durability. Without a doubt he wanted to be in the lineup—day in and day out. When he wasn't in the lineup, either due to hip, back, or other problems, the slugger wished he could have been.

Carlos Juan Delgado Jr. was born to Carlos Sr. and Carmen Delgado in Aquadillo, Puerto Rico, on June 25, 1972. His father worked as an alcohol and drug counselor, and his mother assisted in a medical laboratory. While his parents understood the importance of becoming well educated, they also appreciated their son's formidable athletic ability and willingness to work hard, and they encouraged him to succeed in any sport he chose.

Carlos Jr. grew up alongside three siblings, and as a child he had numerous athletic and other interests—including, surprisingly, volleyball. Another interest was baseball, and even as a child he became a capable catcher. He would remain a catcher until he advanced to the major leagues, eventually settling in as a power-hitting first baseman, dependable designated hitter, and sure-handed outfielder.

Delgado became more and more serious about baseball while in high school, and at the age of 16 he was chosen by the Toronto Blue Jays in the 1988 amateur free agent draft. Meanwhile, he continued to strengthen his muscles and hone his menu of skills in anticipation of the major-league career that he believed was inevitable.

After being drafted by Toronto, Delgado was sent to play for the team's St. Catharines Blue Jays in the New York–Pennsylvania League, a Single-A club. He didn't exactly set the league on fire, hitting just .180 with zero home runs in 1989; however, he recalibrated himself and in 1990 hit 100 points higher with six home runs and 39 RBI. He was rewarded with a promotion to the Myrtle Beach Hurricanes, a higher-level Single-A team for whom he hit 18 home runs in 1991. By year's end he was playing for the Triple-A Syracuse Chiefs.

After returning to the lower minor leagues in 1992 Delgado came into his own, hitting 30 home runs for the Single-A Dunedin Blue Jays and slugging 25 homers for the Double-A Knoxville Smokies the following year. He was elevated to the Blue Jays at the end of the 1993 season.

Delgado bounced between the Blue Jays and Triple-A Syracuse in the next couple of years before finally hitting his stride in 1996, blasting 25 home runs and driving in 92 runners. He would hit 30 home runs in 1997 followed by 38 in 1998 and 44 in 1999. During the next decade Delgado was virtually unstoppable.

"I was a kid in a candy store," he said. "I'm at the big-league level, I'm hitting, I'm hitting home runs, and it's great. I was on cloud nine."[3]

When the 2003 season rolled around Delgado, then in his 30s, was at the peak of his baseball ability and coming off a 33-homer, 108-RBI season. His "cloud nine" ascended into the stratosphere when the Blue Jays played the Devil Rays on September 25 as the season wound to a close.

"I was sick and I almost didn't play that game. I went out and took batting practice and I took a couple of rounds, I took it in, I went to the trainer's table, I laid down, took some medicine," he said.[4]

Fortunately Delgado did play that day and he played unforgettably well, although only 13,408 fans were in attendance as witnesses. His landmark performance was arguably the finest that Toronto's SkyDome, now called the Rogers Centre, has seen in all the years of its existence. It may have been the best display of power the ballpark will *ever* see.

Hailed as an architectural wonder, the SkyDome opened to the public on June 3, 1989. On that day some 60,000 fans watched excitedly as the stadium's acclaimed retractable dome, weighing 20 million pounds, opened to reveal the skies above and all their splendor. Two days later the Toronto Blue Jays played their first game at the dazzling stadium in front of 50,000 eager fans.

The ballpark's breezy roof requires 20 minutes to open and close, and that's not the only moving part. There are five seating levels that wind from left-center field around to right-center and all seats on the lower level can be moved to accommodate the formation of a football field—depending on which sport is in season.[5]

For Delgado, playing in one of the final few games of 2003, it was still very much baseball season. And while the Blue Jays were on a path to finish in third place in the American League East Division, there was still a lot more baseball to be played. For Delgado there were home runs to be hit.

Starting on the mound for the Devil Rays that day was Jorge Sosa, a 6-foot-2, 220-pound right-hander from the Dominican Republic. Coming off a mediocre rookie season, Sosa was having a rough sophomore season as well and would finish the year 5–12. His season was about to get even rougher.

Batting cleanup for the Blue Jays, Delgado came to the plate in the bottom of the first inning with two men on base and hit a Sosa fastball deep to center field and over the 400-foot sign, the ball bouncing off the glass that fronted a stadium restaurant and landing back on the field. The home run was Delgado's 300th career blast, and just like that the Blue Jays had a 3–0 lead.

With Toronto continuing to lead, 3–1, and Sosa still on the mound, Delgado led off the bottom of the fourth inning in similar fashion. Sosa served up another fastball and this time Delgado sent it sailing over the right-field fence, again some 400 feet away. Just like that he was 2-for-2, with two home runs and four RBI.

The Blue Jays added another run that inning to increase their lead to 5–1; however, the Devil Rays rallied for five runs in the top of the sixth to take a 6–5 lead. It was still 6–5 when Delgado led off in the bottom of the sixth inning looking for his third home run of the afternoon.

As Delgado came to bat, Sosa was replaced by little-known Joe Kennedy, a third-year pitcher coming off an 8–11 season in 2002. At 6-foot-4 Kennedy was big and strong, but on that day he was no match for the formidable Delgado. The left-handed Kennedy tried to sneak a curveball by him and Delgado tagged it, again sending the ball over the right-field fence and into the lower-level seats. With three innings left to play the Blue Jays had tied the score at 6–6—and Delgado had three home runs.

Toronto was behind, 8–7, when Delgado came to bat in the bottom of the eighth, leading off an inning for the third time in the ballgame. This time he faced Lance Carter, a third-year player who had posted a cumulative 2–1 record in his first two major-league seasons. Against Carter the outcome was the same as it had been against Sosa and Kennedy.

Carter came at him with a fastball and Delgado again hit it to deep center field, where it bounced high off the upper deck to give him his fourth home run of the game. A broad smile crossed the popular Delgado's face as he stepped on home plate, already on a path toward his 400th career home run.

Toronto went on to win, 10–8, and Delgado finished the game with 4 home runs, 6 RBI, 4 runs scored, and 16 total bases in just 4 at-bats. On that day he became the 15th player to join the Four Home Runs Club and was applauded the following morning in a newspaper dispatch that read as follows: "Carlos Delgado sure woke up in a big hurry. The Toronto slugger took cold medicine and a nap before the game, then hit four home runs Thursday night to become the 15th player in major-league history to accomplish the feat."[6]

On that day Delgado hit both his 300th career home run and four homers in one game at the ripe old age of 31, a period in a ballplayer's career that sometimes marks the tail end of his peak years.

"It was pretty awesome," Aubrey Huff, Tampa Bay's designated hitter, laughed. "We lost 100 games for several years around that time, so if we saw someone do something awesome it was interesting to us."

Added Huff, who at 6-foot-4 and 225 pounds drove in 107 runs that season to complement a .311 batting average,

When I was a kid I saw Juan Gonzales hit three home runs in a game and I thought to myself, "Man, that would be awesome to do one day." Then, I found myself in a game watching Carlos Delgado hit four. It was one of those rare feats—definitely more rare than hitting for the cycle or pitching a no-hitter or even a perfect game.

Vinnie Chulk, a 6-foot-2, 200-pound right-hander, pitched to five batters in the sixth inning for Toronto, giving up a triple and a single and walking two before finally being pulled with three earned runs to his credit and only one out. Despite the rough outing he recalls the game in a good light.

"That was one of the first games I pitched in, and I gave up the lead," said Chulk, who as a rookie that season appeared in only three games. He continued,

> Honestly, it went from being a really, really terrible third of an inning and prob-
> ably [a terrible] rest of the night for me to one of the better celebrations in the
> clubhouse afterwards. It was a good experience to be a part of. Just being in the
> big leagues alone was enough, then to see that after only a few days in the majors
> was incredible.

Chulk said he watched Delgado's fourth home run as he walked from the clubhouse, where he had briefly retreated following his short stint on the mound, back to the dugout.

"That was pretty cool, pretty unreal," he said.

After his perfect performance against Tampa Bay, Delgado would put together five more solid seasons, averaging 33 home runs. During his second-to-last season he would drive in 115 runs before calling it quits after 2009, when he hit 4 homers, drove in 23 runners, and still managed to hit .291. His career accomplishments included more than 2,000 hits, a respectable lifetime batting average of .280, and a 9-RBI game. For 17 years Delgado had played the game with patience and finesse, and now it was over. For the first time in decades he would miss the challenge of opposing pitchers.

"You have to be prepared for that one time [that pitchers] make a mistake," Delgado said toward the end, adding, "You have to be patient. You can't make outs on pitchers' pitches. If they're not throwing strikes, that doesn't mean you have to expand your strike zone and be a bad hitter."[7]

Delgado's retirement followed years of injuries, including back and hip problems, and was not a complete surprise. Finally, after 22 seasons at various levels in professional baseball, he had suffered enough.

"I always said I would try to return until my body had enough," he said. "And my body could take no more. I've been training two years and recently tried yet again to increase the routine of work, but the swing was not there to compete at the level I want."

He added, "There comes a moment when you have to have the dignity and the sense to recognize that something is not functioning—you can't swim against the current."[8]

In 2012, three years after he retired, Delgado became only the 10th Blue Jay honored with the club's Level of Excellence Award for on-field achievement. Three years later he was inducted into the Canadian Baseball Hall of Fame. Along the way he coached his son's Little League team, attended his daughter's swimming lessons and school plays, dabbled on social media (his Twitter account has 73,000 followers), and maintained an involvement with charity work, including his Extra Bases Foundation, which assists people in need. At least outwardly the Hall of Fame snub doesn't define Delgado.

"I played the game the way it should be played," he said. "I enjoyed it. I gave 100 percent. At the end of the day that's all I can do."[9]

16

JOSH HAMILTON

May 8, 2012

O f all the players enrolled in the Four Home Runs Club, none is a bigger mystery than Josh Hamilton. That is largely due to his longstanding battle with substance abuse, a battle that throughout time diminished his potential for all-time greatness. Even considering his drug problems Hamilton performed magnificently throughout much of his nine-year major-league career—not nearly as magnificently, however, as he might have.

Still, Hamilton is a former Most Valuable Player who won the award in 2010, his fourth season in the big leagues. His batting average that season was a league-leading .359, although his other statistics, while excellent, were arguably less than worthy of an MVP player, at least for that season: 186 hits (sixth in the league), 32 home runs (tied for fifth), and 100 RBI (not even in the top 10). It appears that Hamilton may have received the award largely on the strength of the batting title, although 32 home runs and 100 RBI are certainly commendable accomplishments and helped earn him the distinction.

By comparison, in 2008, his second season in the big leagues, Hamilton punched out 190 hits, drilled 32 home runs, drove in a league-leading 130 RBI, and batted a more-than-respectable .304. Despite those numbers he finished a disappointing seventh in the MVP balloting.

"If he made the pitchers throw him a strike he was usually going to hit the ball a lot harder than just about anyone I've seen," said former teammate Scott Feldman, a pitcher who played alongside Hamilton the day he hit four home runs.

A clean-living young man throughout his high school years, Hamilton's troubles began in 2001 as his third season in the minor leagues was about to

Josh Hamilton. *Brad Newton,* © Texas Rangers

begin. After suffering lower back injuries in an automobile accident, Hamilton, who was just 20, had time on his hands and money in his pocket. With those liabilities working against him it is no surprise that he eventually got into trouble, falling victim to alcohol and drugs.

Largely due to the back injury, Hamilton only appeared in 83 games during the 2001 and 2002 baseball seasons, when he played Single-A and Double-A ball for three different clubs. In the years that followed he was suspended for drug violations numerous times and banned from baseball for three consecutive seasons—2003 through 2005. By the time the game reinstated him he was in his mid-20s and had not yet worn a major-league uniform.

"In 1999 [the year he was drafted by the Tampa Bay Devil Rays], baseball and my parents were the only two things I had," Hamilton said. "When I was separated from them . . . I started looking for things to fill that hole."[1]

He found them. While out of baseball Hamilton got married. Then the couple separated. After that they had a baby. Finally, Hamilton made it to the major leagues in 2007 and appeared to have a bright future. On the surface success and happiness were his for the taking. So was calamity.

In 2015, Hamilton appeared to get it all together. But not before a highly publicized relapse, one that eventually got him traded from the Los Angeles Angels of Anaheim to the Texas Rangers. At last, Hamilton was back where he'd had his greatest successes, including the MVP Award, consecutive World Series appearances in 2010 and 2011, a 40-homer/130-RBI season, and the four-home run game that same year.

What's more, Hamilton had God in his corner. Things were literally—and finally—looking up for the 6-foot-4, 240-pound Hamilton.

"It's amazing I'm still alive after all I've done to my body," Hamilton told the magazine *Christianity Today*. "My granny told me during those days that God had something special planned for me, otherwise I would have died."[2]

Joshua Holt Hamilton was born in tobacco country, Raleigh, North Carolina, a region that some might argue is the birthplace of addiction, on May 21, 1981. His father Tony worked at an outdoor machinery dealership, and together with his wife Linda worked diligently to raise their two sons.

Hamilton played baseball from his earliest memory and he always wanted to compete in the sport professionally. That dream didn't stop him from enjoying other sports, and he also played soccer and football. In the end baseball presided over his future.

At Athens Drive High School, Hamilton was a star athlete, and he broke school records seemingly with ease. As a pitcher and center fielder on the

Jaguars' baseball team he was a dominating force, boasting a 96-mile-per-hour fastball and a strong, quick bat. His bat was so strong and quick that as a senior he hit over .500 with 13 home runs and 35 RBI. As a flame-throwing pitcher he experienced similar success, going 7–1 with 91 strikeouts in just 56 innings. To reward him for his brilliant season, *Baseball America* put Hamilton on its cover and he was named Player of the Year for the state of North Carolina.

When the 1999 amateur draft rolled around it was widely reckoned that Hamilton would be selected high. That's exactly what happened, as the Devil Rays chose him first in the first round—at least on paper Hamilton was the top prospect in the country. He signed with the organization for a hefty $3.96 million bonus, and his future seemed secure.

Top prospect or not, newly drafted players often require seasoning, and Tampa Bay sent Hamilton to the Princeton Devil Rays, a Rookie League team in the Appalachian League. He caught fire almost immediately. Before the season was over Hamilton had hit 10 home runs, driven in 48 RBI, and hit .347. He was promoted to the Hudson Valley Renegades in low Single-A ball for the remainder of the season and then on to the Charleston River Dogs in Single-A for the 2000 season. While with Charleston he hit a healthy .302 with 13 home runs.

After that things started to unravel. Following the automobile accident Hamilton began experimenting with substances, and later on he failed some drug tests. As things came to a head he was suspended for three consecutive seasons during what should have been big baseball years. Then he wised up and quit using substances in 2004 while he sat on the sidelines and out of baseball. That same year he got married.

Then, things "raveled" back. Hamilton returned to baseball in 2006, playing briefly again with Hudson Valley. He opened the 2007 season with the Triple-A Louisville Bats, hitting .350 before his newest organization—the Cincinnati Reds had acquired his services through a series of personnel moves—called him up. After the toil and turmoil he had endured, Josh Hamilton was finally a major leaguer.

Hamilton completed a year in Cincinnati before being traded to the Rangers, where he quickly became a star. In 2008, his first season with Texas, he hit .304 with 32 home runs and 130 RBI. Josh Hamilton, it seemed, had at last found a baseball home.

Things were up and down after his rookie season in the majors: Hamilton hit .268 with just 10 home runs in 2009, had the MVP year in 2010, and hit just under .300 with 25 homers and 94 RBI in 2011. With most of his baggage seemingly behind him, it appeared there was no stopping Josh Hamilton. On May 8, 2012, there really was no stopping him.

"Hamilton was seeing [the ball] big as a grapefruit that day," recalled Baltimore Orioles pitcher Troy Patton, an eyewitness to history who played in the game.

Oriole Park at Camden Yards opened in 1992 under a blanket of bluegrass. The prime mover to build a stadium was then-mayor William Schaefer, who began lobbying for the park in the 1980s. Construction finally began in 1989 and work took almost three years before the stadium was opened at a cost of more than $100 million.

The ballpark includes a number of unique features: double-deck bullpens, a playing field situated below ground level, and aisle seats adorned with a nineteenth-century Orioles logo. The stadium is situated just two blocks from the site where Babe Ruth was born.[3]

In 2012, Facebook made its first public offering, the London Olympics were held with great fanfare, and Queen Elizabeth celebrated six decades on the throne. In baseball, the average value of the teams rose 16 percent, a second wild-card team was added to each league for postseason play, and the Houston Astros agreed to move to the American League, where they would win the World Series in 2017. Josh Hamilton was about to make some history of his own,

On the mound for Baltimore on May 8, 2012, was Jake Arrieta, who at 6-foot-4 and 225 pounds was downright intimidating and a future Cy Young Award winner. A right-hander all the way, after two seasons in the big leagues he had posted a 16–14 record and was only 2–3 when he faced Hamilton during his third season in the big leagues.

Hitting third in the lineup, Hamilton came to bat in the top of the first inning with a man on first base and hit Arrieta's first pitch deep to dead center field, where it bounced on top of the wall and landed on the other side for a two-run home run. After one inning of play Texas led Baltimore 2–0.

With his team still leading 2–0 in the top of the third, Hamilton once again faced Arrieta, again with a man on first. In the first inning he'd hit a curveball for a home run, but this time Arrieta served up a fastball and Hamilton smacked it over the left-center-field fence near the 364-foot mark for another two-run home run. After Adrian Beltre followed with a home run, Texas was ahead 5–0.

Batting second in the fifth inning with Arrieta still on the mound, Hamilton drilled a shot that bounced off the right-field wall. By the time outfielders could chase down the ball, Hamilton had coasted into second base with a stand-up double and his third extra-base hit of the game.

Baltimore scored a run in the sixth, and with his team leading 6–1 Hamilton came up in the seventh inning for his fourth at-bat. With a runner on base, the Orioles brought in a new pitcher, Zach Phillips, to face Hamilton, who by then clearly had starting pitcher Arrieta's number. He soon got Phillips's number as well, greeting the left-hander with a shot that again cleared the center-field wall for his third two-run homer of the game. By the end of the inning Texas had increased its lead to an insurmountable 8–1.

The following inning Hamilton came to bat with a teammate on base, now facing sidearmer Darren O'Day. He greeted O'Day as he had the other Baltimore pitchers, hitting another two-run blast over the fence in the deepest part of center field for his fourth home run of the contest. The homer was his fifth in six appearances in two days and earned him a standing ovation from the Baltimore crowd.

"You don't expect somebody to hit four home runs, much less in a big-league game," said Toronto Blue Jays pitcher Vinnie Chulk, who had watched Carlos Delgado hit four in 2003. He described the experience as "amazing."

What a day it had been for Hamilton: 4 home runs in 6 at-bats, 18 total bases, 8 RBI, and 4 runs scored. Texas won the game, 10–3.

"Other than being in the World Series [it's] the highlight of my big-league career," Hamilton said. "I was saying after I hit two I've never hit three in a game before, and what a blessing that was. Then to hit four is just an awesome feeling, to see how excited my teammates got."

He continued, "It reminds you of when you're in Little League and a little kid, and just the excitement and why we play the game. Things like that. You never know what can happen. It was just an absolute blessing."[4]

The blessing was described by a reporter the following morning:

> There are few times when a visiting player comes to Camden Yards and puts on such a spectacular show that he turns the fans in his favor. But Texas slugger Josh Hamilton, the former number-one overall pick who overcame the depths of drug and alcohol abuse to become one of the game's top sluggers, orchestrated one of the most magnificent power displays in baseball history in the Rangers' 10–3 win over the Baltimore Orioles Tuesday night. He gained a share of fans along the way. When Hamilton rounded the bases in the eighth inning—becoming the 16th player in major-league history to hit four home runs in one game—those who remained of the 11,263 on hand offered their appreciation by giving him a standing ovation.[5]

A bright spot for Baltimore that day was pitcher Patton, who enjoyed his best season in 2012, posting a 1–0 record with a 2.43 ERA in 54 appearances.

Patton, who struck out two in pitching the ninth inning for the Orioles, was the only Baltimore hurler not to give up either a home run or a run.

"All of them were well-hit balls," Patton said of Hamilton's blasts. "None of them were cheapies."

Was it exciting for Patton to witness baseball history? In one respect, no. In another, yes.

"It was pretty demoralizing," he said of the four-home run game and 10–3 blowout. "Hamilton single-handedly beat us. I remember sitting back in the clubhouse and feeling pretty good because I didn't give up any home runs."

He continued, "I felt special being a part of something that was history."

Teammate Scott Feldman, who closed out the game for Texas pitching a scoreless ninth inning, also was amazed.

"The whole first half of that season he was incredible, and that night when he hit four homers was pretty amazing," said Feldman. "When he hit the fourth I think most people were just shaking their heads at how easy and effortless he made things look."

On the season, Hamilton would hit 43 homers and drive in 123 runners. His MVP year notwithstanding, the 2012 season may have been Hamilton's best.

After that, however, things soured. In 2013 he sank to 21 home runs and 79 RBI. In 2014 he hit just 10 home runs and drove in 44. And in 2015, a tumultuous season in which he was abruptly refunded to Texas from the Angels, Hamilton hit eight home runs with 25 RBI.

Finally, the Rangers gave Hamilton his unconditional release after he suffered a knee injury that required surgery before the 2016 season even began. Although they later resigned him, he underwent knee surgery again in 2017 and was optioned to the minors. His future is in limbo.

Still, Hamilton has long been at peace with his journey, as a sports column he once wrote underscores:

This may sound crazy, but I wouldn't change a thing about my path to the big leagues. I wouldn't even change the 26 tattoos that cover so much of my body, even though they're the most obvious signs of my life temporarily leaving the tracks. . . .

If I hadn't gone through all the hard times, this whole story would be just about baseball. If I'd made the big leagues at 21 and made my first All-Star Team at 23 and done all the things expected of me, I would be a big-time baseball player, and that's it.

Baseball is third in my life right now, behind my relationship with God and my family. Without the first two, baseball isn't even in the picture. Believe me, I know.[6]

SCOOTER GENNETT

June 6, 2017

Just hours after Scooter Gennett humbled the national pastime by hitting four home runs against the St. Louis Cardinals, the sporting world was abuzz. The questions asked by sportswriters and fans throughout the country were predictable: Who *is* Scooter Gennett, and how does that performance by a little-known utility ballplayer rank among the all-time great single-game offensive accomplishments in the 140-year history of Major League Baseball? After all, Gennett, playing for the Cincinnati Reds, had accomplished something that most of baseball's greatest stars never had, and the disparity between his and their careers was stark and almost incomprehensible in the context of his torrid hitting display.

The answers to those questions were straightforward: When morning broke the day of his mind-boggling home run rampage, Gennett was two months into his fifth season as a major-league ballplayer. His "lifetime" batting average was an acceptable .281; however, his resume claimed only 37 home runs—roughly nine per year in the four-plus seasons he had played in the major leagues. By day's end only five players in the history of baseball had collected more RBI in a single game than Gennett, whose four home runs more than doubled the three he had hit during the first two months of 2017.

On that day, 73 years to the day after America's allies invaded France and five months into Donald Trump's unanticipated presidency, Gennett emerged as a baseball wonder boy as he eclipsed Pat Seerey to become, at that moment, the least productive offensive player ever to hit four home runs in a game, nonetheless standing tall alongside Hall of Famers Ed Delahanty, Lou Gehrig, Chuck Klein, Willie Mays, and Mike Schmidt as a member of the coveted Four Home

Runs Club. Least productive, that is, until his ensuing years in baseball enhance his statistics or someone with lesser credentials comes along to take his place.

Even Gennett conceded that his success was unlikely. "That's something I never thought I would do," he said of the four dingers. "Even three home runs would be too crazy for me."[1]

"Crazy" was an understatement. Gennett drove in more runs—10—than 80 percent of the 30 major-league *teams* scored in their entirety that day. His four homers and one single translated to 17 total bases collected, just two shy of Shawn Green's all-time major-league mark of 19. Paradoxically, the spree marked only the second multihomer game of his career.

Gennett's success couldn't have occurred at a better time for the likable 27-year-old, who was waived by the Milwaukee Brewers following spring

Scooter Gennett. *Minda Haas*

training and claimed by the utility player–hungry Reds just days before the 2017 season was to begin. The game would occur just 17 days before the United Kingdom would initiate divorce proceedings from the European Union, called Brexit, and 96 years to the day following the first no-hitter in Negro League history.

"It was a good night, being from here, born here . . . to do something that's never been done [by a Reds player]," he said. "I can't put it into words—it's an honor, for sure."

Gennett's departure from the Brewers followed what had been his most productive season as a player. In 2016 the native Ohioan hit 14 home runs and drove in 56 runners, both of them career highs at the time. Still, Milwaukee may have lost interest after he transacted just 21 homers and 104 RBI during his first three seasons, an average of seven home runs and 35 RBI—not exactly statistics that commend greatness.

Everything changed with the four-homer bender. The national media played the story big and within 24 hours almost everyone who followed baseball had heard of Scooter Gennett and viewed his performance on the internet, although his last name still failed to resonate metronomically. In time, depending on the remainder of Gennett's career, the name familiarity may come.

Ryan Joseph Gennett was born on May 1, 1990, in—where else?—Cincinnati, Ohio, to Joe and Tina Gennett. Although his love for baseball began in the Queen City, it soon migrated south. When he was just 10 his father asked Scooter how badly he wanted to play baseball. The answer was a definitive . . . badly! So, his father resigned from his position at a trucking company and moved the Gennetts to Sarasota, Florida, where the weather was favorable throughout the year and the boy could play baseball from January through December. Play he did.

"I got to play way more baseball there," he said. "My dad was a scout with the Astros before I was born, and he knew how important it was to play a lot."[2]

By then the nickname "Scooter" had emerged. When the child got wind that his mother planned to take him to the local police station for a lecture on the importance of buckling up in the car, something he had apparently failed to do, he borrowed the alias from the orange-toned Muppets character "Scooter" in hopes it would throw local authorities off track and keep him out of jail. Thereafter the youthful seat belt offender continued answering to the name Scooter, still fearful of ending up in the slammer for the harness violation.

"I thought I was going to be arrested," he said. "So I told the policeman my name was Scooter. After we left there I didn't answer to Ryan because I thought if I answered to my real name I'd get arrested."[3]

As a boy Gennett was small, and he always played as one of the shortest members of any team he was on. Conscious of his limited stature, Gennett took advantage of the benefits that being small, light, and, as a result, speedy presented even early on, working hard to excel at everything that a player of his limited dimensions was expected to do. He was fast and could steal bases. His speed also enabled him to beat out infield hits. And he could bunt, both to get on base and move runners along. In fact, Gennett found that bunting for hits added an element of excitement to not only the game of baseball, but also his own game, and he became exceedingly adept at it.

"When I played baseball as a young boy, my game was built around my quickness," he said. "I was always among the shortest and lightest on my teams, so power wasn't a thing. I was the speed guy."[4]

As a teen Gennett attended Sarasota High School and was chosen by the Brewers in the 16th round (496th pick overall) of the 2009 major-league draft. Unbeknownst to him, just four years later he would hit his first major-league home run off Bronson Arroyo, a big, tall right-hander who joined the Reds the same year as Gennett and started against the Cardinals the day after his teammate made baseball history.

After signing with the Brewers for a reported $260,000, Gennett began his professional career in 2010 with the Single-A Wisconsin Timber Rattlers, batting .309, making the All-Star Team, and earning a promotion the following season to the Single-A Brevard County (Florida) Manatees. There he hit an even .300. In 2012 Gennett made the leap to Double-A, playing for the Huntsville (Alabama) Stars and hitting .293. While he demonstrated consistency at the plate, Gennett was anything but a long-ball threat. In three seasons of minor-league play he had connected for just 29 home runs and 12 triples, although he did average 32 doubles in that same period.

With those statistics, Gennett was elevated to the Triple-A Nashville Sounds in 2013. Facing stronger pitching than he had in Double-A his batting average understandably dropped to a still-respectable .280 with three home runs and 22 RBI. That was good enough to earn him a spot with the major-league Milwaukee Brewers in 2014, where a spark of home run power flickered: He hit his first grand slam on June 25, 2014, off Washington Nationals ace Stephen Strasburg. But despite nine home runs he once again found himself in Triple-A at the start of the 2015 season, eventually moving back up to the parent club as the season continued on. Later that season, on a Brewers day off, he was married, appropriately, at a Brewery.

Through it all, Gennett, an avid potter in his spare time, remained a conundrum, a player who hit for a fair average but had limited power, hit mostly singles and doubles, and maintained average RBI totals at best. As June 2017 rolled around, Gennett's average-ness would only be magnified when his record-tying home run outing appeared out of nowhere.

In their long and colorful history, the Cincinnati Reds have been involved in three four-homer games—twice on their home turf. The first time was in 1993 when Mark Whiten did it at Riverfront Stadium; Gennett accomplished it the second time at Great American Ball Park, which is situated on the Ohio River not far from the city center. He's the only Red to hit four home runs in a game.

Christened in time for the 2003 season, Great American Ball Park replaced Cinergy Field, better known as Riverfront Stadium, where the Reds played for 32 seasons. Skillfully interweaving the Reds history of excellence, the ballpark features statues of players who once graced old Crosley Field, forerunner to Riverfront Stadium, including Johnny Bench, Ted Kluszewski, Ernie Lombardi, Joe Morgan, Joe Nuxhall, and Frank Robinson, with each image artfully lit. A seating gap between home plate and third base allows passersby to peer into the stadium, a generous touch that invites the "passing" interest of pedestrians. The "new" aspect of the ballpark includes a 40-foot LED video scoreboard and the stadium's Machine (as in Big Red Machine) Room Grill pub.

To players those amenities mean little. What does matter are the field dimensions: an easily reachable 325 feet to right field, 328 feet to left, and a respectable 404 feet to dead center. On his big day Gennett found those distances to his liking, hitting two balls over the right-field fence, one to right-center, and another down the left-field line.

On game day Gennett was mired in an 0-for-19 slump but heartened by the fact that Cincinnati would be playing the slumping Cardinals. On the mound that day for St. Louis was Adam Wainright, a 6-foot-7, 235-pound right-hander who at that point early in the season was among the league leaders in wins with a 6–3 record and had a scoreless streak of 17 innings going for him.

The left fielder's slump ended modestly enough in the first inning when Gennett, batting fifth in the lineup, came to the plate with runners on first and second and two out and promptly blooped a single to shallow left field, scoring Billy Hamilton and giving the Reds an early 1–0 lead. Then the fun began.

After setting the Reds down in order in the bottom of the second inning, Wainright surrendered two walks and a single to load the bases with one out in the third. Still trailing 1–0, the big right-hander watched as Gennett strode to the plate, anxious to help his team build on its narrow lead. Gennett worked the pitcher to a full count before powering a 92-mile-per-hour fastball deep into the right-center-field bleachers for a grand slam, the second of his career. Just like that the Reds led 5–0 and Gennett had his first home run of the game.

In the fourth inning Wainright got two quick outs on ground balls to second baseman Jose Peraza before things began to unravel for the second straight inning. An infield single and a double put runners on second and third before an intentional walk loaded the bases. Eugenio Suarez then tripled to drive in three runners and send Wainright to the showers. He was replaced by right-hander John Gant, who at 6-foot-3 and 200 pounds was almost as intimidating as his predecessor.

The first batter Gant faced was Gennett, who promptly sent another fastball over the center-field fence where it bounced onto a strip of grass. Suarez scored from third and Cincinnati led 10–0, thanks largely to Gennett's two home runs and five RBI.

Gant held the Reds scoreless in the fifth inning, but the sixth was a different story. After Suarez struck out looking, Gennett came to the plate. The right-hander threw him a fastball that trailed away and the feisty outfielder tagged it down the left-field line and over the fence, where a fan caught it just beyond the 328-foot mark. The 18,620 fans in attendance requested a curtain call following Gennett's third home run, and Cincinnati led 11–0.

By the eighth inning Gant was gone, replaced on the mound by John Brebbia after completing a scoreless seventh inning. With two outs, a runner on first base, and the crowd on its feet, Gennett came to bat on the verge of making baseball history. With the count 0–2, Brebbia delivered a 93-mile-per-hour high fastball and Gennett dumped it two rows deep into the right-field bleachers for his fourth home run of the game. Prior to that game Gennett had never hit four home runs in a month.

As he passed first base Gennett shook his head once as if in disbelief, and after touching home plate—no teammates were there to congratulate him—he tipped his cap to the appreciative crowd. Gennett, whose totals on the day included 5 hits in 5 at-bats, 4 home runs, and 10 RBI, had given those in attendance a game to remember while leading his teammates to a 13–1 trouncing of the Cardinals and tying a club record for RBI. What's more, the Four Home Runs Club had just increased its membership, adding to its ranks the only player to ever hit 4 home runs, drive in 10 runners, and collect 5 hits in a single game.

"Usually when I hit a home run I consider myself lucky," Gennett said after the game. "But it's hard to get lucky four times in a row."[5]

In its account after the game, the Associated Press put Gennett's performance in proper light:

> Scooter Gennett hit four home runs, matching the major-league record, and finished with 10 RBIs as the Cincinnati Reds routed the slumping St. Louis Cardinals, 13–1, on Tuesday night. Gennett became the 17th player to homer four times in one game—and perhaps the least likely. A scrappy second baseman who was claimed off waivers from Milwaukee in late March, he began the night with 38 career home runs in five seasons, including three this year.[6]

After the game, Gennett spent considerable time talking with the news media, reiterating to various reporters how thrilled he was to tie the record and do it in front of his hometown fans. Then, with the record and baseball immortality packed away in his Reds duffle bag, he stepped from the spotlight to prepare for another game against the Cardinals the following day. After all, unlike most of his brethren in the Four Home Runs Club, Gennett remains an active player—one of two players in either league who can boast of matching such a historic record. The following day, moving over from left field to play second base, he went 1-for-4, with a single and one run scored. Scooter Gennett had come back to earth.

During the two weeks after he tied the single-game mark, Gennett reverted to his former self as a singles and doubles hitter, platooning at several positions in the infield and outfield, sitting out several games, and failing to hit another home run until he delivered a three-run shot against the Dodgers on June 19. After the four-homer experience Gennett remained a utility player, although he finished the 2017 season with 27 home runs.

"It's amazing, especially since he's not an everyday player for us," manager Bryan Price said. "He's got power, but four homers in one game? I don't know what to tell you." He added, "It's very emotional. It was an honor to witness that."[7]

Wainright, the losing pitcher, agreed. "He had a career night, a great night," he said. "Guys do that now and then."[8]

18

J. D. MARTINEZ

September 4, 2017

As the Los Angeles Dodgers endured one of the worst losing streaks in the club's 134-year history, watching as what *Sports Illustrated* described as perhaps the best season ever faded into oblivion, journeyman J. D. Martinez was there to rub it in. The Arizona Diamondback did so with his bat. Playing at Dodger Stadium, one of the most picturesque ballparks ever built, Martinez made things ugly for the Dodgers by socking four home runs off an array of four frustrated LA pitchers, some of whom would continue to suffer until the team's streak, which had begun two days earlier with a doubleheader loss to the lowly San Diego Padres, ended more than a week after his onslaught. It was the team's worst slump since the Allies stormed Normandy on D-Day.

"It's a blessing," Martinez said of his record-tying performance, putting it more spiritually than the Dodgers probably deserved.[1]

For the Dodgers the game was anything but a blessing. Not only did the team lose its fourth consecutive game en route to dropping 11 in a row and 15 of 16, but also it marked the first time that a player had hit four home runs in one game against the Dodgers at Dodger Stadium. (Joe Adcock of the Milwaukee Braves hit four home runs against the Dodgers in a game at Brooklyn's Ebbets Field in 1954.)

What's more, in the 13–0 drubbing Martinez recorded more home runs (four) than the entire Dodgers team had hits (three). Not bad for a guy who was traded midseason from the Tigers to the Diamondbacks despite having hit 16 home runs.

Like Cincinnati's Scooter Gennett, who had hit four home runs in a game just 59 days earlier, Martinez was a somewhat unlikely hero. At the age of 30 he tied Willie Mays, Shawn Green, and Josh Hamilton as players having accomplished the feat after the age of 30—only Chuck Klein and Carlos Delgado, who both achieved it at age 31, were older when they entered the record books. And

J. D. Martinez. *KeithAllisonPhoto.com*

in six previous major-league seasons Martinez had averaged just 18 homers per campaign, although he did earn a spot on the American League All-Star Team in 2015 when he hit 38 home runs and knocked in 102 RBI. Still, he wasn't exactly Babe Ruth, and of the 18 players who hit four home runs in a game, Martinez ranked 13th in career blasts at the time he tied the mark.

"I don't know how to explain it," Martinez said after the game. "It's one of those things where you work real hard and find that perfect swing and find one of those days where everything just kind of lines up. Today, I felt like, was one of those days. I was seeing the ball well, and when I was swinging I was hitting them."[2]

Indeed he was. By season's end Martinez had posted 45 home runs, although his name did not appear among the National League home run leaders because 16 of those blasts were hit when he played for the American League's Detroit Tigers. Still, his overall statistics made it obvious that at least in 2017 Martinez was one of the game's premier home run threats, a fact punctuated by his four-homer game.

"I'm watching his swing and I'm thinking if this is a strike I think this is a homer," teammate A. J. Pollock prophesied seconds before Martinez connected on his fourth slam. "It's obviously the most impressive thing I've ever been a part of. It was awesome."[3]

Julio Daniel Martinez was born in Miami, Florida, of Cuban heritage on August 21, 1987, and reared in South Florida. The son of Julio and Mayra Martinez, he attended Charles W. Flanagan High School in Pembroke Pines, where he graduated in 2006—the same year that the school's baseball team won its second consecutive state title. Martinez played on both the 2005 and 2006 Florida state championship teams, although in retrospect he did not perform up to his own lofty expectations.

"I can honestly say I never really developed until I was in college," said Martinez. "In high school I did well, but I didn't do really, really well. I always hit fourth on the state championship team, but I never really stood out and made a big impression."[4]

Despite his self-proclaimed mediocrity, at least relative to what he believed he might have accomplished, the Minnesota Twins selected Martinez late in the 2006 draft as a 36th-round afterthought; however, he chose to attend college instead of turn professional. At Nova Southeastern University in Florida, hardly a household name or a college baseball powerhouse, Martinez made the best of things, hitting .428 during his final season, earning Division II All-America honors, and increasing his value exponentially from high school. But the Houston

CHAPTER 18

Astros still only selected him in the 20th round of the 2009 major-league draft. In short, Martinez was a longshot to make it to the big leagues, and his future lay in his own ability to dig down deep to grow and develop.

Thus began a long schlep through the minor leagues, first with the Greeneville Astros in rookie ball and then the Tri-City ValleyCats in low A-ball, hitting .403 and .326, respectively, before jumping up to the Corpus Christi Hooks in Double-A and again hitting above .300, but with limited power. Finally, in 2011, Martinez made his major-league debut with the Astros, hitting .274 on the season with six home runs.

"My heart was racing 100 miles an hour," Martinez said of his major-league debut. "Everything seemed so big. It was the first time I ever caught a ball with stands in the stadium as a background. Usually you have the sky as a background. It was so weird. I felt so tiny on the field."[5]

While his overall performance that year was impressive enough, Martinez bounced around the minor leagues for two more seasons before the Detroit Tigers claimed him on waivers in 2014. He debuted with the Tigers that same season, slugging 23 home runs, driving in 76 runs. and hitting .315. Martinez appeared to be in Detroit for the long haul; however, it turned out to be for the relatively short haul.

The Tigers traded Martinez to Arizona midway through the 2017 season. Despite hitting 16 home runs for Detroit in only 200 at-bats, the team had sent him packing. But as the 2017 season came to a satisfying close, Martinez appeared to once again have found a baseball home, this time in Phoenix.

"I like to get the ball up in the air," Martinez said in 2014, presenting a hint of things to come. "If I get the ball in the air, there's a chance it will go out or be a double."[6]

Constructed between 1959 and 1962 as a means of moving the recently transplanted Brooklyn Dodgers out of cavernous Los Angeles Memorial Coliseum and into their own digs, Dodger Stadium is a baseball anomaly. Situated in the heart of Chavez Ravine, the stadium affords fans a soothing view of waving palm trees and the low hills that meander through one of many barrios that dot Los Angeles County. There is no nearby downtown to crowd the stadium. There is no effective public transportation system to reel fans in. And there are no nearby restaurants to greet fans before a typical 7:10 p.m. weekday start time.

The team has called Dodger Stadium, the third-oldest ballpark in the major leagues, home for more than 55 years, one more than timeless announcer Vin Scully did during his legendary broadcast career. With Scully's departure after the 2016 season, the cathedral ballpark boasts an appropriate new address:

1000 Vin Scully Avenue. Scully, believe those who were reared taking their transistor radios to the stadium to hear him call the game, was the face and voice of Dodger Stadium from the day the ballpark began welcoming fans.

Opened to the public on April 10, 1962, the ballpark quickly developed—and has maintained—a reputation for cleanliness and beauty. Even so, the seating capacity hasn't changed much—roughly 56,000 fans are allowed to enjoy that beauty in any given game, the same approximate number that could enjoy a game on Opening Day 1962. Memorable moments in the stadium's history include Sandy Koufax's perfect game in 1965 and Kirk Gibson's walk-off home run that turned the tide in the 1988 World Series.

The field dimensions haven't changed much, either: 330 feet down the lines and 395 feet to dead center field. On September 4, 2017, those dimensions were perfect for what was about to happen.

When Arizona visited Dodger Stadium to open a three-game series on September 4, 2017, the Dodgers held a comfortable 12 1/2-game lead over the Diamondbacks in the National League West Division. The Dodgers had been winning at a .670 clip, and on the mound that day was Rich Hill, a 6-foot-5 left-hander who just 12 days earlier had thrown a perfect game into the ninth inning and a no-hitter into the 10th, eventually losing the game on a walk-off home run. A year earlier, Dodgers manager Dave Roberts had pulled Hill from a game after seven hitless innings.

Despite the potential for perfection, Hill, who at age 37 was a 13-year major-league veteran, was inconsistent. Going into the September 4 game he was 9–6 with an earned run average of 3.71.

Martinez began his record-tying game ingloriously by striking out on a 2–2 pitch in the second inning; however, he exacted his revenge against Hill in the fourth inning when he came to bat again eager to make something happen. With one out and Kristopher Negron on first following a single, Martinez broke a scoreless tie by smacking a grooved fastball over the left-center-field fence to give the Diamondbacks a 2–0 lead. The home run was Martinez's 34th of the season.

By the time Martinez came to bat in the seventh inning the Diamondbacks were still ahead 2–0 and the thought of a four-home run game was far from anyone's mind. Then along came reliever Pedro Baez, who would suffer through a disastrous September while watching his chances of making the Dodgers' playoff roster disintegrate in a volley of home runs and earned runs allowed in several appearances. Martinez led off the inning by slugging a 3–1 Baez fastball over the right-field fence and well up into the Dodger Stadium pavilion. He would give up a home run to the next batter, Brandon Drury, and two consecutive singles before being replaced by Edward Paredes, who would quickly give up two more singles. By the time the dust of the seventh inning had settled, the Diamondbacks led the Dodgers 6–0.

Reliever Paredes was long gone by the time Martinez came to bat again in the eighth inning, replaced by Robbie Ray and then Josh Fields. With one out and none on base, Fields fell behind in the count, 2–0, before serving up a thigh-high fastball that Martinez sent deep to right field and over the fence. The home run, his third of the game, was hit off the third pitcher that Martinez faced.

At that point the Diamondbacks led comfortably, 7–0. Although only one inning was left to play, there remained a glimmer of hope that Martinez would come to bat once more. Thanks to a single by Jake Lamb and a home run by Adam Rosales, both of them coming after Martinez's homer in the eighth inning, the odds increased substantially. Rosales's home run boosted Arizona's lead to 9–0.

Martinez was due to bat fifth in the ninth inning, and he needed two teammates to get on base if his shot at a fourth home run were to happen. Fortunately for him Dodgers reliever Wilmer Font walked Rey Fuentes, Negron doubled, and Pollock singled, bringing Martinez to the plate with one out and Pollock on first. With the count 1–0 and fans squirming nervously in their seats, Martinez, facing Font, walloped a 1–0 slider over the left-field fence for his fourth home run of the game. In five at-bats Martinez had done the improbable: He had hit home runs in the seventh, eighth, and ninth innings, on top of his first blast in the fourth inning, to tie the major-league mark for home runs in a game. He had homered off four different pitchers, only the third time that had been done.

In addition to the home runs, Martinez's statistics on the day included four runs scored and six RBI.

Oddly, Martinez had been in the position of swinging for a fourth home run on one previous occasion. On June 21, 2015, playing for the Tigers against the Yankees at Yankee Stadium, he flew out to right field in his final at-bat, leaving him with three home runs. There would be no record-tying performance on that day.

"In my last at-bat [that game], I started thinking about it, and that's when it didn't happen," said Martinez.[7]

Things were different against the Dodgers.

"This at-bat, I came up and I was like, just go up here and try to have a good at-bat," he said. "Just keep doing what you've been doing all day. You know what, if it's meant to be, it's meant to be. It's going to happen. There's no point in trying to force it. Just go up there and have a good at-bat."[8]

Martinez's fourth home run was his 11th in 16 games. On the year the slug-ger drove in 104 runs for two different teams, a formidable achievement for a man who was sent packing halfway through the season.

That evening the *Sporting News* portrayed Martinez's accomplishment matter-of-factly:

Diamondbacks outfielder J. D. Martinez on Monday became the 18th player in major-league history to hit four home runs in a game. Martinez connected against Dodgers reliever Wilmer Font in the top of the ninth inning for homer number four. He homered earlier versus Rich Hill, Pedro Baez, and Josh Fields.

"Was I shocked?" Martinez asked. "No. Going up there and hitting it, it didn't really shock me. I was just happy it went over."[9]

More surprised was teammate Archie Bradley, a pitcher. "We went nuts down there [in the bullpen]," he said.[10]

Unlike 16 of the 18 players in the Four Home Runs Club, Martinez's story, like that of Scooter Gennett, is unfinished. At the age of 30 he could very well play for another decade, or at least through a ballplayer's peak years—ages 30 to 35. He was highly productive in 2017, and as content as he appears to be in Arizona, there is no reason to believe that Martinez will be any less productive in 2018, although many ballplayers show a slight decline in their early 30s.

Whatever happens, one thing is certain: The name J. D. Martinez will never become vieux jeu—yesterday's news. Instead, it will resonate for as long as base-ball fans debate the merits of home run hitters and, in particular, the select few who have hit four home runs in a single Major League Baseball game.

APPENDIX A

MEMBERS OF THE FOUR HOME RUNS CLUB

Rankings

Ranked by Career Home Runs

Willie Mays	660
Mike Schmidt	548
Lou Gehrig	493
Carlos Delgado	473
Rocky Colavito	374
Gil Hodges	370
Joe Adcock	336
Shawn Green	328
Chuck Klein	300
Mike Cameron	278
Bob Horner	218
Josh Hamilton	200*
Mark Whiten	158
J.D. Martinez	152*
Ed Delahanty	101**
Pat Seerey	86
Bobby Lowe	71
Scooter Gennett	62*

*Still active.
**Died while active.

Ranked by Years of Service

Willie Mays	22
Bobby Lowe	18
Mike Schmidt	18
Gil Hodges	18
Joe Adcock	17
Lou Gehrig	17
Carlos Delgado	17
Chuck Klein	17
Mike Cameron	17
Ed Delahanty	16
Rocky Colavito	14
Shawn Green	15
Mark Whiten	11
Bob Horner	10
Josh Hamilton	9
Pat Seerey	7
J. D. Martinez	7
Scooter Gennett	5

Age at Which They Achieved the Feat

Pat Seerey	25
Gil Hodges	26
Rocky Colavito	26
Scooter Gennett	27
Mike Schmidt	27
Joe Adcock	27
Mark Whiten	27
Bob Horner	28
Lou Gehrig	28
Ed Delahanty	28
Bobby Lowe	29
Mike Cameron	29
Willie Mays	30
Shawn Green	30
Josh Hamilton	30
J. D. Martinez	30
Carlos Delgado	31
Chuck Klein	31

APPENDIX B

MEMBERS OF THE FOUR HOME RUNS CLUB

Major-League Statistics

Key
AB = at-bats
H = hits
2B = doubles
3B = triples
HR = home runs
RBI = runs batted in
AVG = batting average

BOBBY LOWE'S MAJOR-LEAGUE STATISTICS

Years in Major League Baseball: 18
Teams: Boston Beaneaters, Chicago Orphans, Pittsburgh Pirates, Detroit
    Tigers
Total At-Bats: 7,078
Hits: 1,934
Doubles: 230
Triples: 85
Home Runs: 71
Runs Batted In: 989
Career Batting Average: .273

Year	Team	League	AB	H	2B	3B	HR	RBI	AVG
1890	BSN	NL	207	58	13	2	2	21	.280
1891	BSN	NL	497	129	19	5	6	74	.260
1892	BSN	NL	475	115	16	7	3	57	.242
1893	BSN	NL	526	157	19	5	14	89	.298
1894	BSN	NL	613	212	34	11	17	115	.346
1895	BSN	NL	417	124	12	7	7	62	.297
1896	BSN	NL	306	98	11	4	2	48	.320
1897	BSN	NL	499	154	24	8	5	106	.309
1898	BSN	NL	559	152	11	7	4	94	.272
1899	BSN	NL	559	152	5	9	4	88	.272
1900	BSN	NL	474	132	11	5	3	71	.278
1901	BSN	NL	491	125	11	1	3	47	.255
1902	CHI	NL	480	119	13	3	0	35	.248
1903	CHI	NL	105	28	5	3	0	15	.267
1904	PIT	NL	1	0	0	0	0	0	.000
1904	DET	NL	506	105	14	6	0	40	.208
1905	DET	NL	181	35	7	2	0	9	.193
1906	DET	NL	145	30	3	0	1	13	.207
1907	DET	NL	37	9	2	0	0	5	.243

Source: "Bobby Lowe," BaseballReference.com, http://www.baseball-reference.com/players/l/lowebo01
.shtml (8 February 2017).

ED DELAHANTY'S MAJOR-LEAGUE STATISTICS

Years in Major League Baseball: 16
Teams: Philadelphia Phillies, Cleveland Infants, Washington Senators
Total At-Bats: 7,510
Hits: 2,597
Doubles: 522
Triples: 186
Home Runs: 101
Runs Batted In: 1,466
Career Batting Average: .346

Year	Team	League	AB	H	2B	3B	HR	RBI	AVG
1888	PHI	NL	290	66	12	2	1	31	.228
1889	PHI	NL	246	72	13	3	0	27	.296
1890	CLE	PL	517	153	26	13	3	64	.296
1891	PHI	NL	543	132	19	9	5	86	.243
1892	PHI	NL	477	146	30	21	6	91	.306
1893	PHI	NL	595	219	35	18	19	146	.368
1894	PHI	NL	494	200	39	19	4	133	.404
1895	PHI	NL	480	194	49	10	11	106	.404
1896	PHI	NL	499	198	44	17	13	126	.397
1897	PHI	NL	530	200	40	15	5	96	.377
1898	PHI	NL	548	183	36	9	4	92	.334
1899	PHI	NL	581	238	55	9	9	137	.410
1900	PHI	NL	539	174	32	10	2	109	.323
1901	PHI	NL	542	192	38	16	8	108	.354
1902	WSH	AL	473	178	43	14	10	93	.376
1903	WSH	AL	156	52	11	1	1	21	.333

Source: "Ed Delahanty," *BaseballReference.com*, http://www.baseball-reference.com/players/d/delahed
01.shtml (8 February 2017).

LOU GEHRIG'S MAJOR-LEAGUE STATISTICS

Years in Major League Baseball: 17
Team: New York Yankees
Total At-Bats: 8,001
Hits: 2,721
Doubles: 534
Triples: 163
Home Runs: 493
Runs Batted In: 1,995
Career Batting Average: .340

Year	Team	League	AB	H	2B	3B	HR	RBI	AVG
1923	NY	AL	26	11	4	1	1	8	.423
1925	NY	AL	437	129	23	10	20	68	.295
1926	NY	AL	572	179	47	20	16	109	.313
1927	NY	AL	584	218	52	18	47	173	.373
1928	NY	AL	562	210	47	13	27	147	.374
1929	NY	AL	553	166	32	10	35	125	.300
1930	NY	AL	581	220	42	17	41	173	.379
1931	NY	AL	619	211	31	15	46	185	.341
1932	NY	AL	596	208	42	9	34	151	.349
1933	NY	AL	593	198	41	12	32	140	.334
1934	NY	AL	579	210	40	6	49	166	.363
1935	NY	AL	535	176	26	10	30	120	.329
1936	NY	AL	579	205	37	7	49	152	.354
1937	NY	AL	569	200	37	9	37	158	.351
1938	NY	AL	576	170	32	6	29	114	.295
1939	NY	AL	28	4	0	0	0	1	.143

Source: "Lou Gehrig," BaseballReference.com, http://www.baseball-reference.com/players/g/gehrilo01 .shtml (8 February 2017).

CHUCK KLEIN'S MAJOR-LEAGUE STATISTICS

Years in Major League Baseball: 17
Teams: Philadelphia Phillies, Chicago Cubs, Pittsburgh Pirates
Total At-Bats: 6,486
Hits: 2,076
Doubles: 398
Triples: 74
Home Runs: 300
Runs Batted In: 1,201
Career Batting Average: .320

Year	Team	League	AB	H	2B	3B	HR	RBI	AVG
1928	PHI	NL	253	91	14	4	11	34	.360
1929	PHI	NL	616	219	45	6	43	145	.336
1930	PHI	NL	648	250	59	8	40	170	.386
1931	PHI	NL	594	200	34	10	31	121	.337
1932	PHI	NL	650	226	50	15	38	137	.348
1933	PHI	NL	606	223	44	7	28	120	.368
1934	CHI	NL	435	131	27	2	20	80	.301
1935	CHI	NL	434	127	14	4	21	73	.293
1936	CHI	NL	109	32	5	0	5	18	.294
1936	PHI	NL	492	152	30	7	20	86	.309
1937	PHI	NL	406	132	20	2	15	57	.325
1938	PHI	NL	458	113	22	2	8	61	.247
1939	PHI	NL	47	9	2	1	1	9	.191
1939	PIT	NL	270	81	16	4	11	47	.300
1940	PHI	NL	354	77	16	2	7	37	.218
1941	PHI	NL	73	9	0	0	1	3	.123
1942	PHI	NL	14	1	0	0	0	0	.071
1943	PHI	NL	20	2	0	0	0	3	.100
1944	PHI	NL	7	1	0	0	0	0	.143

Source: "Chuck Klein," *BaseballReference.com*, http://www.baseball-reference.com/players/k/kleinch01 .shtml (8 February 2017).

PAT SEEREY'S MAJOR-LEAGUE STATISTICS

Years in Major League Baseball: 7
Teams: Cleveland Indians, Chicago White Sox
Total At-Bats: 1,815
Hits: 406
Doubles: 73
Triples: 5
Home Runs: 86
Runs Batted In: 261
Career Batting Average: .224

Year	Team	League	AB	H	2B	3B	HR	RBI	AVG
1943	CLE	AL	72	16	3	0	1	5	.222
1944	CLE	AL	342	80	16	0	15	39	.234
1945	CLE	AL	414	98	22	2	14	56	.237
1946	CLE	AL	404	91	17	2	26	62	.225
1947	CLE	AL	216	37	4	1	11	29	.171
1948	CLE	AL	23	6	0	0	1	6	.261
1948	CHI	AL	340	78	11	0	18	64	.229
1949	CHI	AL	4	0	0	0	0	0	.000

Source: "Pat Seerey," BaseballReference.com, http://www.baseball-reference.com/players/s/seerepa01.shtml (8 February 2017).

GIL HODGES'S MAJOR-LEAGUE STATISTICS

Years in Major League Baseball: 18
Teams: Brooklyn Dodgers, Los Angeles Dodgers, New York Mets
Total At-Bats: 7,030
Hits: 1,921
Doubles: 295
Triples: 48
Home Runs: 370
Runs Batted In: 1,274
Career Batting Average: .273

Year	Team	League	AB	H	2B	3B	HR	RBI	AVG
1943	BRO	NL	2	0	0	0	0	0	.000
1947	BRO	NL	77	12	3	1	1	7	.156
1948	BRO	NL	481	120	18	5	11	70	.249
1949	BRO	NL	596	170	23	4	23	115	.285
1950	BRO	NL	561	159	26	2	32	113	.283
1951	BRO	NL	582	156	25	3	40	103	.268
1952	BRO	NL	508	129	27	1	32	102	.254
1953	BRO	NL	520	157	22	7	31	122	.302
1954	BRO	NL	579	176	23	5	42	130	.304
1955	BRO	NL	546	158	24	5	27	102	.289
1956	BRO	NL	550	146	29	4	32	87	.265
1957	BRO	NL	579	173	28	7	27	98	.299
1958	LA	NL	475	123	15	1	22	64	.259
1959	LA	NL	413	114	19	2	25	80	.276
1960	LA	NL	197	39	8	1	8	30	.198
1961	LA	NL	215	52	4	0	8	31	.242
1962	NY	NL	127	32	1	0	9	17	.252
1963	NY	NL	22	5	0	0	0	3	.227

Source: "Gil Hodges," *BaseballReference.com*, http://www.baseball-reference.com/players/h/hodgegi 01.shtml (8 February 2017).

JOE ADCOCK'S MAJOR-LEAGUE STATISTICS

Years in Major League Baseball: 17
Teams: Cincinnati Reds, Milwaukee Braves, Cleveland Indians, Los Angeles
   Angels, California Angels
Total At-Bats: 6,606
Hits: 1,832
Doubles: 295
Triples: 35
Home Runs: 336
Runs Batted In: 1,122
Career Batting Average: .277

Year	Team	League	AB	H	2B	3B	HR	RBI	AVG
1950	CIN	NL	372	109	16	1	8	55	.293
1951	CIN	NL	395	96	16	4	10	47	.243
1952	CIN	NL	378	105	22	4	13	52	.278
1953	MIL	NL	590	168	33	6	18	80	.285
1954	MIL	NL	500	154	27	5	23	87	.308
1955	MIL	NL	288	76	14	0	15	45	.264
1956	MIL	NL	454	132	23	1	38	103	.291
1957	MIL	NL	209	60	13	2	12	38	.287
1958	MIL	NL	320	88	15	1	19	54	.275
1959	MIL	NL	404	118	19	2	25	76	.292
1960	MIL	NL	514	153	21	4	25	91	.298
1961	MIL	NL	562	160	20	0	35	108	.285
1962	MIL	NL	391	97	12	1	29	78	.248
1963	CLE	AL	283	71	7	1	13	49	.251
1964	LA	AL	366	98	13	0	21	64	.268
1965	CAL	AL	349	84	14	0	14	47	.241
1966	CAL	AL	231	63	10	3	18	48	.273

Source: "Joe Adcock," BaseballReference.com, http://www.baseball-reference.com/players/a/adcocjo 01.shtml (8 February 2017).

ROCKY COLAVITO'S MAJOR-LEAGUE STATISTICS

Years in Major League Baseball: 14

Teams: Cleveland Indians, Detroit Tigers, Kansas City Athletics, Chicago
   White Sox, Los Angeles Dodgers, New York Yankees

Total At-Bats: 6,503

Hits: 1,730

Doubles: 283

Triples: 21

Home Runs: 374

Runs Batted In: 1,159

Career Batting Average: .266

Year	Team	League	AB	H	2B	3B	HR	RBI	AVG
1955	CLE	AL	9	4	2	0	0	0	.444
1956	CLE	AL	322	89	11	4	21	65	.276
1957	CLE	AL	461	116	26	0	25	84	.252
1958	CLE	AL	489	148	26	3	41	113	.303
1959	CLE	AL	588	151	24	0	42	111	.257
1960	DET	AL	555	138	18	1	35	87	.249
1961	DET	AL	583	169	30	2	45	140	.290
1962	DET	AL	601	164	30	2	37	112	.273
1963	DET	AL	597	162	29	2	22	91	.271
1964	KC	AL	588	161	31	2	34	102	.274
1965	CLE	AL	592	170	25	2	26	108	.287
1966	CLE	AL	533	127	13	0	30	72	.238
1967	CLE	AL	191	46	9	0	5	21	.241
1967	CHI	AL	190	42	4	1	3	29	.221
1968	LA	NL	113	23	3	0	3	11	.204
1968	NY	AL	91	20	2	2	5	13	.220

Source: "Rocky Colavito," *BaseballReference.com,* http://www.baseball-reference.com/players/c/colavro
   01.shtml (8 February 2017).

WILLIE MAYS'S MAJOR-LEAGUE STATISTICS

Years in Major League Baseball: 22
Teams: New York Giants, San Francisco Giants, New York Mets
Total At-Bats: 10,881
Hits: 3,283
Doubles: 523
Triples: 140
Home Runs: 660
Runs Batted In: 1,903
Career Batting Average: .302

Year	Team	League	AB	H	2B	3B	HR	RBI	AVG
1951	NY	NL	464	127	22	5	20	68	.274
1952	NY	NL	127	30	2	4	4	23	.236
1954	NY	NL	565	195	33	13	41	110	.345
1955	NY	NL	580	185	18	13	51	127	.319
1956	NY	NL	578	171	27	8	36	84	.296
1957	NY	NL	585	195	26	20	35	97	.333
1958	SF	NL	600	208	33	11	29	96	.347
1959	SF	NL	575	180	43	5	34	104	.313
1960	SF	NL	595	190	29	12	29	103	.319
1961	SF	NL	572	176	32	3	40	123	.308
1962	SF	NL	621	189	36	5	49	141	.304
1963	SF	NL	596	187	32	7	38	103	.314
1964	SF	NL	578	171	21	9	47	111	.296
1965	SF	NL	558	177	21	3	52	112	.317
1966	SF	NL	552	159	29	4	37	103	.288
1967	SF	NL	486	128	22	2	22	70	.263
1968	SF	NL	498	144	20	5	23	79	.289
1969	SF	NL	403	114	17	3	13	58	.283
1970	SF	NL	478	139	15	2	28	83	.291
1971	SF	NL	417	113	24	5	18	61	.271
1972	SF	NL	49	9	2	0	0	3	.184
1972	NY	NL	195	52	9	1	8	19	.267
1973	NY	NL	209	44	10	0	6	25	.211

Source: "Willie Mays," BaseballReference.com, http://www.baseball-reference.com/players/m/mayswi 01.shtml (8 February 2017).

MIKE SCHMIDT'S MAJOR-LEAGUE STATISTICS

Years in Major League Baseball: 18
Team: Philadelphia Phillies
Total At-Bats: 8,352
Hits: 2,234
Doubles: 408
Triples: 59
Home Runs: 548
Runs Batted In: 1,595
Career Batting Average: .267

Year	Team	League	AB	H	2B	3B	HR	RBI	AVG
1972	PHI	NL	34	7	0	0	1	3	.206
1973	PHI	NL	367	72	11	0	18	52	.196
1974	PHI	NL	568	160	28	7	36	116	.282
1975	PHI	NL	562	140	34	3	38	95	.249
1976	PHI	NL	584	153	31	4	38	107	.262
1977	PHI	NL	544	149	27	11	38	101	.274
1978	PHI	NL	513	129	27	2	21	78	.251
1979	PHI	NL	541	137	25	4	45	114	.253
1980	PHI	NL	548	157	25	8	48	121	.286
1981	PHI	NL	354	112	19	2	31	91	.316
1982	PHI	NL	514	144	26	3	35	87	.280
1983	PHI	NL	534	136	16	4	40	109	.255
1984	PHI	NL	528	146	23	3	36	106	.277
1985	PHI	NL	549	152	31	5	33	93	.277
1986	PHI	NL	552	160	29	1	37	119	.290
1987	PHI	NL	522	153	28	0	35	113	.293
1988	PHI	NL	390	97	21	2	12	62	.249
1989	PHI	NL	148	30	7	0	6	28	.203

Source: "Mike Schmidt," *BaseballReference.com*, http://www.baseball-reference.com/players/s/schmimi 01.shtml (8 February 2017).

BOB HORNER'S MAJOR-LEAGUE STATISTICS

Years in Major League Baseball: 10
Teams: Atlanta Braves, St. Louis Cardinals
Total At-Bats: 3,777
Hits: 1,047
Doubles: 169
Triples: 8
Home Runs: 218
Runs Batted In: 685
Career Batting Average: .277

Year	Team	League	AB	H	2B	3B	HR	RBI	AVG
1978	ATL	NL	323	86	17	1	23	63	.266
1979	ATL	NL	487	153	15	1	33	98	.314
1980	ATL	NL	463	124	14	1	35	89	.268
1981	ATL	NL	300	83	10	0	15	42	.277
1982	ATL	NL	499	130	24	0	32	97	.261
1983	ATL	NL	386	117	25	1	20	68	.303
1984	ATL	NL	113	31	8	0	3	19	.274
1985	ATL	NL	483	129	25	3	27	89	.267
1986	ATL	NL	517	141	22	0	27	87	.273
1988	STL	NL	206	53	9	1	3	33	.257

Source: "Bob Horner," *BaseballReference.com*, http://www.baseball-reference.com/players/h/hornebo 01.shtml (8 February 2017).

MARK WHITEN'S MAJOR-LEAGUE STATISTICS

Years in Major League Baseball: 11

Teams: Toronto Blue Jays, Cleveland Indians, St. Louis Cardinals, Boston Red Sox, Philadelphia Phillies, Atlanta Braves, Seattle Mariners, New York Yankees

Total At-Bats: 3,104

Hits: 804

Doubles: 129

Triples: 20

Home Runs: 105

Runs Batted In: 423

Career Batting Average: .259

Year	Team	League	AB	H	2B	3B	HR	RBI	AVG
1990	TOR	AL	88	24	1	1	2	7	.273
1991	TOR	AL	149	99	18	7	9	45	.221
1991	CLE	AL	258	66	14	4	7	26	.256
1992	CLE	AL	508	129	19	4	9	43	.254
1993	STL	NL	562	142	13	4	25	99	.253
1994	STL	NL	334	98	18	2	14	53	.293
1995	BOS	AL	108	20	3	0	1	10	.185
1995	PHI	NL	212	57	10	1	11	37	.269
1996	PHI	NL	182	43	8	0	7	21	.236
1996	ATL	NL	90	23	5	1	3	17	.256
1996	SEA	AL	140	42	7	0	12	33	.300
1997	NY	AL	215	57	11	0	5	24	.265
1998	CLE	AL	226	64	14	0	6	29	.283
1999	CLE	AL	25	4	1	0	1	4	.160
2000	CLE	AL	7	2	1	0	0	1	.286

Source: "Mark Whiten," BaseballReference.com, http://www.baseball-reference.com/players/w/whitema 01.shtml (8 February 2017).

MIKE CAMERON'S MAJOR-LEAGUE STATISTICS

Years in Major League Baseball: 17
Teams: Chicago White Sox, Cincinnati Reds, Seattle Mariners, New York
  Mets, San Diego Padres, Milwaukee Brewers, Boston Red Sox, Florida
  Marlins
Total At-Bats: 6,839
Hits: 1,700
Doubles: 383
Triples: 59
Home Runs: 278
Runs Batted In: 968
Career Batting Average: .249

Year	Team	League	AB	H	2B	3B	HR	RBI	AVG
1995	CHI	AL	38	7	2	0	1	2	.184
1996	CHI	AL	11	1	0	0	0	0	.091
1997	CHI	AL	379	98	18	3	14	55	.259
1998	CHI	AL	396	83	16	5	8	43	.210
1999	CIN	NL	542	139	34	9	21	66	.256
2000	SEA	AL	543	145	28	4	19	78	.267
2001	SEA	AL	540	144	30	5	25	110	.267
2002	SEA	AL	545	130	26	5	25	80	.239
2003	SEA	AL	534	135	31	5	18	76	.253
2004	NY	NL	493	114	30	1	30	76	.231
2005	NY	NL	308	84	23	2	12	39	.273
2006	SD	NL	552	148	34	9	22	83	.268
2007	SD	NL	571	138	33	6	21	78	.242
2008	MIL	NL	444	108	25	2	25	70	.243
2009	MIL	NL	544	136	32	3	24	70	.250
2010	BOS	AL	162	42	11	0	4	15	.259
2011	BOS	AL	94	14	2	0	3	9	.149
2011	FLA	NL	143	34	8	0	6	18	.238

Source: "Mike Cameron," BaseballReference.com, http://www.baseball-reference.com/players/c/camermi 01.shtml (8 February 2017).

SHAWN GREEN'S MAJOR-LEAGUE STATISTICS

Years in Major League Baseball: 15
Teams: Toronto Blue Jays, Los Angeles Dodgers, Arizona Diamondbacks,
New York Mets
Total At-Bats: 7,082
Hits: 2,003
Doubles: 445
Triples: 35
Home Runs: 328
Runs Batted In: 1,070
Career Batting Average: .283

Year	Team	League	AB	H	2B	3B	HR	RBI	AVG
1993	TOR	AL	6	0	0	0	0	0	.000
1994	TOR	AL	33	3	1	0	0	1	.091
1995	TOR	AL	379	109	31	4	15	54	.288
1996	TOR	AL	422	118	32	3	11	45	.280
1997	TOR	AL	429	123	22	4	16	53	.287
1998	TOR	AL	630	175	33	4	35	100	.278
1999	TOR	AL	614	190	45	0	42	123	.309
2000	LA	NL	610	164	44	4	24	99	.269
2001	LA	NL	619	184	31	4	49	125	.297
2002	LA	NL	582	166	31	1	42	114	.285
2003	LA	NL	611	171	49	2	19	85	.280
2004	LA	NL	590	157	28	1	28	86	.266
2005	ARI	NL	581	166	37	4	22	73	.286
2006	ARI	NL	417	118	22	3	11	51	.283
2006	NY	NL	113	29	9	0	4	15	.257
2007	NY	NL	446	130	30	1	10	46	.291

Source: "Shawn Green," BaseballReference.com, http://www.baseball-reference.com/players/g/greensh
01.shtml (8 February 2017).

CARLOS DELGADO'S MAJOR-LEAGUE STATISTICS

Years in Major League Baseball: 17
Teams: Toronto Blue Jays, Florida Marlins, New York Mets
Total At-Bats: 7,283
Hits: 2,038
Doubles: 483
Triples: 18
Home Runs: 473
Runs Batted In: 1,512
Career Batting Average: .280

Year	Team	League	AB	H	2B	3B	HR	RBI	AVG
1993	TOR	AL	1	0	0	0	0	0	.000
1994	TOR	AL	130	28	2	0	9	24	.215
1995	TOR	AL	91	15	3	0	3	11	.165
1996	TOR	AL	488	132	28	2	25	92	.270
1997	TOR	AL	519	136	42	3	30	91	.262
1998	TOR	AL	530	155	43	1	38	115	.292
1999	TOR	AL	573	156	39	0	44	134	.272
2000	TOR	AL	569	196	57	1	41	137	.344
2001	TOR	AL	574	160	31	1	39	102	.279
2002	TOR	AL	505	140	34	2	33	108	.277
2003	TOR	AL	570	172	38	1	42	145	.302
2004	TOR	AL	458	123	26	0	32	99	.269
2005	FLA	NL	521	157	41	3	33	115	.301
2006	NY	NL	524	139	30	2	38	114	.265
2007	NY	NL	538	139	30	0	24	87	.258
2008	NY	NL	598	162	32	1	38	115	.271
2009	NY	NL	94	28	7	1	4	23	.298

Source: "Carlos Delgado," *BaseballReference.com,* http://www.baseball-reference.com/players/d/delgaca
01.shtml (8 February 2017).

JOSH HAMILTON'S MAJOR-LEAGUE STATISTICS

Years in Major League Baseball: 9
Teams: Cincinnati Reds, Texas Rangers, Los Angeles Angels
Total At-Bats: 3,909
Hits: 1,134
Doubles: 234
Triples: 24
Home Runs: 20
Runs Batted In: 701
Career Batting Average: .290

Year	Team	League	AB	H	2B	3B	HR	RBI	AVG
2007	CIN	NL	298	87	17	2	19	47	.292
2008	TEX	AL	624	190	35	5	32	130	.304
2009	TEX	AL	336	90	19	2	10	54	.268
2010	TEX	AL	518	186	40	3	32	100	.359
2011	TEX	AL	487	145	31	5	25	94	.298
2012	TEX	AL	562	160	31	2	43	128	.285
2013	LA	AL	576	144	32	5	21	79	.250
2014	LA	AL	338	89	21	0	10	44	.263
2015	TEX	AL	170	43	8	0	8	25	.253

Source: "Josh Hamilton," *BaseballReference.com*, https://www.baseball-reference.com/players/h/hamiljo 03.shtml (8 February 2017).

SCOOTER GENNETT'S MAJOR-LEAGUE STATISTICS

Years in Major League Baseball: 5
Teams: Milwaukee Brewers, Cincinnati Reds
Total At-Bats: 1,987
Hits: 562
Doubles: 112
Triples: 13
Home Runs: 62
Runs Batted In: 257
Career Batting Average: .283

Year	Team	League	AB	H	2B	3B	HR	RBI	AVG
2013	MIL	NL	213	69	11	2	6	21	.324
2014	MIL	NL	440	127	31	3	9	54	.289
2015	MIL	NL	375	99	18	4	6	29	.264
2016	MIL	NL	498	131	30	1	14	56	.263
2017	CIN	NL	461	136	22	3	27	97	.295

Source: "Scooter Gennett," *BaseballReference.com*, http://www.baseball-reference.com/players/g/gennesc 01.shtml (13 June 2017).

J. D. MARTINEZ'S MAJOR-LEAGUE STATISTICS

Years in Major League Baseball: 7
Teams: Houston Astros, Detroit Tigers, Arizona Diamondbacks
Total At-Bats: 2,828
Hits: 805
Doubles: 168
Triples: 13
Home Runs: 152
Runs Batted In: 476
Career Batting Average: .285

Year	Team	League	AB	H	2B	3B	HR	RBI	AVG
2011	HOU	NL	208	57	13	0	6	35	.274
2012	HOU	NL	395	95	14	3	11	55	.241
2013	HOU	NL	296	74	17	0	7	36	.250
2014	DET	AL	441	139	30	3	23	76	.315
2015	DET	AL	596	168	33	2	38	102	.282
2016	DET	AL	460	141	35	2	22	68	.307
2017	DET	AL	200	61	13	2	16	39	.305
2017	ARI	NL	232	70	13	1	29	65	.302

Source: "J. D. Martinez," *BaseballReference.com*, https://www.baseball-reference.com/players/m/martijd 02.shtml (30 November 2017).

SELECTED
BIBLIOGRAPHY

As of December 19, 2017, Baseball-Reference.com listed statistical information, available elsewhere from numerous sources, for each player profiled in this book.

As of December 20, 2017, Ballparksofbaseball.com described many major-league ballparks described in this book.

The Society for American Baseball Research, SABR.org, provided background information for several players discussed in this book.

As of December 23, 2017, several quotes used in this book were posted at LouGehrig.com.

Baseball Almanac. "Willie Mays Quotes." Accessed 8 February 2017. http://www .baseball-almanac.com/quotes/quomays.shtml.

MLB.com. "JD-Back, Back, Back, Back! Martinez: 4 HRs." Accessed 14 September 2017. http://m.mlb.com/news/article/252494292/d-backs-jd-martinez-hits-four-home-runs/.

Oliphant, Thomas. *Praying for Gil Hodges.* New York: Thomas Dunne/St. Martin's Griffin, 2005.

Society for American Baseball Research. "Chuck Klein." Accessed 8 February 2017. http://sabr.org/bioproj/person/8dd27865.

———. "Rocky Colavito." Accessed 8 February 2017. http://sabr.org/bioproj/person/ 8899e413.

Sowell, Mike. *July 2, 1903: The Mysterious Death of Hall of Famer Big Ed Delahanty.* New York: Macmillan, 1992.

Stewart, Wayne. *The Gigantic Book of Baseball Quotations.* New York: Skyhorse Publishing, 2007.

SELECTED BIBLIOGRAPHY

Torres, John A. *Home Run Hitters: Heroes of the Four-Home Run Game*. New York: Macmillan for Young Readers, 1995.

Zachter, Mort. *Gil Hodges: A Hall of Fame Life*. Lincoln: University of Nebraska Press, 2015.

NOTES

PROLOGUE

1. Michael Agnes, *Webster's New World College Dictionary*, 4th ed. (Cleveland, OH: Wiley Publishing, 2002), 683.

2. Stuart Miller, *Good Wood: The Story of the Baseball Bat* (Chicago: ACTA Sports, 2011).

3. Wayne Stewart, *The Little Red Book of Baseball Wisdom* (New York: Skyhorse Publishing, 2012), 68.

4. Stewart, *The Little Red Book of Baseball Wisdom*, 69.

5. "Homerun History," *Ennisdailynews.com*, http://www.ennisdailynews.com/sports/archive-1218/ (8 February 2017).

6. *Star-Ledger* staff, "Bobby Thomson, Former N.J. Resident Known for 'Shot Heard 'Round the World' Home Run, Dies at 86," *New Jersey Star-Ledger*, http://www.nj.com/news/index.ssf/2010/08/bobby_thomson_former_jersey_re.html (17 August 2010).

CHAPTER 1: BOBBY LOWE

1. "Robert Lincoln Lowe Made Four Homers in a Row and Was a Wonderful Player in the '90s—Now a Scout," *Pittsburgh Press*, 16 February 1913, 20.

2. George V. Tuohey, *A History of the Boston Base Ball Club . . . A Concise and Accurate History of Base Ball from Its Inception* (Boston: M. F. Quinn, 1897), 156.

3. Tuohey, *A History of the Boston Base Ball Club*, 158.

4. Charlie Bevis, "Congress Street Grounds, Boston," *SABR.com*, http://sabr.org/bioproj/park/33169c79 (8 February 2017).

5. "South End Grounds," *Ballparks.com*, http://www.ballparks.com/baseball/national/sthend.htm (8 February 2017).

6. Harold Kaese, *The Boston Braves* (New York: Putnam, 1948), 74.

7. Bill Felber, *Inventing Baseball* (Phoenix: SABR, 2013), 249.

8. "Brilliant Player: Story of How Bobby Lowe Was Discovered in 1882," *Boston Daily Globe*, 11 December 1915, 15.

9. "Lowe Can Manage If He Gets the Place: Detroit Will Not Hold Newcastle Man to His Contract If He Gets Position to Manage Team," *Detroit News*, 13 November 1907.

10. "Bobby Lowe: Visits Mrs. Stahl, Mother of His Former Teammate," *Fort Wayne News*, 30 March 1908.

11. Kaese, *The Boston Braves*, 74.

12. "Bobby Lowe Dead; Baseball Star, 83," *New York Times* (Associated Press), 9 December 1951.

CHAPTER 2: ED DELAHANTY

1. "Box Score of Four-Home Run Game by Ed Delahanty," *Baseball-Almanac.com*, http://www.baseball-almanac.com/boxscore/07131896.shtml (8 February 2017).

2. Daniel Okrent and Steve Wulf, *Baseball Anecdotes* (New York: Diversion Books, 1989), 37.

3. "The Life and 1903 Death of Ed Delahanty," *Misc. Baseball*, https://miscbaseball.wordpress.com/2011/12/27/the-life-and-1903-death-of-ed-delahanty/ (30 November 2017).

4. Mike Sowell, *July 2, 1903: The Mysterious Death of Hall of Famer Big Ed Delahanty* (New York: Macmillan, 1992), 74.

5. "Ed Delahanty," *SABR.com*, http://sabr.org/bioproj/person/d835353d (accessed 8 February 2017).

6. Jerrold Casway, "Ed Delahanty's Four-Home Run Game," *SABR.com*, http://sabr.org/gamesproj/game/july-13–1896-ed-delahanty-s-four-home-run-game (8 February 2017).

7. Harold Kaese, "Ed Delahanty's Four-Home Run Game," *SABR.com*, http://sabr.org/gamesproj/game/july-13–1896-ed-delahanty-s-four-home-run-game (8 February 2017).

8. Kaese, "Ed Delahanty's Four-Home Run Game."

9. Sowell, *July 2, 1903*, 112.

10. "The Life and 1903 Death of Ed Delahanty," *Cleveland Plain Dealer*, https://miscbaseball.wordpress.com/2011/12/27/the-life-and-1903-death-of-ed-delahanty/ (20 December 2017).

11. Sowell, *July 2, 1903*, 181.

12. Sowell, *July 2, 1903*, 263.

13. "Delahanty's Body Found," *New York Times*, 10 July 1903.
14. David Fleitz, *Napoleon Lajoie, King of Ballplayers* (Jefferson, NC: McFarland, 2014), 19.
15. "Ed Delahanty," *Baseballhall.org*, http://baseballhall.org/hof/delahanty-ed (8 February 2017).
16. "Ed Delahanty," http://baseballhall.org/hof/delahanty-ed.

CHAPTER 3: LOU GEHRIG

1. "Quotes by Lou Gehrig," *Lougehrig.com*, http://lougehrig.com/about/quotes.html (8 February 2017).
2. "Quotes by Lou Gehrig."
3. "Quotes by Lou Gehrig."
4. "Quotes by Lou Gehrig."
5. "Shibe Park," *Ballparksofbaseball.com*, http://www.ballparksofbaseball.com/ballparks/shibe-park/ (8 February 2017).
6. Matt Kelly, "Lou Gehrig Hits Four Consecutive Home Runs," *Baseballhall.org*, http://baseballhall.org/discover/inside-pitch/lou-gehrig-hits-four-consecutive-home-runs (8 February 2017).
7. Harvey Frommer, *Five O'Clock Lightning: Babe Ruth, Lou Gehrig, and the Greatest Team in Baseball, the 1927 New York Yankees* (Hoboken, NJ: John Wiley & Sons, 2008), 93.
8. "Quotes by Lou Gehrig."
9. Brad Engel and Wayne Stewart, *Tales From First Base: The Best, Funniest, and Slickest First Basemen Ever* (Lincoln, NE: Potomac Books, 2013), 60.
10. Dave Anderson, *The New York Times Story of the Yankees* (New York: Black Dog and Levanthol, 2012), 97.
11. "Gehrig, 'Iron Man' Of Baseball, Dies at the Age of 37," *New York Times*, 3 June 1941, 1, 26.
12. Joseph Vecchione, *New York Times Book of Sports Legends* (New York: Touchstone Books, 1992), 74.
13. "Yankee Legend Lou Gehrig Dies at 37," *Los Angeles Daily Mirror* (Associated Press), http://latimesblogs.latimes.com/thedailymirror/2011/06/yankee-legend-lou-gehrig-dies-at-37.html (20 December 2017).
14. "Quotes by Lou Gehrig."

CHAPTER 4: CHUCK KLEIN

1. James Lincoln Ray, "Chuck Klein," *SABR.com*, http://sabr.org/bioproj/person/ 8dd27865 (8 February 2017).
2. Ray, "Chuck Klein."
3. Ray, "Chuck Klein."
4. Ray, "Chuck Klein."
5. "Chuck Klein," *Baseballhall.org*, http://baseballhall.org/hof/klein-chuck (8 February 2017).
6. Ray, "Chuck Klein."
7. Leslie Avery, "Chuck Klein Smacks Four Homers in Pirates Game," *Altoona Mirror*, 11 July 1936, 10.
8. "Chuck Klein Found Dead," *Holland Evening Sentinel* (United Press), 29 March 1958.
9. "Chuck Klein," *Baseballhall.org*.

CHAPTER 5: PAT SEEREY

1. John A. Torres, *Home Run Hitters: Heroes of the Four-Home Run Game* (New York: Macmillan for Young Readers, 1995), 32.
2. Torres, *Home Run Hitters*, 33.
3. Lew Freedman, *A Summer to Remember: Bill Veeck, Lou Boudreau, Bob Feller, and the 1948 Cleveland Indians* (New York: Skyhorse Publishing, 2014).
4. Carl Lundquist, "Twin Bill Loss to Braves Drops Pirates to Fourth Place," *Altoona Mirror*, 19 July 1948.
5. Joe Reichler, "Today's Sports Parade," *Mansfield News Journal* (United Press), 19 July 1948.
6. Fred Schuld, "Pat Seerey," *SABR.org*, http://sabr.org/bioproj/person/b393a0e4 (8 February 2017).
7. "White Sox Option Seerey to LA," *St. Petersburg Times* (Associated Press), https://news.google.com/newspapers?nid=888&dat=19490513&id=fdtOAAAAIBAJ &sjid=G04DAAAAIBAJ&pg=2919,1362923 (20 December 2017).
8. Russell Schneider, *The Cleveland Indians Encyclopedia* (Champaign, IL: Sports Publishing, 2004), 247.
9. Schneider, *The Cleveland Indians Encyclopedia*, 237.
10. Torres, *Home Run Hitters*, 37.
11. Bob Dolgan, "Fat Pat Gave His All or Nothing at Plate," *Cleveland Plain Dealer*, 15 May 2001.

CHAPTER 6: GIL HODGES

1. Houston Mitchell, "The 20 Greatest Dodgers of All Time: Gil Hodges," *Los Angeles Times*, http://www.latimes.com/sports/dodgers/dodgersnow/la-sp-20-greatest-dodgers-all-time-fan-vote-htmlstory.html (20 December 2017).
2. Lyle Spatz, *The Team That Forever Changed Baseball and America* (Lincoln: University of Nebraska Press, 2012), 142.
3. Wayne Stewart, *The Gigantic Book of Baseball Quotations* (New York: Skyhorse Publishing, 2007), 345.
4. Thomas Oliphant, *Praying for Gil Hodges* (New York: Thomas Dunne/St. Martin's Griffin, 2005), 35.
5. Oliphant, *Praying for Gil Hodges*, 21–22.
6. Mort Zachter, *Gil Hodges: A Hall of Fame Life* (Lincoln: University of Nebraska Press, 2015), 69.
7. "Ebbets Field," *Ballparksofbaseball.com*, http://www.ballparksofbaseball.com/ballparks/ebbets-field/ (8 February 2017).
8. Joseph Vecchione, *New York Times Book of Sports Legends* (New York: Touchstone Books, 1992), 124.
9. Deborah Wiles, *The Aurora County All-Stars* (New York: HMH Books for Young Readers, 2016), 190.
10. Joe Reichler, "Gil Hodges Hits Four Home Runs as Dodgers Trounce Braves, 19–3," *Massillon* (Ohio) *Evening Independent* (Associated Press), 1 September 1950.
11. Zachter, *Gil Hodges*, 305.
12. Zachter, *Gil Hodges*, 247.
13. Mort Zachter, "Excerpt: How Gil Hodges Helped Turn the 1969 Mets into an Amazin' Team," *Sports Illustrated*, https://www.si.com/mlb/2015/03/20/gil-hodges-book-excerpt-mort-zachter-1969-mets (20 December 2017).
14. *Oh, God!* Film. United States: Carl Reiner, 1977.
15. "Gil Hodges Dies of Heart Attack," *Victoria* (Texas) *Advocate* (Associated Press), 3 April 1972, 1(B).
16. "Gil Hodges Dies of Heart Attack."
17. Oliphant, *Praying for Gil Hodges*, 35.

CHAPTER 7: JOE ADCOCK

1. Richard Goldstein, "Joe Adcock, 71, Power Hitter for Milwaukee Braves in the '50s," *New York Times*, http://www.nytimes.com/1999/05/04/sports/joe-adcock-71-power-hitter-for-milwaukee-braves-in-50-s.html (20 December 2017).
2. Gregory Wolf, "Joe Adcock," *SABR.org*, http://sabr.org/bioproj/person/0999384d (8 February 2017).

3. Gregory Wolf, *Thar's Joy in Braveland* (Phoenix, AZ: Society for American Baseball Research, 2014).

4. "Joe Adcock," *Lasportshall.com*, http://www.lasportshall.com/inductees/baseball/joe-adcock/?back=inductee (8 February 2017).

5. Wolf, *Thar's Joy in Braveland*.

6. "Joe Adcock Smashes Four Homers," *Charleston Gazette* (Associated Press), 1 August 1954.

7. Wolf, "Joe Adcock," http://sabr.org/bioproj/person/0999384d.

8. Goldstein, "Joe Adcock, 71," http://www.nytimes.com/1999/05/04/sports/joe-adcock-71-power-hitter-for-milwaukee-braves-in-50-s.html.

CHAPTER 8: ROCKY COLAVITO

1. "Harold Friend," *Bleacherreport.com*, http://bleacherreport.com/users/104240-harold-friend (8 February 2017).

2. David Zingler, "Rocky Colavito," *Simply Baseball Notebook's Forgotten in Time*, http://z.lee28.tripod.com/sbnsforgottenintime/rockycolavito.html (8 February 2017).

3. Terry Pluto, "At 82, Former Cleveland Indian Rocky Colavito Faces a New Challenge—Losing a Leg," *Cleveland Plain Dealer*, http://www.cleveland.com/pluto/index.ssf/2015/09/at_82_rocky_colavito_faces_a_n.html (20 December 2017).

4. Joseph Wancho, "Rocky Colavito," *SABR.org*, http://sabr.org/bioproj/person/8899e413 (8 February 2017).

5. "Memorial Stadium," *Ballparksofbaseball.com*, http://www.ballparksofbaseball.com/ballparks/memorial-stadium/ (8 February 2017).

6. Andy Knobel, "Looking Back: Rocky Colavito Hit Four Homers against Orioles in 1959," *Baltimore Sun*, http://www.baltimoresun.com/sports/orioles/blog/bal-rocky-colavito-hit-4-homers-against-orioles-in-1959–20120509-story.html (20 December 2017).

7. Knobel, "Looking Back."

8. Knobel, "Looking Back."

9. Wancho, "Rocky Colavito."

10. Wancho, "Rocky Colavito."

11. Pluto, "At 82."

CHAPTER 9: WILLIE MAYS

1. Wayne Stewart, *The Little Red Book of Baseball Wisdom* (New York: Skyhorse Publishing, 2012), 169.

2. "Willie Mays Quotes," *Baseball-almanac.com*, http://www.baseball-almanac.com/quotes/quomays.shtml (8 February 2017).

3. "Willie Mays Quotes."

4. "Willie Mays Quotes."

5. "Jackie Robinson Quotes," *Baseball-almanac.com*, http://www.baseball-almanac .com/quotes/quojckr.shtml (8 February 2017).

6. "Willie Mays Quotes," *BrainyQuote.com*, https://www.brainyquote.com/quotes/ quotes/w/williemays139962.html (8 February 2017).

7. "Milwaukee County Stadium," *Ballparks.com*, http://www.ballparks.com/baseball/ national/county.htm (8 February 2017).

8. Bruce Weber, "Willie Mays, at 78, Decides to Tell His Story," *New York Times*, 30 January 2010, (SP)1.

9. Leo Durocher, *Nice Guys Finish Last* (Chicago: University of Chicago Press, 1975), 431.

10. Patrick Reusse, "Willie Mays: An All-Star for All Time," *Minneapolis Star Tribune*, http://www.startribune.com/willie-mays-an-all-star-for-all-time-july-13/ 266888711/ (20 December, 2017).

11. "Willie Mays Breaks Out of Minor Slump with Bang: Four Home Runs," *Janesville Daily Gazette* (Associated Press), 1 May 1961, 14.

12. Sandy Foster, *Say What?* (Morrisville, NC: Lulu, 2011), 99.

13. Paul Marcus, *Creating Heaven on Earth: The Psychology of Experiencing Immortality in Everyday Life* (London: Karnac Books, 2015), 93.

14. Larry Moffi and Jonathan Kronstadt, *Crossing the Line: Black Major Leaguers, 1947–1959* (Winnipeg, Canada: Bison Books, 2006), 60.

CHAPTER 10: MIKE SCHMIDT

1. "Mike Schmidt," *Baseballhall.org*, http://baseballhall.org/hof/schmidt-mike (14 March 2017).

2. Wayne Stewart, *The Gigantic Book of Baseball Quotations* (New York: Skyhorse Publishing, 2007), 189.

3. "Quotes from Mike Schmidt," *Baseball-almanac.com*, http://www.baseball -almanac.com/quotes/quoschm.shtml (14 March 2017).

4. "Quotes from Mike Schmidt."

5. "Cubs History," *Cubs.com*, http://chicago.cubs.mlb.com/chc/ballpark/information/ index.jsp?content=history (8 February 2017).

6. Stewart, *Gigantic Book of Baseball Quotations*, 489.

7. "Schmidt's Four-Straight Homers Modern NL Record," *Kingston* (New York) *Daily Freeman* (United Press), 18 April 1976, 29.

8. "Schmidt: Four Homers in a Row," *New York Times* (Associated Press), 18 April 1976, 131.

9. "Schmidt's Four-HR Rampage Makes History," *St. Louis Post-Dispatch*, 18 April 1976, 25.

10. Jayson Stark, "With Phillies Having Fun, Schmidt Wonders What If," *Philadelphia Inquirer*, 27 May 1990.

11. Brian Smith, "Ex-Phillies Great Mike Schmidt on Comeback Trail from Cancer," *York Dispatch*, 24 April 2014.

CHAPTER 11: BOB HORNER

1. Ronald Yates, "Horner Parting Shots Stun Fans in Japan," *Chicago Tribune*, http://articles.chicagotribune.com/1988–02–11/sports/8803290509_1_japanese-teams-japanese-pastime-top-sports-columnists (20 December 2017).

2. Yates, "Horner Parting Shots Stun Fans in Japan."

3. Yates, "Horner Parting Shots Stun Fans in Japan."

4. Matt Levin, "Horner's Game Grew through Four Years at Apollo," *Arizona Republic*, 22 August 2009.

5. "Atlanta Fulton County Stadium," *Ballparksofbaseball.com*, http://www.ballparksofbaseball.com/ballparks/atlanta-fulton-county-stadium/ (8 February 2017).

6. "Atlanta Fulton County Stadium."

7. Kyle Taylor, "Bob Horner, Home Run Hitter and Food Pantry Volunteer," *Irving Cares*, 2015, 1.

8. Jack Wilkinson and Carroll Rogers, *Game of My Life* (New York: Sports Publishing, 2013), 62.

9. "Horner's Four Homers Go to Waste," *New Castle* (Pennsylvania) *News* (United Press), 7 July 1986, 15.

10. Charles F. Faber, *Major-League Careers Cut Short* (Jefferson, NC: McFarland, 2010), 33.

11. Ken Sugiura, "Nine Questions: Bob Horner," *Atlanta Journal-Constitution*, http://www.ajc.com/sports/baseball/nine-questions-bob-horner/14EYM7unrVdHqxml2Rrg0N/ (20 December 2017).

12. Sugiura, "Nine Questions."

CHAPTER 12: MARK WHITEN

1. "How a Tragic Accident Brought Mark Whiten to Cardinals," *Retrosimba.com*, http://retrosimba.com/2013/03/18/how-a-tragic-accident-brought-mark-whiten-to-cardinals/ (8 February 2017).

2. Bill Jauss, "Sox Win Wild One over Blue Jays," *Chicago Tribune*, http://articles.chicagotribune.com/1991–05–20/sports/9102150354_1_mark-whiten-sox-manager-jeff-torborg-punch (20 December 2017).

3. Dom Amore, "Whiten Gets It Going at Latest Stop," *Hartford Courant*, 13 April 1997.

4. "Riverfront Stadium," *BallparksofBaseball.com*, http://www.ballparksofbaseball .com/ballparks/riverfront-stadium/ (8 February 2017).

5. Joe Kay, "Superstar Whiten Revels," *Iowa City Iowan*, 9 September 1993, 48.

6. "Riverfront Stadium."

7. R. Cory Smith, "RBI Program Continues Strong Tradition at USA Base-ball's AEBC Tournament," *Usabaseball.com*, http://web.usabaseball.com/article.jsp ?ymd=20150813&content_id=142986276&vkey=news_usab (8 February 2017).

CHAPTER 13: MIKE CAMERON

1. "Mets' Cameron Breaks Cheekbones and Nose in a Horrifying Collision," *Washington Post*, https://www.washingtonpost.com/archive/sports/2005/08/12/mets -cameron-breaks-cheekbones-and-nose-in-a-horrifying-collision/2bb5bfca-0b2f -4f71-8c83-bab44682c7af/?utm_term=.62d79f9b4292 (20 December 2017).

2. "Mets' Cameron Breaks Cheekbones and Nose."

3. "Guaranteed Rate Field," *Ballparksofbaseball.com*, http://www.ballparksofbaseball .com/ballparks/guaranteed-rate-field/ (8 February 2017).

4. "Cameron's King of the Hill," *Walla Walla Union Bulletin* (Associated Press), 3 May 2002.

5. "Cameron's King of the Hill."

6. "Fast Facts," *Baseball-almanac.com*, http://www.baseball-almanac.com (30 November 2017).

7. Joe Halverson, "Mike Cameron Retires: A Look at an Underrated Legacy," *BleacherReport.com*, http://bleacherreport.com/articles/1072320-mike-cameron-retires -a-look-at-an-underrated-legacy (8 February 2017).

8. Halverson, "Mike Cameron Retires."

9. Stephen Cannella, "Homerunner Center Fielder Mike Cameron Is a Star in Seattle but Loves Being with the Folks Back Home in Georgia," *Sports Illustrated*, 14 January 2002, 73–75.

10. Evan Drellich, "After Disappointment Early in Draft, Cameron and Dad Bull-ish on Astros," *Houston Chronicle*, http://www.houstonchronicle.com/sports/astros/ article/After-early-disappointment-Daz-Cameron-and-dad-6317156.php (20 December 2017).

CHAPTER 14: SHAWN GREEN

1. Mike DiGiovanna, "Shawn Green's Record Day: Slugger Smashes Four HRs," *Los Angeles Times*, http://www.sfgate.com/sports/article/SHAWN-GREEN-S-RECORD-DAY-Slugger-smashes-4-HRs-2818757.php (20 December 2017).

2. Murray Chass, "At Yom Kippur, Green Opts to Miss at Least One Game," *New York Times*, http://www.nytimes.com/2004/09/23/sports/baseball/at-yom-kippur-green-opts-to-miss-at-least-one-game.html (20 December 2017).

3. "Miller Park," *Ballparksofbaseball.com*, http://www.ballparksofbaseball.com/ballparks/miller-park/ (8 February 2017).

4. David Schoenfield, "Vote: Best Single-Game Performance Ever," *ESPN.com*, http://www.espn.com/blog/sweetspot/post/_/id/23774/vote-best-single-performance-of-all-time (16 March 2017).

5. DiGiovanna, "Shawn Green's Record Day."

6. Mike DiGiovanna, "Green's Fantastic Four," *Los Angeles Times*, http://articles.latimes.com/2002/may/24/sports/sp-dodgers24 (20 December 2017).

7. "Shawn Green Biography," *Internet Movie Database*, http://www.imdb.com/name/nm1684693/bio (15 February 2017).

8. Johnathan E. Briggs, "Dodger Goes to Bat for Literacy," *Los Angeles Times*, http://articles.latimes.com/2000/jun/01/local/me-36244 (1 June 2000).

9. "Green Breaks Slump with Four HRS vs. Brewers," *Racine* (Wisconsin) *Journal Times* (Associated Press), 24 May 2002.

10. "Shawn Green Slams Record Four Homers," *CBC Sports*, http://www.cbc.ca/sports/baseball/shawn-green-slams-record-four-homers-1.342464 (8 February 2017).

CHAPTER 15: CARLOS DELGADO

1. "Delgado Matches History with His Bat," *USA Today* (*Associated Press*), 26 September 2003.

2. Joseph Wancho, "Carlos Delgado," *SABR.org*, http://sabr.org/bioproj/person/8899e413 (8 February 2017).

3. Ben Nicholson-Smith, "Carlos Delgado Talks Career, Retirement," *Mlbtraderumors.com*, http://www.mlbtraderumors.com/2011/04/carlos-delgado-talks-career-retirement.html (8 February 2017).

4. Shi Davidi, "Delgado on Four-HR Game: 'I Was in La-la Land,'" *Sportsnet.ca*, http://www.sportsnet.ca/baseball/mlb/delgado-on-4-hr-game-i-was-in-la-la-land (8 February 2017).

5. "Rogers Centre," *Ballparksofbaseball.com*, http://www.ballparksofbaseball.com/ballparks/rogers-centre/ (8 February 2017).

6. "Delgado Ties Record, Hits Four Home Runs," *Arizona Republic* (Associated Press), 26 September 2003, 32.

7. Wayne Stewart, *The Gigantic Book of Baseball Quotations* (New York: Skyhorse Publishing, 2007), 199.

8. "Carlos Delgado Retires from Baseball," *Espn.com*, http://www.espn.com/mlb/news/story?id=6343791 (8 February 2017).

9. Brendan Kennedy, "Blue Jays Legend Carlos Delgado Makes Case for Hall of Fame," *Toronto Star*, https://www.thestar.com/sports/bluejays/2014/12/01/blue_jays_legend_carlos_delgado_makes_case_for_hall_of_fame.html (20 December 2017).

CHAPTER 16: JOSH HAMILTON

1. Mike DiGiovanna, "The Fall and Rise of Josh Hamilton," *Los Angeles Times*, http://articles.latimes.com/2013/feb/04/sports/la-sp-0205-josh-hamilton-addiction-20130205 (20 December 2017).

2. Dan Reed, "Super Natural: Josh Hamilton's Comeback," *Christianity Today*, 15 June 2011, 34.

3. "Oriole Park at Camden Yards," *Ballparks.com*, http://www.ballparks.com/baseball/american/oriole.htm (8 February 2017).

4. "Josh Hamilton Hits Four Two-Run HRs as Rangers Bury O's," *Espn.co.uk* (Associated Press), http://www.espn.co.uk/mlb/recap?gameId=320508101 (8 February 2017).

5. David Ginsburg, "Rangers' Hamilton Blasts Four in Romp," *Clovic News Journal* (Associated Press), 9 May 2012.

6. Tim Keown, "I'm Proof That Hope Is Never Lost," *ESPN.com*, http://www.espn.com/mlb/news/story?id=2926447 (8 February 2017).

CHAPTER 17: SCOOTER GENNETT

1. C. Trent Rosecrans, "Reds Outfielder Scooter Gennett Makes History with Four-Home Run Game," *USA Today*, https://www.usatoday.com/story/sports/mlb/2017/06/06/reds-scooter-gennett-makes-history-hitting-four-home-runs/102572182/ (24 January 2018).

2. Tom Haudricourt, "Brewers Prospect Scooter Gennett More Than Measures Up," *Milwaukee Journal Sentinel*, http://archive.jsonline.com/sports/brewers/brewers-prospect-scooter-gennett-more-than-measures-up-fv6212e-161777805.html/ (20 December 2017).

3. Haudricourt, "Brewers Prospect Scooter Gennett More Than Measures Up."

4. "The Sacrifice of Others—Scooter Gennett—Milwaukee Brewers," *Christophera page.com*, http://christopherapage.com/uncategorized/the-sacrifice-of-others-scooter-gennett-milwaukee-brewers/ (13 June 2017).

5. Tyler Kepner, "Scooter Gennett Hits Four Home Runs, Joining an Exclusive Club," *New York Times*, 6 June 2017, (B)11.

6. "Scooter Gennett Ties MLB Record with Four-Homer Game," *Los Angeles Times* (Associated Press), http://www.latimes.com/sports/mlb/la-sp-scooter-gennett -20170606-story.html (20 December 2017).

7. "Scooter Gennett Hits Four Home Runs for Reds to Tie MLB Record," *U.S. News & World Report*, https://www.usnews.com/news/sports/articles/2017-06-06/ scooter-gennett-hits-4-home-runs-for-reds-to-tie-mlb-record (20 December 2017).

8. "Scooter Gennett Hits Four Home Runs for Reds."

CHAPTER 18: J. D. MARTINEZ

1. Beth Harris, "Diamondbacks' J. D. Martinez Hits Four Home Runs, Ties MLB Record," *Chicago Tribune*, http://www.chicagotribune.com/sports/baseball/ ct-diamondbacks-jd-martinez-hits-4-home-runs-ties-mlb-record-20170904-story.html (20 December 2017).

2. "Diamondbacks' J. D. Martinez Hits Four Home Runs against Dodgers," *USA Today*, https://www.usatoday.com/story/sports/mlb/2017/09/04/jd-martinez-4-home -runs/631912001/ (20 December 2017).

3. Steve Gilbert, "J. D.-Back, Back, Back, Back! Martinez: Four HRs," *Mlb.com*, http://m.mlb.com/news/article/252494292/d-backs-jd-martinez-hits-four-home-runs/ (14 September 2017).

4. Tony Capobianco, "Former Flanagan High Player J. D. Martinez Regroups after Signing Minor-League Deal with Detroit Tigers," *Miami Herald*, http://www .miamiherald.com/sports/high-school/prep-broward/article1962630.html (20 December 2017).

5. Capobianco, "Former Flanagan High Player J. D. Martinez Regroups."

6. "Where Did Tigers Slugger J. D. Martinez Come From?" *Foxsports.com*, http://www.foxsports.com/detroit/story/where-did-tigers-slugger-j-d-martinez-come -from-062314 (18 September 2017).

7. Gilbert, "J. D. Back, Back, Back, Back!"

8. Gilbert, "J. D. Back, Back, Back, Back!"

9. Tom Gatto, "J. D. Martinez Hits Four Home Runs in Game for Diamondbacks vs. Dodgers," *Sporting News*, http://www.sportingnews.com/mlb/news/jd-martinez -four-home-runs-in-a-game-diamondbacks-dodgers-mlb-records/2vdxr9fm6zt 71f4suvd5zprpk (20 December 2017).

10. Gilbert, "J. D. Back, Back, Back, Back!"

INDEX

ABOUT THE AUTHOR

Steven K. Wagner, author of *Perfect: The Rise and Fall of John Paciorek, Baseball's Greatest One-Game Wonder* (2015) and *Seinsoth: The Rough-and-Tumble Life of a Dodger* (2016), has worked as a freelance journalist since 1989. He began his career as a staff writer and later as assistant bureau chief with legendary news organization United Press International. Wagner then worked for the Portland *Oregonian* as the newspaper's Vancouver, Washington, bureau chief and its night crime reporter. The author has freelanced extensively for the *Los Angeles Times*, and his work also has appeared in the *New York Times*, the *Washington Post*, and *Baseball America*. Wagner is married and resides in southeastern Pennsylvania.

The author, c. 1960.